BLING, BOAS AND BALLS!

BLING, BOAS AND BALLS!

Joanne Copeman

Disclaimer

Some names and identifying details have been changed to protect the privacy of certain individuals in order to maintain their anonymity.

DEDICATION

*I dedicate this book to the two most important people in my world;
my mother Patricia, who is not only a wonderful mother but my best friend,
and my precious daughter Pearl, the best thing that has ever happened to me.
I adore them both.*

CONTENTS

PROLOGUE

I was slouching around a table after a gig, having a few drinks with Elvis, Tina, Cher and Elton. We were merrily swapping amusing tales about life on the road.

'Somebody should write a book,' Cher said.

I nodded in agreement. 'Do you know what? I might give it a whirl.'

Now, I'm not an overly ambitious person, or in any way arrogant, but I'm sure it will be a bestseller and I'll be a millionairess within a year. I'll have a huge mansion, acres of sprawling grounds, Jaguars, Porsches, an abundance of waiting staff, an offensive amount of cash and an endless supply of king prawns. I will then write the sequel, they'll turn it into a movie, I'll make a few billion then retire to a remote part of Italy to eat fine quality pasta and drink my own body weight in Barolo.

* Disclaimer *

Should anybody consider suing, you are welcome to my Y reg Ford Focus estate. Please don't leave any personal belongings inside as the central locking went years ago. You can also take my 32-inch Blaupunkt TV (with Freeview), although it should be called Defunct as the delay is just awful (if you need to watch something on Wednesday, may I suggest you make your selection on Tuesday).

CHAPTER ONE

THE NEXT BIG THING

Paphos, Cyprus, 1993

'Ladies and Gentlemen, your attention please! Next on stage, a couple of real crackers from Nuneaton, England… It's Jo and Steph!'

It was the summer of 1993. Steph and I were best friends working in Cyprus throughout the blistering hot holiday season. We adopted various roles; anything from chambermaids and receptionists to pool cleaners and barmaids – you name it, we did it. We were regulars at a lively little joint called Boogies Karaoke Bar in Paphos. Steph was clearly tone deaf but she thought she was Aretha Franklin after three Orange Zombies, most of which she spilt down her. Each weekend we rode our little moped, which we affectionately named Revin Kevin, to Boogies Bar, took to the stage and enthusiastically performed our little drunken duets. We had a ball and it was during that heady period in Paphos that I decided I was a fabulous singer and should become a global superstar…

Birmingham, England, 1995

From: <Copeman, Joanne>
To: <Morris, Jason>
Sent: 30 November 1995 13.28
Subject: Inane drivel of utmost importance
Mr Morris,
I have decided to relieve my overwhelming boredom in your absence by keeping what can only be described as a sort of diary: Copeman the Cappuccino Years. *I will, over the next three days, enter snippets of info whenever I please. I will log*

things that amuse me, disturb me or affect me in any way. I shall forward my diary entries for your perusal upon your return to the workplace (how dare you feck off to France and take three days holiday!).

I shall now begin…

Wednesday 28/11

Have just arrived to be met by a letter from HR stating that as the company has gone through, and continues to go through, big changes, we need to individually elect a staff representative for each department. We have no union as such so they require us to nominate someone and hand our slips back to the head of HR, Miss Rhiannon Rees. Now, one does not need a brain equivalent to that of Sherlock Holmes to conclude that this spells REDUNDANCIES for our sunny branch. We have been given a choice of Paul Derrick or Ray Whitmore to represent the operations department. Is this any choice at all? Jaysus Mary Mother of God, what will become of us? We are doomed, doomed! I shall, of course, nominate Paul Derrick. We are all aware that as a member of the transport department, Ray cannot put his trousers on in the morning without a little help.

The sense of boredom today is immense. I am signing off now as I have planned to kill myself at 3pm and I have not got much time to prepare. I have decided that the warehouse is where I shall meet my fate and I am going to throw myself off the racking. I may need a bit of help climbing up the racking as my popped facet joint limits me greatly, although I should be able to jump off without too much assistance.

For now and forever, I remain the queen of your genitals.
Until next time,
Copeman, the utterly depressed.

Thursday 29/11

Suicide attempt failed. Bloody agency staff caught me on the forks of a reach truck. I have, however, succeeded in damaging my spleen, vertebrae, all remaining facet joints, discs, cornea, retina, colon and I badly chafed my chin, which means that my beard will always grow patchy.

Anyway, something far more disturbing has happened today. Ray has been elected to be our staff representative. We may as well clear our desks now. Nobody who sports fawn slacks should be trusted in such a position of power. I am too upset to continue with this diary entry. I will go for a ciggie and see if topping up my nicotine levels helps to suppress my anxiety…

…It did. Until I returned to hear 'Old Fawn Slacks' talking of strikes and picket lines. He is taking his role far too seriously already. Honestly, anything to get out of actually doing some work. No wonder this company is on its arse. Ray has said he needs to speak to me regarding my package – oh God I despair! I demand an election recount. They say that with a bit of hard work and the right guidance, Ray could be a solid and inspiring representative of our workforce but, as I said to a colleague in French exports this morning, you cannot polish a turd…

Ray says a crisis meeting must be held tomorrow night at the Denbeh Arms public house. I'm certain that he will speak in tongues and tell mistruths. He has said that we must all help to choose the playlist for the Christmas party. He also wants to perform a short dance routine to Teenage Dirtbag *– apparently he has been practising all week. He has already* *sewn some silver sequins onto a pair of his best fawn slacks and says he wants this year's Christmas party to be special.*

I must go now. I simply cannot function this pm. I have tried everything listed in my How to Improve Mood list but to no avail.

Bye bye my little oven chip…
Your European Correspondent,
Miss Copeman

Friday 30/11

It's mayhem. Ray is up there now in a meeting with all senior management. The word in the depot is that a few people are being made redundant but I'm not one of them. Bastards! I was ready for the off. Damn it. I am too weary to write anymore. I hope I have given you some insight into the chronic events of the past three days. You will no doubt get the factual version of events from your colleagues in the Bournemouth depot. I must dash now. It's all been a bit much today. I'm on the edge.

On a serious note, I have now got to do the paperwork for three Stuttgart import trailers that have managed to pull into the depot at the same time again. Shits. The bloody drivers do it on purpose. It's 3.45pm already and the transport department delight in telling me on a daily basis that if I don't get my delivery notes in before 4.30pm I can shove it up my arse.

This has been Joanne Copeman, next to the German Import Desk, Midlands Depot. Goodbye.

This is what I spent much of my day doing. I was 21 years old working as a European shipping co-ordinator for a large freight forwarding company in the Midlands. I use the term 'working' extremely loosely. My post on the German Import Desk was beginning to bore the life out of me and I felt the need for change. The year had been very dull and the tedious, bleak UK weather was only adding to my sense of boredom. I felt that I had seen enough of the shipping industry and knew I really should get cracking if I was to become the next Whitney or Mariah.

I had secretly wanted to be a singer from the very first time I picked up a microphone at a karaoke in 1992. My father Barry performed at local pub gigs and I was only nine years old when I first saw him sing in front of an audience; even then it seemed so exciting to me. After all the drinking, smoking and general arsing about with Steph, my plan was to become the next great diva and move to LA where I would start the recording of my first album. At this stage one would have expected me to have put a great deal of thought into this huge decision, after all I was about to leave a steady office job to try my luck in the competitive and ruthless world of showbiz. I'm not sure if I was fearless, naïve or stupid but I would be lying if I said that the prospect frightened me. Perhaps my gung ho attitude towards the career change was simply due to my age but as I saw it, shipping was boring and showbiz was exciting. It was as simple as that.

Yes I expected it to be a difficult business to break into but it didn't phase me at all. (Little did I know at the time that my gung ho attitude was not merely down to my young age; it was actually a personality trait that was to stay with me throughout my adult life.)

I hadn't told many people about my master plan in case they didn't share my optimism and thought I was slightly deluded, however I'd told Steph as soon as the thought entered my mind. We were out during one of our drunken karaoke evenings whilst working in Cyprus when I made my grandiose announcement. Steph was wacky so I felt perfectly at ease sharing my plan with her. She was, by her own admission, a terrible singer, so when I told her she laughed and said, 'It's a great plan Jo but, alas, I fear you must go it alone. I will of course, support you from the bar!'

Steph was working in the administration department at Triton Showers, a major UK shower manufacturer based in Nuneaton, and she made it very clear that although LA sounded appealing, she felt that she was actually the backbone of the entire Triton operation and couldn't possibly desert them. I told her I understood and said it was highly likely that Whitney had a best friend who worked in the shower manufacturing industry too.

With the knowledge that Steph would be faithfully supporting me from the bars of the UK, I felt brave enough to tell the people close to me whom I thought it might really affect. Firstly, I made my mum fully aware as I suspected I would need funding somewhat and I thought she should know straight away to enable her to start saving. Secondly, I told my boyfriend Steve (everybody called him Robbo, me included, as his surname was Roberts). I informed him that, depending on his behaviour, he may or may not be able to become my manager (we hadn't been seeing each other long and he tended to go along with anything in the early days). Thirdly, I told my dad Barry (Bazza) who had helped inspire my newly chosen career.

Bazza no longer lived with us but was still very much around. My mum and Bazza separated when I was only a baby but they had remained great friends and Mum found him as amusing as the rest of us. There were no hard feelings regarding their parting. Both maintained that they were young and it was a mutual decision. They actually got along just like old mates. Bazza was a sales representative for a large brewery by day and a club singer by night (some allege that he was a pimp at weekends). He had a deep, rich singing voice that was as smooth as velvet. Not only did he have a wonderful tone, he was also pitch perfect. He had been singing for many years and performed at some large venues. He had worked alongside named acts and made some life-long friends. Bazza was actually good friends with the American soul singer Edwin Starr and they had performed a version of Ben E King's *Stand By Me* together when I was in my teens (I loved it and I still have the footage today).

Bazza's father, Reg, who I called Grandad Copeman, had also been a singer in his day and performed around the local clubs most of his adult life. I had never seen him sing as I was too young but I had been told by elder family members that his voice was fabulous and he was quite the showman. Bazza said Grandad Copeman sang with live bands and he covered most of the well-known swing numbers that were popular in that era. He was renowned for having a big voice and his impersonation of Al Jolson belting out *Mammy* was one his favourite party tricks. Bazza recalled first getting up on stage with his dad when he was just nine years old. Singing was obviously in my blood. When I told Bazza about my career plan he decided that firstly I needed to get some 'live' experience.

'Jo you need to join me on a few of my gigs and there's no time like the present!'

This was ideal as he already had the PA equipment and knew where to get my backing tracks done. I was on my way. He had an old contact by the name of Mark Lewen who produced all of his tracks for him so he introduced me. A few months later I had printed out some lyrics and Bazza had given his honest opinion on my chosen songs. I was slowly getting a set list together. Mum was supportive but incredibly nervous about the prospect, as one would expect any sensible mother to be. However, she knew that once I had made a decision to do something, good or bad, little could be done to change my mind. She was also a believer in the 'whatever you choose to do, make sure you do it well' attitude. She was a dedicated grafter and if she said she was in, she was in. It was a case of, 'Are you sure about this singing thing? Right, well let's bloody well do it then!'

Bazza was enthusiastic, and I think a little proud, that I appeared to have singing in my Copeman blood. It was early 1996 and I was still working at the shipping company. I was being a little careful whilst making the transition in order to keep earning money. I was aware that there would need to be a definite crossover period financially. I expected to be able to secure some gigs over the following few months and leave my job by Christmas of that year. I was still 21 years old so I felt no need to panic timing wise.

***

'Hello love. Go upstairs, make yourself comfortable and pop your clothes on the stool. I'll be up in a minute. Tea?'

It was the summer of 1996 (not to be confused with the Summer of '69). Mark Lewen greeted me at the door of his house in the same daft way as he had done the last time and the time before that. Mark's house was a pretty detached place in Polesworth near Atherstone, which was an ideal location for me because Polesworth was a 10-minute drive away from where we lived. He stood at the door, bulging out of his little jodhpurs with a silly grin on his face.

'Yes please,' I replied, smiling at his wife Marlene as I passed her and trotted up the stairs.

I was at Mark's house to get some more backing tracks to add to my expanding repertoire. He had already produced many a 'strange and macabre arrangement' for me in his spare bedroom. I'd quickly noticed that the tracks all came complete with screaming backing vocals, huge guitar solos and fade out endings but in those days Bazza and I thought they sounded great.

Mark always answered the door in tight-fitting jodhpurs. I'm not even sure he had a horse but he did tell me that the tight jodhpurs helped him hit the high notes when laying down his backing vocals. His spare bedroom was decorated in a strange Cowboy and Indian theme with every country and western prop going. This should have started alarm bells ringing as Billy the Kid he was not. Mark was in his early fifties and fitted PVC windows for a living. His recording equipment was a little makeshift but it did the trick. He had a microphone stand of sorts, which comprised of a long bit of pipe, a coat hanger and an old microphone that was covered in a pair of tights. He used this to record what he liked to call his 'close harmonies'.

'Right love, here's your tea. I'll play you what I've got so far,' Mark said as he entered the room. I could hear Marlene talking to him from downstairs but he wasn't listening.

'Mark? Did you hear what I said? I'm talking about our Lisa's mate's mother, Michelle. She got four numbers and the bonus. What do you reckon she'll get for that? ... Mark I'm talking to you!' Mark took his headphones out of a drawer and smiled.

'I think Marlene's talking to you,' I said.

'Marlene talking? No!' He replied sarcastically.

'Well it's nice that she's still chatty,' I replied as I took a slurp of the very milky-tasting brew.

'Jo, I haven't spoken to Marlene in 18 months because I didn't want to interrupt her,' Mark said dryly. He switched the gear on and was just about to play my part-finished backing track when Marlene bustled into the room with a face like thunder.

'I'm going out, not that you listen to a fucking word I say,' she barked. She smiled at me, rolled her eyes at him and then she was gone.

'Bye Marlene!' I shouted as she went back down the stairs still chuntering about putting the lottery on.

'She still looks well and is full of energy Mark.'

He was still flicking switches and altering levels on his mixer. 'Yeah she's a good gal our Marlene. She's no show pony but she'll do to ride around the house.' I laughed even though I knew I shouldn't. He was such a chauvinist.

'Last weekend she asked what I thought of her outfit and I said that her arse and mammaries were still decent but that's about it. That's the downside with Marlene. She's got the body of *Baywatch* but the face of *Crimewatch* I'm afraid.' I laughed again.

He and Marlene had actually been married for over 25 years and were quite happy. Mark reminded me that this was due to the fact that he had been wearing his headphones for the last 15 years. He played me part of the track and promised to have it finished for the following week. This was exciting as I was due to join Bazza on a few of his pub gigs later that month.

Atherstone was my hometown and Bazza performed in many of the local pubs. Long Street in Atherstone was predominantly pubs and greasy cafés. There were far too many drinking establishments for Atherstone's small and odd population, although the residents did their best to drink regularly in all of them. This explained why the majority who lived there were fat, alcoholic or both. Atherstone didn't host any groups such as AA or Overeaters Anonymous. Why waste ground space on that self-help rubbish when you can squeeze in another take-away or alehouse? The only 12-step programme that these folk completed was the 12 steps it took them to waddle to the chippy or the nearest boozer. No pub singer would ever be out of work in Atherstone. It may have been a far cry from LA but it was a start.

My first gig with Bazza was late that same summer in a pub called The Clock. I was an absolute bag of nerves on the night and remember being so scared that my hands were shaking when I was trying to apply my eyeliner before we started. However I refused to let the nerves get the better of me and got up there. It didn't really help matters when a bloke called Jason, who worked at Mum's factory, shouted, 'Copeman get your tits out!' during a particularly nerve-racking rendition of Celine Dion's *Think Twice* (if I had thought twice, I'd have stayed at home). I swiftly downed four Bacardi and Cokes, continued performing (without getting my tits out) and got through my first booking. I'd also managed to do it cock-up free, which I was rather pleased about. I began performing with Bazza regularly and as the next few months passed I realised that most of the small pubs that Bazza and I performed in were like clones of one another. We were paid £80 per gig in those days, sometimes £100.

There were occasionally a few fights whilst we sang, some were brawl-free, but in the main they were all the same.

Bazza did not get involved in fights. Ever. If a fight broke out in ye olde public house, Bazza was gone. The term 'I'm a lover not a fighter' never applied to anyone more than it did to Bazza. He'd had many women during his life but he had never ever had a fight (he was in fact on wife number three at that point, having had numerous wenches in between). He used to say as far as women were concerned, he tried to cover most of the Warwickshire postcodes and his mate Woody would cover Leicestershire. I could rest assured that if a fight ever got under way on any booking, anywhere, Bazza could usually be found sneaking out of a well-hidden fire exit, hiding in the toilets or comforting the women. In his own words, he was always ready 'to split the scene and rescue the chicks!' The pubs could be a little rough and ready but on the upside I was approaching the grand old age of 22 that very October and my departure from 9am–5pm existence was only a few months away.

***

'For fuck's sake these sheets are like ice!' Robbo grumbled as he got into the freezing cold bed.

'It's not just the sheets, it's the whole room. We could rent this place out to those geezers that are into cryopreservation. Give that bloke who runs Alcor a bell and tell him we've got just the gaff for freezing dead bodies.' I said, whilst hesitantly waiting for Robbo to warm the bed up a bit.

'What are you on about you weirdo and who the buggery feck are Alcor?' Robbo asked.

'It's a company in California who freeze dead folk then bring them back to life. Well I think they have mastered the freezing bit but I'm not sure they have sorted the bringing them back to life part actually. Anyway, they freeze them to minus 196 degrees and I reckon it's colder than that in here,' I replied, through chattering teeth.

'Nothing will come back to life in this bedroom Jo. I'm investing in an electric blanket. Now stop fucking about and get in!' Robbo tossed and turned frantically trying to get warm.

Our bedroom was, without a doubt, the coldest bedroom I have ever encountered. It had an old, rotten bay window that simply was not fit for purpose and central heating made no difference. We had to really build ourselves up just to get into bed at night. Once we had thrown ourselves in bed we sounded like a couple that had an unfortunate case of Tourette syndrome for at least the first 20 minutes.

Let me describe my boyfriend Robbo. I just couldn't seem to do 'mundane' in anything and somehow always managed to have off-the-wall friends. I was always at the extreme end of the spectrum and I could forgive just about anything other than boring, predictable and dull. Even though I had not lived with Bazza, he had been around all of my formative years and he entertained from the moment he walked through the door. He had everyone in hysterics so I suppose it was not difficult to understand why I would be drawn to someone who would keep me constantly laughing and Robbo was simply hilarious. However when he was not being hilarious he could be very edgy. We both loved a drink; he with his lager, me with my vino. At this stage we were young and carefree so we had a ball.

It was around this time that Robbo and I made a plan. Firstly we had decided to move into our own place. Secondly, we had cleverly decided that Robbo should pack up work and arrange more performing engagements for me. We concluded that he would have to put his suit on, take his briefcase and visit venues in Birmingham to secure bookings. It was very similar to Rene managing Celine or Tommy Mottola running the day-to-day affairs of Mariah, only Robbo had no experience, no contacts, no money and an empty briefcase. Still, I think he did surprisingly well. It was now the spring of 1997 and I'd left my shipping job the previous December. Robbo and I had recently moved into a one-bedroom, ground floor flat in a big, old three-storey house that had been converted into three flats in Sutton Coldfield, Birmingham. He was 26 years old and I was 22 so we felt like it was the adult thing to do.

The very day we moved in three policemen met us near the front door. They seemed to be escorting a cowering creature, wrapped in a curtain, up the stairs. I was told by one of the coppers that it was the guy who lived on the third floor. Apparently, he had escaped from a local loony bin after trying to hang himself in the flat. We also had the pleasure of living below a dysfunctional, mentally unstable Irish family who resided on the second floor. Jeremy Kyle's guests looked like pillars of the community in comparison with this family. They would have struggled to remain sufficiently sober for their lie detector tests or their DNA results. There was also a huge Alsatian dog next door called Molly, who used to take great delight in terrifying us to within an inch of our lives whenever we tried to make it down the back garden path. It was a strange place.

In addition to Robbo visiting potential bookers, we each, in turn, spent one hour a night on the phone in that icy bedroom (it was the only place that had a phone point I'm afraid and at that time cordless phones were a luxury that were only owned by the upper class) and tried to secure work. One of us would do one hour on the phone whilst the other thawed out in the kitchen and vice versa. After three months we decided that perhaps Robbo should do a little bit of part-time work to keep us afloat, despite having done fairly well and establishing a solid little client base of around

20 venues that were independent of Bazza's. Robbo got a job at Magnet Kitchens through a friend and even though securing gigs wasn't an easy ride, not once did we consider that I should give up or return to 'real work'.

***

'Get him out!' John shouted over to two of the barmaids. 'Forget it, I'll do it! You lot get out... and you. Go on fuck off, we don't have any of that in here.'

It was a lie. They did have lots of that in there. I peered over at the bar area where John, the landlord, was systematically removing two blokes who were getting physical with a third man. Bazza and I had just finished *Every Breath You Take* so there was a quiet pause between tracks.

Hearing the break in music, John looked over in our direction and bellowed, 'Just keep singing! I don't pay you pair to stand gawping!'

Bazza turned to me and said, 'What do you reckon? *When The Going Gets Tough, the Tough Get Going?*'

'Yeah why not.' I queued up the track and the music began to play.

The Plough pub in Mancetter village was small compared to most, holding around 25 people. Bazza and I were performing at one of our regular Friday night bookings when a scuffle at the bar broke out. I had been performing on the pub circuit weekly for around six months by this point and The Plough stood out as being the smallest pub. In fact, the area where we had to perform was no bigger than somebody's lounge – we could hardly fit any of the PA equipment inside. We had to set it up in such a position that we blocked the front entrance and people could only get in from the back, which is also where they got thrown out. We were situated so that we were blocking the access to the toilets too so everybody had to walk right in front of us, whilst we were singing, whenever they needed a slash. We only had two little speakers, a mixer, an amp and a monitor but it was bloody tight.

John was a lecherous sod and always smacked my arse whenever he saw me. He thought he was paying the earth when he parted with his £80 at the end of the evening. There were always a few scraps occurring at The Plough but luckily they tended to be in the bar area not the lounge. The Plough was a little claustrophobic and all you could hope for was that nobody lobbed a pint all over your mixing desk or pissed on your extension leads. In those days our mixing desk was as big as a house. We only needed two channels (it was not as if we were playing with a live band) but it still looked like something you could land planes with. The content of our shows varied and the sets were mixed but there were rules as with any naff pub set. In those days it had to include *Simply The Best* and *Sweet Caroline* and if Bazza refused to sing *You'll Never Walk Alone* as an encore I doubt he would have left the building with his limbs intact.

***

'Right Joanne, the contract is signed. See you on the 1st and don't forget the suspenders you fine young filly! It will be a filthy affair,' Tim said with a beaming grin.

I tried to get back in the van before he could clip me on the arse but, as usual, he was too quick for me. Wheelrights garage in Long Street was a little car dealership full of unique characters. The most legendary of them all was one of the directors, a chap called Tim Smythe. He booked Bazza and I on many occasions to perform at what he liked to call his little 'forums'. These sordid affairs always turned out to be held in either The Black Horse or The Hat & Beaver, two of Atherstone's finest drinking establishments. His forums basically consisted of himself, Pete Lemming, the financial director, (Pete had a dodgy limp and dribbled a lot) and the rest of the dubious Wheelrights clan, getting absolutely paralytic until about 2am. They always had three or four reasonable looking women present who obviously did not work for them at the dealership. These ladies appeared to be 'contracted' to be there and many told me that the girls were hired for Pete and Tim's pleasure. Apparently the dribbling duo liked to receive a good whipping late on in the evening, après forum, when they retired to their room at The Chapel House Hotel.

Tim's bookings were always a laugh and he paid a decent fee in those days (my services were strictly limited to singing, although I never judged the other 'performers'). He always signed the contract with a silly comment stating he would pay an extra £20 if I sang *Black Velvet* in suspenders. Luckily he never double checked the suspender situation once I was in situ because he had his 'whipping girls' to take his mind elsewhere. Having had the pleasure of spending an evening in the company of dribbling Pete Lemming I knew that those girls earned every penny.

Tim was a great car salesman. He chatted to his punters about every subject matter under the sun, apart from purchasing a car. I think nearly everybody in Atherstone bought their vehicles from Tim and I always purchased my gigging vans from him. Sadly the last I heard, Tim had fleeced Wheelright's garage for thousands of pounds. The word on Long Street was that poor Timothy had suffered a nervous breakdown, endured a lengthy spell in a psychiatric unit and then started up again solo. I haven't seen him for a long time although there have been apparent sightings of him driving up and down Long Street. People say he now has a bewildered look on his face. Perhaps it's the medication.

***

'Ahh shit,' I gasped. 'I've left the backing track tape in the car. Will someone nip down and get it out of the cassette player?' Mum obliged and in no time she was back in the corridor of doom handing me my cassette. A door opened.

'Joanne Copeman please,' called the bored, young girl with her clipboard.

'Good luck Jo!' called Mum and Robbo in unison.

It was mid-summer of 1997 and I was auditioning for *Stars in Their Eyes*. As any auditionee knows, it is a long and lonely walk to an audition room and the sound of my heels on the tiled floor seemed unusually loud. Bored Clipboard Girl held the door open and in I went. At the top end of the room, positioned in the centre, was a Formica table with two men and one woman sat behind. In one corner of this extremely depressing and unwelcoming room sat an elderly man at an electric keyboard that looked for all the world as if he may actually have been asleep.

'Ok Joanne, I have you down as doing Alannah Myles on backing track. Your tape please.'

The woman at the desk held out her hand and I gave her my tape. She put it in the player, pressed play and all three faces looked up at me expectantly. You could literally have heard a pin drop and time seemed to stand still.

Then the most bizarre and ridiculous of things happened. As clear as a bell and loud enough to wake up the old geezer on the keyboards…

Peter Cook: … *I had the same bloody trouble about two nights ago. I come in, about half past eleven at night… I come in, I get into bed, you see, feeling quite sleepy. I could feel the lids of me eyes beginning to droop, you see – a bit of droop in the eyes. I was about to drop off when suddenly – tap, tap, tap at the bloody window pane. I looked out. You know who it was?*

Dudley Moore: *Who?*

Peter Cook: *Bloody Greta Garbo. Bloody Greta Garbo, stark naked save for a shortie nightie, hanging on to the window sill and I could see her knuckles all white, saying 'Peter, Peter'. You know how those bloody Swedes go on…*

'Eh? No, that's not right,' I stammered. 'Switch it over, it must be on the other side.'

I knew of course it wasn't but panic was welling. Where the fuck was *Black Velvet* and why were we all listening to Peter Cook and Dudley Moore? I must have entered some sort of parallel universe.

The woman looked at me sympathetically. 'No problem I'll pop it in on the other side.' She glared disapprovingly at the man on her left who was shamelessly laughing at the Pete and Dud sketch.

Peter Cook: *Now, Mr Spiggott, you are, I believe, auditioning for the part of Tarzan.*

Dudley Moore: *Right.*
Peter Cook: *Now, Mr. Spiggott, I couldn't help noticing almost at once that you are a one-legged person.*
Dudley Moore: *You noticed that?*
Peter Cook: *I noticed that, Mr Spiggott… you, a one-legged man, are applying for the role of Tarzan – a role which, traditionally, involves the use of a two-legged actor.*
Dudley Moore: *Correct.*
Peter Cook: *And yet you, a unidexter, are applying for the role.*
Dudley Moore: *Right.*
Peter Cook: *A role for which two legs would seem to be the minimum requirement.*
Dudley Moore: *Very true.*
Peter Cook: *Well, Mr. Spiggott, need I point out to you where your deficiency lies as regards landing the role?*
Dudley Moore: *Yes, I think you ought to.*
Peter Cook: *Need I say without overmuch emphasis that it is in the leg division that you are deficient.*
Dudley Moore: *The leg division?*
Peter Cook: *Yes, the leg division, Mr. Spiggott. You are deficient in it to the tune of one.*

The woman stopped the tape and I simply stood there bewildered. She could have stopped it sooner for fuck's sake. I noticed both men seated either side of her were trying desperately not to laugh. I felt nauseous as the reality of what had happened dawned on me. We had driven to Robbo's parents' house a few hours earlier, left my mums car there and jumped in Robbo's car, as he knew his way around Birmingham. I had left my backing track in my mum's car when we had swapped vehicles. The tape I had given them was Robbo's *The Best of Peter Cook and Dudley Moore* from his car. I stared at the three faces behind the desk.

At that point, even the woman was laughing. 'Ok Joanne. I am not sure what has happened here. That is the best thing I have listened to today (suppressed chuckle) but it is not *Black Velvet*. Do you have any sheet music as back up? It's always a good idea you know.' I could see the mens' shoulders shaking and knew they were struggling. I didn't trust myself to speak so I just shook my head like some retarded idiot. I left the room and stomped down the corridor of doom, red faced.

As I passed Robbo and Mum on the plastic chairs I heard Robbo say sarcastically, 'That went well then.' I didn't stop.

'Oh Joanne, you have left Peter Cook and Dudley Moore!' shouted Bored Clipboard Girl from the top of the corridor.

As astute as ever, Robbo immediately realised what had happened and went back up the corridor towards Bored Clipboard Girl. 'Thanks,

Pete and Dud are sheer class. Was it the one about the one-legged man? That one kills me...'

'ROBBO!' I shouted, banging through the exit swing doors.

Arsehole of the day, however, was most definitely me so off I went home, with no hope of walking through those smoky double doors or meeting Matthew Kelly.

***

It would be sinful if I did not talk briefly about agents. I often worked for a slightly crazy agent called Geoff Laird in the early days. I probably worked for him on a monthly basis over a 12-month period and that was more than enough as he was difficult to deal with. He was a temperamental old bloke with a huge beard. Other than giving me work, the only way Geoff helped was to make me very choosy about who I worked for in the future. He really was a controlling nightmare. Some of his bookings were nearly as bad as his attitude. The last engagement Geoff ever secured for me was one that I'll never forget. It was for a 'venue' in Huntingdon in Cambridgeshire. I had been booked (through Geoff) by a little agency called Crystal Entertainments to do a solo gig in a nasty joint called The Truck Stop. It didn't sound much cop as venues go, but I was assured that it was a popular night and all the truckers bought their wives along for an evening out. I was told that they were actually a friendly crowd.

I persuaded a very reluctant Robbo to load up our knackered old white Ford Escort Van and off we went. At this point can I ask that you don't pity us, we also had a second family car – a Nissan Micra. It only had first and fourth gear, second and third had long gone, and could be heard screaming around the roundabouts in first gear then rumbling down the road in fourth. It also had a nice 'shit brown' coloured plastic interior. Still, I couldn't have complained, we bought it for £50 and it lasted six months. I have spent more than that on a pair of trainers. Robbo was working full time for Magnet Kitchens during this dodgy stage in my singing career. By this point he was getting slightly pissed off with driving up and down the A14 (well all over the country in fact) and for some reason many of my gigs in the early days seemed to be in East Anglia.

I must admit the A14 was a drag and always really foggy (even in the height of summer). It was the A road equivalent to the Bermuda triangle. I'm quite sure that acts would often load up and set off down the A14 on a misty Saturday night and never return. I continuously told Robbo that he must suffer for my career but I felt that was wearing thin.

The A14 seemed longer and foggier than ever on that particular night. When we finally arrived The Truck Stop looked totally horrid and the aroma of fried food and fags filled our nostrils. We hesitantly started to unload some of the gear from the van. Whilst lugging a bass bin up the stairs, I spotted a poster on the grubby wall advertising the evening's entertainment. It read:

Tuesday at The Truck Inn
Park Up
Eat Up
Watch the Football
See the Girl Reveal All
Come Along and Have a Ball!

'What the fuck does that mean?' Robbo asked, quickly turning a funny shade of green.

'I don't know but I'm revealing nowt. We better ask somebody,' I replied, hoping there was a perfectly reasonable explanation. It was indeed Tuesday, I noticed that the posters were everywhere and the sweaty, greasy drivers were all beginning to come inside. We briskly walked over to a blonde-haired woman standing behind a kiosk near the entrance.

'Excuse me? Can I just confirm that you have booked a singer for tonight? I'm the entertainment and I'm a little concerned about those posters on the wall. They appear to be advertising a stripper.'

The woman looked up at me and seemed a little sheepish. 'Oh hello love. You must be Joanne. My name is Jan and I usually organise the bookings. There's been a bit of a fuck up, excuse my French!' She laughed nervously. I didn't laugh at all. 'I've been on holiday and one of our young gals was running the diary. She's messed up the advertising in relation to the rotas. The stripper is on next week but advertised this week. I didn't know until I came back in this morning,' she said, glancing at me then Robbo with a worried look on her face.

'Ah that's a shame because there are loads of hefty drivers coming in expecting some bird to get their kit off and I've had a wasted journey along the A14. I take it that's why there is not one single trucker's wife in sight?' I replied abruptly.

'Let's just get the stuff back in the van and do one Jo,' Robbo cut in, with his eyes still fixed on the entrance. To our horror, more of the hairy creatures were making their way in.

'Joanne could you just explain the situation to them over the microphone and say I've made a mistake? We still need some entertainment and you're already here now. Please?' Jan pleaded. She was panicking.

'Jan I'm sorry but I'm not about to announce to 150 fat, egg-stained vests, 'the stripper isn't coming but don't worry lads, I'll sing you a few Whitney Houston power ballads instead!''

Jan looked defeated. 'But what will I do?'

Robbo was obviously having visions of his balls being wedged between two slices of thick-cut white bread as punishment for taking their stripper away and was getting fidgety. 'I don't know Jan but I know what I'm doing. Sorry but we're off.'

We quickly loaded the speakers back into the van and crawled off back down the foggy A14. We'd got a sweat on whilst making our get away and the van was backfiring beautifully. The atmosphere in the van was not good. Robbo was thoroughly pissed off and I was £120 light. Needless to say I had a few choice words for Crystal Entertainments the following morning. I told them they were getting 15% of sweet feck all. I was annoyed but I chose to leave Geoff Laird and his unruly beard alone. I saw no point in berating the irrational, wonky sod. I simply made a mental note to never work for the crazy man again.

***

'Jo there will always be a need for spuds. They're one of life's basic necessities. Everything you need is in the potato and everything you want is in the pint,' Steph said smugly as if she had just stumbled upon the key to a happy and carefree existence.

'I agree me old mucka but do you not think that the retail outlets of the 21st century could possibly have the spud market sewn up? And whilst we're at it Stephanie, I think you need to introduce something else into your own diet other than crisps and pints of Carling.'

Steph was busily jotting down her potato round route on the back of an envelope, whilst ignoring my negativity. 'Ah yes, then there's crisps! How hard can it be to slice a few spuds up and fry them? I could market my homemade crisps like that farm shop up the road. They take the piss on their crisps at 70p a packet!' I looked at her in bewilderment but she lost no enthusiasm. 'Right lets go down the pub and discuss my business plan. I may need a bank loan for a spud truck.'

My chosen career path may have been proving a little bumpier than I originally anticipated in terms of climbing up the ladder and moving away from pub venues. The transition was proving slow but I had vowed to stick with it. It was now the winter of 1997 and the year was drawing to a close. I had been singing in pubs for nearly 18 months, which, in my opinion, was long enough. I felt I'd completed my 'bootcamp' style live training period and was beginning to think about performing in better venues.

In the meantime, my best mate Steph had come up with her own revolutionary career plan in the form of a potato round. She claimed that eventually she would be a renowned female entrepreneur and make a small fortune. She was fed up at Triton Showers and had been complaining that the hours didn't suit her for sometime. She said she found the hours to be very unsociable but I knew that this simply meant she resented having to turn up on Monday mornings with a hangover. Apparently she had thought long and hard about it and decided that a potato round was the way forward. She was confident that after a year or two she would make Sir Alan Sugar look like a very small businessman (which is actually true, if describing his physical form). All of this was coming from a woman who thought our general election was an annual thing, that Reagan was still president of the USA and when asked during a quiz to name two wonders of the world, she looked slightly blank, then gave 'gas and electricity' as her answer (she was absolutely not joking).

Steph was indeed a gem. We had been best friends since we met at college when we were 17 years old and she had been as mad as a box of frogs from the very first day that I clapped eyes on her. We were invited to a wedding once and we both received a written invitation. Steph read hers and immediately called me. She said she didn't understand what was 'suspicious' about the occasion. I asked her what she was wittering on about and read mine to her. 'We would be delighted to invite you to this auspicious occasion.' Auspicious not suspicious! I then explained what the word 'auspicious' meant. Once I had explained the situation she simply said, 'Good. I didn't think it was a great start to a marriage if the bride and groom were suspicious of each other before they'd even got hitched.' Classic Stephanie.

Now I have to say that around this time her behaviour was becoming more and more bizarre. She amused the life out of me but I was beginning to notice that she was not in the sanest of minds. She had always been a bit of a party girl (myself included) but now she was, how can I put it? She was sort of 'missing weekends' to the extent that she would go out on Friday night and not recollect a thing until she woke up in her bed on Monday afternoon (hence the career change). Picture George Best on a particularly heavy bender and you'll get the idea. Rather than address her drinking and make it out of bed on a Monday morning, she decided to stay in bed and get her new venture off the ground so she could work afternoons. When she set her mind on something, little could be done to change it. What can one do when one's bestest chum has decided to knock on people's doors flogging vegetables for a living?

I have to say that she has always had a special bond with vegetables and loves nothing more than a good vegetable patch. She had her own little veggie patch and it did seem to stimulate her. I was told living off the land was often challenging and she called me numerous times to tell me about the perils of 'growing your own'. She visited me absolutely distraught one evening because a big insect was roaming the patch during the night and eating her runner beans. I hadn't known her to be that upset since The Backstreet Boys split up. I told her to focus on the positives, such as the quality of her onions, but she's hard to talk around once she gets emotional. Anyway, I had my own uncertain career to take care of so I couldn't spend too much time worrying about my bubbly, although slightly erratic, Stephanie.

Grandad Copeman singing at 'The Chase' in Chapel End, Nuneaton, in the early 1950s

Mum looking pretty in pink!

CHAPTER TWO

RAISING THE GAME

I had performed in so many pubs during 1996 and 1997, not just local but all over the place. Some gigs were with Bazza but many of them were solo. I had told my old shipping employers a few years prior that I was off to pastures new but not to worry, they could catch me on MTV. It was around the Christmas of 1997 that I realised I was still some way off MTV and LA. I was also aware that money was tight. We simply could not live on my pub gigs and Magnet Kitchens wages alone. Things had to change.

'I need to see you immediately, if not sooner,' I said to Bazza authoritatively. 'I feel this is something we need to discuss in person not over the phone.' I didn't need to explain that it was nothing of a medical nature. Bazza could tell by the urgency in my voice that it was far more important than that and therefore must relate to singing.

'I'll be over in 30 minutes. Get the kettle on,' he keenly replied.

After our lengthy crisis talk Bazza and I had bravely decided to make the giant leap, working both together and alone, into what could loosely be considered one step up from the bowels of hell… social clubs. That was where the real money was.

I decided I should buy new PA equipment, new backing tracks, new costumes, improved promotional material and a slightly more sophisticated set (note I use the word 'slightly'). I first had to beg and plead with Jodhpur Man (who had started calling himself The Anal Intruder) to produce backing tracks that actually had a performance ending and did not contain layer upon layer of screeching backing vocals. Bazza came with me and it really was a hard slog. Bazza and I had said many times that if we had anybody else local to us that could custom produce backing tracks we would burn Mark Lewen's house down with him in it.

Every time we entered that little bedroom, we knew exactly what was coming and this occasion would be no different. Jodhpur Man would tell us that he had been up all night because it was a really 'complex arrangement'. He would have said the very same thing if it was a version of *Jingle Bells*, he was just trying to put the prices up to £30. The performance endings consisted of a great big random thud at the end of the looped chorus and the backing vocals were cut down to 40 double-stacked layers of him squealing as opposed to 80. He would not be told when it came to instrumentals in a track either. We told him time and time again to keep the instrumentals down to an absolute minimum because we were standing on stage alone. We didn't have the luxury of a live band to bounce off so we looked complete tits standing there with nothing to do during a two-minute instrumental. Would he listen? Would he feck.

Bazza had decided to try once more. He cleared his throat. 'Mark listen to me. Please try to picture this scenario. The club has closed, the bar staff have calculated the takings for the night, the lights have gone down, the last punter has left the building and they are locking up, but I am still only half way through *Three Times a Lady* because you have put a marathon instrumental in the backing track. Not ideal is it? The last one you gave me, which was *Stuck On You*, was longer than an extended version of *Bohemian Rhapsody*! If the standard version is good enough for Lionel Richie, it's good enough for me. Please try to understand.'

Bazza was exasperated as he looked out of Mark's bedroom window. He then turned around, looked at Mark and said, 'Jo, how long has he had those fucking headphones on?'

I smiled. 'He popped them on as soon as you started talking.'

Next on the agenda was a trip to performer's paradise, a retail outlet by the name of Sound Academy. I had Mum on board with just about everything at this stage. Mum and Bazza's companionship was helpful because she was now heavily involved in every aspect of my career, from clothes to contracts. Initially she started to get more involved to support me but I could tell that she was actually beginning to enjoy it. She was the director of an engineering company in Atherstone at that stage but she had already reduced her hours (this was actually down to the fact that she had gotten herself a golden retriever puppy and had nothing to do with my singing). She had made it clear that she was keen to retire nice and early as she had been there for 30 years. As far as my own career was concerned, Mum was a great assistant; in fact she was turning out to be a perfect partner.

Updating our gear basically meant that we needed to trade in my existing PA equipment and generally get really confused about new PA equipment. Out with the old and in with the new. I eventually ended up with a nice little Logic system plus the big bloody 'lead bags' full of jacks and XLR's that had to be continuously lugged about. The lead bag was ruthless. We spent what seemed like an eternity, après gigs, at about 1am, coiling the leads up perfectly, only to find the next day that the contents of the whole bag looked like a tin of Heinz spaghetti. It was brutal and if we were pushed for time it could actually bring tears to my eyes. The overnight goings on in the lead bag has always remained a mystery. Cassettes and even CDs were long since a thing of the past – everybody was on MiniDisk now. I could even set up this new PA equipment myself if I had to, although I couldn't haul it around on my own unless I started taking copious amounts of steroids and grew a beard. I usually relied on Bazza or Robbo for the real heavy lifting. Failing that, venue staff would always help to 'get me in' although they didn't give a shite when it came to 'getting me out'.

Agents managed to find me a lot of work in many of the large social clubs. Call them what you will, working men's clubs, ex-service men's clubs, trade and labour clubs, allotment clubs (what's that all about? I never saw a cabbage the whole time I sang in them… apart from a few in the audience), Conservative, Liberal or community clubs. They all fell under the social club umbrella. They all had pictures of Queen Elizabeth II and their relevant political leaders placed all over the furry, dated walls. The clubs were completely archaic and scattered far and wide.

There was a particular agent called Jim O'Donnell Entertainments who had got most of the large Birmingham social clubs tied up. I had noticed over the years that most agents liked to call themselves International Entertainment Consultancies and other fancy names. Jim O'Donnell had something similar printed on his flimsy business cards although I know for a fact that he didn't supply anything internationally – he never went further than Dudley. As with many small agencies Jim worked from 'home', he was another one that worked from his bedroom.

There was a definite process. First, singers had to send him a demo and a picture. If he liked what he heard (or more importantly what he saw), he would rope us into visiting him at his home where he would tell us that he had a present for us (not while I had an ounce of strength he didn't) and he'd say that he kept our poster above his bed. (After speaking to both male and female artists that worked for Jim, I can confirm that this process was only ever followed for the female singers so the boys missed out). He would then show us his pet rabbits, which he kept in the spare room, make us endure his painful rendition of *Wind Beneath My Wings* and a few Alf Garnett impressions and then, hey presto, we were in.

Once the little induction was over he started to give me bookings in the big Birmingham social clubs. Acts had to provide a fair few posters for the large social clubs. Elan Hills Studio was the place to go for promotional pictures – well it was if you wanted to get loads of shots with your head always tilting strangely to the left and a Dynasty Krystle Carrington soft focus over every shot. I didn't know at the time but I soon realised that everybody's promo shot seemed to look like that in those days. I looked like an extra from Dallas who wore too much slap and had a neck disorder. Elan Hills must have been earning a fortune until we all realised that we looked like heavily made-up whiplash victims.

I developed good relationships with agents very quickly and was performing in most of the large social clubs across the country. The clubs paid fairly well compared with pubs and regular work was always available. I performed the standard 2 x 45-minute spots, obviously fitting in around Bingo, The Meat Raffle, Open the Box and Play Your Cards Right (any act who's done the rounds on the club circuit will remember these rituals affectionately). If we made a noise any louder than a sigh during the bingo, we would be shot and if we accused anyone of any funny business during Open The Box we would have had our heads removed. Talk about focused. Have you ever seen 300 social club members playing bingo? They are ferocious with their big dobby pen thingies. I would prefer to have a dispute with a 12-foot grizzly bear or tell Peter Sutcliffe face-to-face that what he did to those 13 women was just not on rather than question Joan from Tysley Ex-serviceman's Club when she shouted, 'House!'

Some of them used to have reams and reams of tickets to mark for one game. For saying most of them couldn't read, write or string a sentence together, they were red hot on the bingo. I remember asking one bloke called Cliff, who one evening had around eight tickets to mark, how he kept up because the numbers seemed to come out so fast.

'That's nowt kid, I usually turn 'em upside down to give me sen a challenge.'

I was often tempted to get a really loud ringtone on my mobile, something like *Firestarter*, then get someone to ring it during the precious bingo session. Once I answered it, I dreamt of arguing with the person on the other end at high volume, then just when the 'bingo bunch' were about to totally lose it with me, I would go over to one of them and say, 'Excuse me can I just borrow a pen?' I would then take one of their bingo dobbing pens as if I needed to jot down a phone number. At this point in my little imaginary scenario, I would apologise for the interruption, put my phone away, give back the pen and tell them to resume bingo. Just as the next number was about to be called, I would open a bag of pork scratchings, noisily rustling and crunching with gay abandon. To complete my delightful dream, I would then pretend to be marking a bingo card myself. Half way through, just as somebody was nearing the climax of a full house I would shout, 'Can you give me the last couple of numbers again please, I needed to send my mate a quick text and I didn't catch them!' Obviously it could only remain a dream because I actually wanted to live.

As depressing as the social clubs were, I was earning regularly. Robbo was still travelling all over the place with me at weekends and I still performed with Bazza whenever I could. Bazza and I often still performed as a double act and were called One & One – I know, I know. At one point we won Coventry Duo of the Year; not exactly a Brit Award but it cheered us up. When we were hanging around in the club dressing rooms, where many acts put their contact details and posters on the wall, we often noticed that our posters had been somewhat defaced. It soon became apparent that this was a popular pastime for acts waiting to go on stage. I noticed on one of our posters Blu-tacked onto a dressing room wall that I had grown a big, bushy moustache and Bazza had formed a pair of breasts on his forehead. Bazza was of the opinion that if you can't beat them join them, so from then on we made it a regular pastime to deface the posters of our cruel competitors whilst waiting for the fat, pissed entertainment secretary to introduce us on stage.

Social clubs were in their own world. Most of the changing rooms in these clubs were filled with broken, plastic orange chairs, old vacuum cleaners, a moose head and mop buckets. The orange chairs were always stacked on top of each other, about eight feet high and could not be separated. It would have been easier to surgically separate Siamese twins than to remove just one chair and, trust me, I have really tried (the chairs, not the twins). If I tried to pull one from the stack, the lot would lift up with it. I would just consider myself lucky that I didn't have to get changed in the disabled toilets or the committee room. Having said that, at least in the disabled loos there was always a toilet. There were so many times that I was sent off to a dressing room or to the committee room to change, only to find that the other act had ran over their time slot or there was some sort of delay.

This was the familiar scenario that we acts experienced; the warm glass of Liebfraumilch or Blue Nun that we had sipped at earlier had now travelled through our system and a trip to the ladies was in order, only the ladies loos were at the other end of the building. We were not supposed to be seen wandering through the audience in costume and it would have been too late anyway because we were due to go on stage at any given minute. In this situation, if the 45-minute spot seemed too long, acts had three options for relief (providing the changing room had a lock that actually worked, which was a rarity); a small sink (in some places), the half-pint glass that had contained the warm, vile wine or a metal mop bucket. Wetting one's self on stage was never an option for me.

***

'Now ladies and gents for tonight's turn...' Entertainment secretaries were (and always will be) a different breed. The majority of them carried a huge bunch of keys attached to their belts (just to show you that they had the power to lock and unlock every door in the club if they wanted to... or indeed every lock in the world), a mobile phone that nobody but their wives rang them on and a look of self-importance that would have put Adolf Hitler to shame. They would tell us how important their Tuesday evening committee meetings were whilst they gulped down a pint of bitter and nibbled on a bag of genetically modified pork scratchings. Did you not know that 'The Committee' in Smethwick Working Mens Club was more important than the G8?

If all went to plan, they would make sure we knew when to have our gear set up by, our times on and off stage and call for us about five minutes before our spot. Many of them were sober until around 9pm and then proceeded to get pissed out of their tiny minds until midnight. They just about managed to introduce the acts through their muffled mics and always (and I mean 99.9% of the time) got the act's name wrong. They may have got it right if your stage name was 'Bill'. They actually came and asked Bazza and I, pen and paper in hand, how we wanted to be introduced. We told them to introduce us as One & One.

'Ok, One Plus One.'

'No, One & One.'

'Right got it,' they replied. Then off they went on stage and said over the microphone something like, 'Ladies and gentlemen, please welcome One and the Other One!'

A place I will never, ever forget was a club called Kingstanding Ex-serviceman's Club in Birmingham. I performed there once a month for around four years. The entertainment secretary there was a little Irish man called Andy Comerford. Andy was about five feet tall and must have only weighed around seven stone. Saturday nights were important for him and he always wore his little brown suit and tie. He was in his mid-sixties but looked about 109 years old.

'You see Jo bab, I can't possibly give you £130 'cus the old club, she ain't doin' well at the minute. You know I would if I could don't you?'

he mumbled as he chain-smoked his way through one of his 30-a-day roll-ups. 'Be back with you in a minute bab, just gonna sort out where this new Jukebox and these bandits are going.'

I shook my head. 'Yeah, really hard up,' I muttered to myself as I jumped out of the way of a couple of big blokes in vests who were wheeling in the new machines.

Andy had stuck to this same line for four years. On this particular Saturday night, he was really milking it. He should have been the buyer for a multinational corporation, the clever old sod, because he would always finish off any negotiation with, 'I bloody hate this job, I do honestly. I don't mind telling you bab, I'm resigning at the end of this month.' He also said that for four years.

Andy never got off his scrawny arse to introduce the acts, he just sat on any random table, on the right-hand side of the stage where he had a clear view of the door, the stage, the bar and every bastard thing. Andy did hot-desking before it was even thought of by corporate management. Being such a tiny specimen, he got where water couldn't get. He was a tight little creature. He did a great job of looking at his watch at the beginning and end of every 45-minute set to make sure we hadn't short changed them. He was always pissed and telling foul jokes by 10pm. Any reference to genitalia after 10.30pm amused the life out of him.

'Me Mam's only come tonight because you're on you know. Her bleeding foots been playing her up like buggery again, she ain't been able to get about all week but she's hobbled down here to see you again. You better sing *Wind Beneath My Wings* for me Mam.' Dawn said as I arrived back at my seat.

'No problem Dawn,' I dutifully responded.

The audience in this club was an absolute cracker. I had never witnessed a funnier crowd in any other club. There were so many dysfunctional characters in one room you would have thought that they had been created for a sitcom. The club was situated on a rough council estate in Kingstanding, Birmingham. We had to get the PA gear in through a side entrance and cart it down a corridor that seemed a mile long. The security had to be tight there so the doors of this entrance were kept firmly locked. This was not achieved by some fancy locking system but by balancing two metal chair legs in the grey bars of the fire exit door. The security man on the desk of the main front entrance looked dead (I don't think anyone ever actually checked for a pulse). He never uttered a word in all the time I performed there. He was a complete mute. As he saw us approach, he would just raise one hand to the buzzer, still staring straight ahead and the door would open.

I knew all the little cliqués in that club, where they sat and their names. They fell out with each other every other week. I would get there at 6pm, get the gear in and get set up for around 7pm. At 7.30pm they started coming in; each group had their own specific time of arrival and I knew every one of them by the second. They had their own seats and god help anyone that tried to pinch them. Most of the regulars and their relatives were on the way to, had just got out of, or were actually in the nick. I was convinced at least a third of the room was electronically tagged.

Dawn and her mother Joan always arrived first. They sometimes had a man called Les with them but most weeks they would have an issue with him and make him sit on his own on the other side of the room. He was often out of favour. If you asked him why they had fallen out with him again he would look confused and shrug his shoulders. Dawn was a thickset don't-mess-with-me type of woman who always wore blue t-shirts and had dark, curly hair. Her mother Joan always had a bad foot and came equipped with loads of sandwiches wrapped in foil. She had a very pale blue rinse and glasses. Joan always packed Robbo some sandwiches to eat on the way home. Dawn could be slightly hostile if ruffled. They sat on the right-hand side of the stage.

'Hello Joanne bab, I hope you've packed them ciggies up with a voice like that. You promised us last time,' John said as he wagged a finger in my face. 'The wife's brought you some bread sauce in foil.'

Margaret and John always arrived a few minutes after Dawn and her mother. They would pride themselves on being the best dressed in the club. Margaret had blonde hair (the tongued and set look) and wore little black trouser suits and gold jewellery. Her husband John was a tall Geordie fella with glasses. Margaret only ever talked about bread sauce recipes and her dog. They sat in the middle of the room and had pride of place near the bar. At 8.15pm Reg, Tracy and Tracy's mother came in with their lad Paul. Tracy steamed over to where I sat as soon as she saw me with her husband Reg in tow.

'Where you bloody been? We've missed you. Our Alesha has done nothing but play your bleeding tape all week ain't she Reg? She's sent you this card. Bastard Comerford and the committee still won't let her in yet, they say she's under age and I've got to bring her passport. Well they can shove it up their arses can't they Reg?'

She then got her little black diary out and made sure she had all my future dates logged in it. This family was an absolute beauty. Tracy was always bright orange (even in December, which led me to think something fishy was going on in the tanning department). She usually wore fluorescent polyester dresses that were lime green and lemon –

the offensive, tight, short, clingy ones. She would never be in danger of getting run over whilst walking home, not in those Hi-Vis frocks. She was in her early forties, wore glasses and carried a fair bit of weight. She wore white stiletto shoes and had as many gold sovereign rings as she could squeeze onto her little fat fingers. She also sported ankle chains with charms hanging off them that dangled clumsily around her chunky orange ankles. To be honest, before bright orange tans and bling became a favourite of WAGs, Tracy already had it going on (apart from false nails, she bit hers).

Tracy only ever spoke out of one side of her mouth. When she was talking to me it always seemed like she was telling me a secret. Reg was 70, nearly 30 years older than Tracy. He actually looked well for his age. He would often smack her on her wobbly arse and say, 'It's this that keeps me young!' Reg was very small and balding with glasses. He got pissed after about two pints and wouldn't leave me alone. This Saturday night would be no different.

Alesha, their youngest, was not allowed in the club so always waited outside for to me finish then jumped up and down squealing like she'd just seen Madonna. Tracy and Reg used to give me greetings cards at Easter and Christmas. They had asked Robbo when my birthday was so that they could celebrate too. They used to take photographs of me and get them developed to show me on the next gig. They seriously didn't miss a trick. Robbo always called them 'the stalkers' and they definitely had potential. They sat on the left-hand side of the stage.

Dawn and Joan didn't get on with Tracy, Reg and co. Dawn said they were all septic. She used to call them 'the septics' and said sliming around the acts was disgusting. I thought it was just me but Dawn said they also stalked a duo called Flash. I had felt special for a while and didn't know Flash were getting similar treatment.

Another class act that used to arrive at about 8.30pm was an odd little man and wife duo, both in their fifties, who met each other at an epilepsy support group. He was bald on top but had long, dark flowing locks at the back. He used to wear black trousers and shiny black boots and he had a huge set of spurs attached to the boots. These impressive spurs had silver wheels that spun round and everything. All of his fingernails were bitten apart from the little fingernail on his left hand that was really long and I never knew why. She looked like something from The Addams Family. She had long, black poker-straight hair that parted down the middle and wore floral blouses with lacy white collars. She had an odd way of looking at people. She would look under her eyes with her head tilted to one side. Not in an attractive or beseeching way like Princess Diana, more like a gloomy Eeyore from *Winnie-the-Pooh*.

When Robbo and I first saw them we thought he was some sort of wife beater. It looked as if they were having a little fight whilst sitting at their table. She was wriggling and squirming about in her seat, kicking him and he was grabbing her wrists and trying to slap her. It was most distracting. I asked Dawn what it was all about and she said they did it all the time. Apparently the woman had epileptic fits and he had to restrain her. Dawn said they often had these outbursts at the club. She said if they ever both had a funny turn at the same time we would all be in trouble. The epileptic duo told me they were very much in love and he had bought her a ring. She said he was a great husband and 'changed her' often, as she didn't have much bladder control. They sat smack bang in the middle of the room and there was always lots of smacking and banging going on.

There was an old guy that always came in late called Fred. He reeked a bit and wore a cap and a long mac. He was generally pissed by the time he got there and, without fail, used to get his grubby kit off every time I sang *Hot Stuff*. He danced around the stage area, removing layer after dirty layer. It took him forever to get down to the nitty gritty because of his age and level of alcohol consumption. Right at the very end of the song he would just stand there in his pants. He thought it was great, especially if he'd timed it right. It used to take him the entire duration of the next two songs to find his clothes and put them back on again. He would sit on the edge of the stage while I was singing, putting his vest back on and trying to do his shoelaces up. One night during *Hot Stuff* a couple of blokes told him to 'Fucking sit down!' He replied in a slurry fashion, 'You can fuck off. You can't dance and you can't even dance!' That made Robbo laugh out loud.

So there you have it. That was Kingstanding Ex-Serviceman's Club at about 10.30pm on a typical Saturday night. There was Dawn and Joan singing along to *Wind Beneath My Wings* whilst nibbling ham salad sandwiches and slagging off the septics; some bloke wandering around selling pink copies of the Sports Argos and some cockles; Tracy and Reg feeling each other's arses whilst smooching to *The Power of Love*; Andy Comerford telling his foul jokes; the epileptics lovingly restraining each other; a few blokes having a scrap near the door; Margaret telling a table of four women something regarding 'bread sauce' whilst John supped an extra pint at the bar before she came back and Fred, the stripper on a budget, giving it some serious rhythm to *Hot Stuff* in his dirty old y-fronts with the pea green trim. At the end of the night, the whole club were on the dance floor, sweating like pigs and strutting about to *Simply The Best*.

As did many acts, I used to have a CD that I sold at gigs for a fiver. I remember an elderly couple called Patrick and Maude at a gig in a club in Nuneaton. I was amazed when, during the break after my first spot, they asked me over to their table and said they wanted to buy a CD (usually club crowds wouldn't part with their money until the end of the night and then the buggers would try and haggle). These two sweet little oldies were ready to pay full price. They were both easily in their 80s and Patrick was wheelchair-bound. I noticed that they were both drinking that horrible looking diluted orange squash, the stuff that cost around 14p for a half, and Maude had three packets of Walkers crisps poking out the top of her handbag. She said she wasn't paying the club's prices for crisps, she could get them cheaper as multipacks in Supercigs. After some brief chitchat, she gave me £5 and took the CD. She asked me how long until my last spot and I told her I had about another 15 minutes of my break left.

She then delivered a pearler. She took some nail clippers and nail files from her bag and asked if I would mind cutting and filing Patrick's nails! She informed me that his hands were badly withered, his fingers were crooked and, with her poor vision, she was likely to take his fingers off entirely. She said she needed a young person with decent eyesight. The first time someone actually asked to buy my CD I had to include a free over-70s manicure. Well what could I do? She was right, Patrick's hands were withered and crooked. It was horrendous; I didn't know where to start. Robbo didn't know whether to laugh or be sick so he went and played a game of pool to get out of the way. It really wasn't how I wanted to spend my break time but I did what I could. At the end of the night, Robbo said we better get out of there quick before Patrick got his socks off and asked me to tidy up his toes. Social clubs were great for keeping entertainers grounded but they were not for the faint hearted and a sense of humour was essential.

A great way (or so we were informed) to get better gigs was to take part in showcases. Now I have to say that there were good and bad. Further on into my career I started to sniff out the real stinkers but in those days I fell into ye olde showcase trap. Club showcases really were dire. The aim for the venues was to fill the room and take money over the bar (they used to let anybody in) and the aim for agents was to all meet up and get pissed. The agents would sit around nibbling on dry roasted peanuts, laughing, yauping and swilling bitter while the acts tried their best to sing over the noise. Even later on in my career when performing at 'proper' showcases, I learned that bookers used it more as a jolly, a chance to meet up, stay overnight and practice a few rounds of golf. At these showcases, however, there was no chance the general public could attend. Oh no, these were serious agents. They would begin the evening trying to look professional, akin to a panel of judges from *The X Factor* but they too turned into red-faced arseholes after a few pints.

CHAPTER THREE

A RECORD DEAL

Whilst I was still performing in some of the large social clubs, by 1999 I was moving along nicely towards cabaret venues. I had gained a good reputation on the circuit and the small social clubs were becoming a thing of the past. This was mainly due to showcases (the decent ones) and the good working relationships that I had built up with agents over those past few years. I was doing more and more cabaret clubs, restaurants, hotel dinner dances, golf clubs and private functions. I wanted a really good quality demo CD to enable me to get even better quality venues/agents and to sell at gigs (no OAP manicures included).

I'd decided that I wanted it recorded by someone other than Jodhpur Man. I was still performing with Bazza on our duo gigs but there was even more call for solo work as it was less costly for venues. Bazza was fine with that as he still had his day job so a few bookings per month was adequate for him. I was doing a few gigs per week and really wanted to work at classier venues. I started to look at professional recording studios and this is where I got my first bit of luck.

Gary Porter lived next door to Mum in Hinckley. How convenient, I hear you say. Well it was. He was around 50 years old, very fit and very bald. He was not the most sociable of neighbours and would just grunt now and again if you passed him in the street. He could often be seen running around the pretty estate in very short, tight aqua marine shorts that seemed to spend most of their time up the crack of his arse. His wife was small and thin with long, dyed blonde hair. She too was very fit and wore lots of baseball caps and wristbands. She reminded me of something out of a 1980s fitness video. She could have easily doubled up for Olivia Newton John in *Let's Get Physical*.

Gary was well known in the Midlands area as he had his own show band so I made my mind up that he must be put to use somehow. I thought he fancied Mum so I told her to flirt with him a little and test the water. She did and, hey presto, after a few chats with her he said he would listen to my existing demo but couldn't promise anything. He said he would listen to my voice and see if he thought it was worth working with me on my new demo. He invited me into his own recording studio a few days later for the verdict and it was a 'yes'. He assured me that this was not merely due to the fact that he fancied my mum. Actually he didn't seem capable of flattery or lies, regardless of whether he fancied a shag or not. In fact as time went on, I learned that his brutal honesty was sometimes socially inconvenient. He said he was impressed with my voice and that I had a unique tone. I later realised that he rarely gave out compliments at all and he often made Simon Cowell look like a pussycat. He was always ultra-critical and ultra-cynical but utterly brilliant.

We got to work in his studio. He said I should record a few well-thought-out covers and possibly think about some original material. I'd found a modern studio in Birmingham and Gary wanted to use it because he said he could get tracks mixed quicker. The Birmingham studio had a digital mixing desk and Gary's was still analogue. Gary told his wife he was playing golf whenever we went to the studio because she would go mad if she knew he was helping some bird record an album for nothing. He used to meet me on the corner of the road with his clubs in the back of his car, wearing the full golfing clobber. He wore long shorts, knee length socks, the whole shebang. I thought it was a little over done but if he needed to get into character and it made him feel better then so be it.

The studio was called Thin Man Studios and the guy who ran it was a little fat man called John. His family were very wealthy and Gary said they had obviously bought the studio for John to have a play with. Gary repeatedly said that John was useless and didn't know what he was talking about. John tended to just get up and bugger off during sessions, which drove Gary insane. He used to say, 'Where is the little fat c**t? We're his only fucking customers and he's fucked off again!' He often strutted off to find him asking him why the place stank of fish. He told him if it was some new diet he was on to forget it because it wasn't working. Gary would then make sure that John knew he was a useless fucker, tell him to sit down and not bloody move until he said so. John would just grin inanely. He didn't seem to take offence and I think he was sort of fascinated by Gary Porter. He certainly respected him and with good reason, Gary was a perfectionist.

At lunchtime Gary would send John out to get dinner from wherever. He would then make me go outside and let him practice playing with his balls (golf balls). He'd whack the ball, I hoped it didn't hit me, then, like an eager golden retriever, I would go to fetch it and throw it back to him. We did this until John came back with the grub, which sometimes felt like a long time. I was no subservient type of female but I was not paying the bloke so if I had to catch his balls at lunchtime then that's what I would do.

We spent a few weeks working on the CD. We had our little spats and differences of opinion but Gary constantly reminded me that he was brilliant and I was not. When we had finished a session John would get the studio diary out and ask us when we wanted to book in again. Gary would say, 'You have no other customers, we don't fucking need to book. We'll just turn up but get rid of that smell of fish before we do.' We chose the track list and got cracking. We included an original track called *Blind Man's Shoes* and decided that is what we should call the CD.

All in all we were very pleased with the finished product. John thought it was great too but as Gary reminded him, nobody gave a shit what he thought. I set to work getting the demo out to quality agencies and secured some great cabaret gigs. In fact the CD was really working for me, the quality of gigs was much better and the money was creeping up nicely. Word was getting around so I sent a copy of *Blind Man's Shoes* to local radio stations as Gary had suggested. Local stations were happy to play certain tracks and have me in for a little chat but getting airplay further a field was proving a little more difficult.

I began working at well-known cabaret venues, such as the main UK holiday piers and variety clubs, opening shows and supporting well-known TV comedians such as Frank Carson and Bernard Manning. The latter definitely had a certain type of audience. As I am sure you are aware, I'm talking hard-drinking, big-mouthed, tattooed, aggressive, pie-eating sods (and that's just a few of the women). Bernard's whole crowd consisted mainly of men and these blokes didn't piss about. They were there to see Manning and didn't want to hear any sad little support act belting out Celine Dion. The bastards actually used to bang the tables shouting, 'Manning! Manning! Manning!' They appeared hostile to say the least and I just had to get out there and be brave. It was hard work but I didn't weaken and I think I sensed a little respect in the end. The 30-minute slot was long enough though; you had to shift before they got fidgety.

Bernard Manning didn't look well the last time I saw him; the poor bugger looked yellow. He had to be driven the length of Hastings Pier in a golf buggy because he couldn't walk very far. He has, of course, now crossed over to the big comedy club in the sky, bless him.

***

It was now 2001 and my gigs were going great guns but time was moving fast. I had been singing for six years and although *Blind Man's Shoes* was doing what I wanted it to, it only contained one original track. I still had my LA dream and wanted more. I felt that I needed to get some sort of real direction and quality original material to send off to UK record labels and management companies. Gary had been brilliant but it's a cruel business and I knew his material was not modern enough. I had to find someone in the business with experience to collaborate with, a songwriter/producer with up-to-date ideas. I had no idea how to find this person but I thought in the meantime I would source the right studio at the very least. I decided it would be a good idea to stick to studios in Birmingham (not London just yet) because it was close to where I lived. I had done my time with John at Thinman Studios so off I went to sniff around other areas of Birmingham. This is where I got my second bit of luck.

During my search I stumbled upon a studio in Handsworth Wood, not to be confused with Handsworth. Although both places are in Birmingham and extremely close to each other, they are two very different areas I can assure you. Handsworth Wood was pretty and affluent. There were large houses, people walking dogs and fundage a plenty. In Handsworth there were guns, boarded-up shops, litter and dog shite. Fortunately for me this studio was in the Handsworth Wood area.

I can't quite recall how I found the place but I do remember it was called Grosvenor studios. At the time I think you could simply hire it and use your own technician/engineer. Obviously that was not my aim but I was not aware that this was the arrangement at the time I visited. I suppose it looked pretty much run-of-the-mill as studios went. A lady who looked to be in her 50s introduced herself; she was pleasant, professional and very well spoken. As I chatted to her she told me that she owned the studio and both of her sons were in the music business. The first, Chris, was apparently in musical theatre and was doing very well in the West End. The second, Richard, also lived in London and was the musical director/keyboard player for the boy band Boyzone amongst other chart-topping acts. Bingo.

I tried to chat to her a little more and explained what I was trying to do. I suggested that Richard might be able to give me a little advice or direction, if he was not too busy of course. She said he was very busy and she was sure he wouldn't appreciate her dishing out his mobile number but she added that I could leave her a CD and she would send it on to him. She said she would ask him to listen to it. I held out little to no hope but called back a couple of weeks later to find that she had passed it on and Richard had listened to it. Her feedback was that he liked my voice and he would like to work with me on some original material. She gave me his mobile number and told me to call him that afternoon.

Richard was great. He knew the business and exactly what I was trying to achieve. We had a chat and arranged for me to meet with him in London. He already had songs that he had written and thought I should record a few. He had a studio in Ealing where he produced arrangements for many chart acts and new bands. His material was well produced, the songs were very catchy and, although his studio was technically a bedroom, there was not a pair of jodhpurs in sight.

This new development with Richard was another cute little story for the local press. '*Leicestershire Girl Works With Boyzone Musical Director*'. They loved it and produced many articles featuring a large photograph of Ronan Keating next to a dodgy picture of me giving the thumbs up in my back garden. I really wanted to know where they found the photographers for these little local papers. No matter what you looked like, the photos were always awful. The photographer always made you look like a John Merrick throwback. It obviously took great skill to make me appear like I had one oversized hand and the freaky camera angle that gave me an alien-like forehead was genius. I learned over the years that small, local tabloids are actually desperate for any story, as are most local radio stations. They seldom have much to talk about. If you bear that in mind, you will understand why I was often featured in local papers and heard rattling away on local radio stations.

I recorded two songs in London that Richard had written. On reflection the songs were perhaps a little too light and breezy for me. They were very 'poppy' but at that point I used them anyway. I hadn't yet developed my own identity and they were all I had. I started to get promotional packages together to send to record companies. I was informed that feedback from them could take months if they bothered giving any at all. They literally got hundreds of demos per day. Over a period of a few months I received many, 'thank you but your material is not for us at this time' letters, just standard typed stuff. I did have a very encouraging, handwritten note back from a guy called Alan Wright who was the artists and repertoire (A&R) manager for Mercury Records at that time.

The note was on letter-headed paper but he had actually taken the time to write down his thoughts. He wrote, 'Good voice! It's a bit too poppy for me but if you do anything that isn't so poppy then bang it out to us'. I agree that his note did not call for cracking open the champagne but it did give me a little hope and determination to continue.

I decided to keep looking in *The Stage* newspaper, the entertainment industry's golden paper. Pretty much everybody in the business read *The Stage*. It was where they advertised auditions for bands, solo vocalists, dancers – the works. We all had to keep our eyes peeled for auditions and opportunities listed. After a month or so I saw that a management company from up north called Rock-IT Music were auditioning singers with the aim of writing and recording their own original material. After the audition, if they decided that you were what they were looking for they would take you on and manage you. I thought I should give it a shot.

Before they would allow anybody to audition we had to send them a picture and a recent demo. I sent the two songs that I had recorded with Richard. After a few weeks they called to say that they had listened to the demo and they wanted me to audition for them. They gave me date and time so I was all set. My audition went well and they were impressed. The manager at Rock-IT stated quite quickly that he wanted me to sign a management contract. They seemed to have good premises, an up-to-date studio, young, bright producers, musicians, vocal coaches and a busy little A&R office.

I didn't really have anything to lose and wanted to write my own songs. I would need help and direction but that's what they were there for. Rock-IT said that my management would be specifically geared towards the main line and independent record labels. The director was called Adam De Cruz. I was informed that I would be signing a three-year management deal. Once I had signed, we got to work. Initially they wanted me to come up with five tracks. There were plenty of development support meetings, vocal assessments and pre-production meetings as we worked through my ideas.

I enjoyed working with the producers in the studio and it was great to create a song from scratch. I had a fair amount of recording studio experience already and I also had no problem laying down harmonies. Once my tracks were complete and everybody was happy, we got to work on photography and cover design. They also invited me to a gig where they were showcasing a talented singer/songwriter to some A&R guys who represented EMI records in London. I needed to see how these showcase gigs worked.

It was nothing like I expected. I don't really know what I expected but these gigs were in no way big or flashy. They were very intimate. They took place in tiny back rooms of bars and clubs and there were just industry people wandering around, along with some dedicated followers of the artist/band. The first little place I went to was packed and all very casual. The guy performing was really good and so cool. I sat and watched him with a JD and Coke. There was also 'coke' of a different variety doing the rounds but that I did expect. After around five minutes somebody pointed out to me that I was sitting next to John Lennon's son, Julian... as one does.

That gig was a new experience and I had an idea what would be expected of me. I was proud of what I had achieved and happy with the result. They were totally happy with the five tracks and we were all ready to approach the labels. We ruthlessly cut five tracks down to three by choosing the three strongest songs, as was standard procedure before approaching the labels. This particular part of the process was passed on to the promotional department and I started to deal with a guy called Geoff Watson. That's when I became somewhat deflated. I'd managed to work well with everybody at Rock-IT up to that point but I admit I had issues with Mr Watson.

Press release:

Joanne Set for Stardom

Burbage-based singer-songwriter Joanne Copeman is ready to hit the big time with the promotional release of a three-track demo CD through Rock-IT Music Company, Colne, Lancashire.

Rock-IT Music Company takes on only the very most talented singers and songwriters and sponsors the recording of demo albums featuring their work, which it then uses to promote them to record companies and publishing houses.

Before being picked up by Rock-IT, Joanne had acquired a firm reputation as a professional singer and was already a well-known face on the pub, club and quality cabaret circuit across the Midlands.

Upon first meeting Joanne at their studios in Lancashire, Rock-IT were knocked dead by the strength of her singing voice and signed her up to a recording and promotional deal on the spot.

Rock-IT Music Promotions Manager Geoff Watson said, 'We knew Jo had a great singing voice when we took her on but as she got to work on original material with our in-house studio production team, we soon learned that she had a keen ear for a killer pop tune too. Joanne's songs are a funky mixture of pop and deep-fried gospel-soul. We'll be promoting her hard to all the right people in the 'biz over the next few months with the ultimate goal of getting her a record deal with a major company.'

In the run up to her promotional campaign Jo has already appeared on [INSERT RADIO STATION HERE] and is set up for future interviews on [SHOW AND TIME] on [RADIO STATION] on [DATE], which will be playing some of her original material during the show.

-Ends-

For further information, please contact Geoff Watson, Promotions Manager, Rock-IT Music Company.

Original Message
From: <Rock-IT Music Company Office>
To: <Joanne Copeman>
Subject: CDs
Dear Jo,
Just a quick note to let you know that I have sent your CDs to the appropriate A&R personnel at all the record companies and publishers on the list previously supplied. I will report back on any feedback received but please bear in mind turnaround time to receiving a response varies vastly from company to company and person to person and can be as little as one or two weeks or as much as four months! As I say though, I will keep you informed of any feedback as we go.
Best regards,
Geoff

From: <Joanne Copeman>
To: <Rock-IT Music Company Office>
Subject: Re: CDs
Geoff,
I am fully aware of the time scale on the R/Companies listening/responding that is to be expected. It was the three-month wait for Rock-IT to get the CDs ready that has been worrying me. I did complete the CD middle of August and we have only just sent them out, mid-November. I was told that they would be ready a couple of weeks from when they were ordered. I know I may come across as a little impatient sometimes but three months is a bit too long to wait and the worry was that we were approaching Christmas and that the r/companies start to slow down, etc. but it can't be helped now. Feedback from them will probably be next year.
Jo

From: <Rock-IT Music Company Office>
To: <Joanne Copeman>
Subject: Re: CDs
Dear Joanne,
Firstly, I must remind you that a large part of the delay in getting the CDs ready came from your end with repeated changes requested to the recordings and to the artwork.

Secondly, and more importantly, I have to point out that, if you are worried about your age, three months makes absolutely no difference whatsoever. Neither would one or two years. We're not recruiting for a Pop Idol-type TV show with a set cut-off age. Outside TV shows, where age makes a difference, is purely in demographics. In marketing, adult demographics are generally divided into 18–24, 25–35 and 35+. When you hit 25 you changed demographic. That's where you'll stay until you're 35. That means you're now in the same age bracket as Natalie Imbruglia, Jennifer Lopez, Shania Twain, Anastasia or Sheryl Crowe (when she had her first hit), rather than Britney Spears, Christina Aguilera or S Club 7.

If you want to be a teeny pop star, yes, you are too old. If you want to have a recording career, you most certainly are not. Yes, you're right, we probably are looking at after Christmas for feedback in a lot of cases but, hypothetically, even if we have no feedback by August, you will be no older in marketing terms than you were last August, or, to be honest, the August before that. Calm down. Stop panicking. I hope you can see my point. Although I obviously understand, and share, your sense of general urgency, when you're 45, we'll panic. Before that, we'll carry on plugging away until we get there.

Best regards
Geoff

__From:__ <Joanne Copeman>
__To:__ <Rock-IT Music Company Office>
__Subject:__ Re: CDs
Dear Geoff,
Never mind 'demographics' I can bet you all the tea in china that Madonna would not have settled for the response, 'when you're 45 we'll panic'. She would not be where she is today with that attitude. I think that says it all!
Bestest Regards
Jo

__From:__ <Rock-IT Music Company Office>
__To:__ <Joanne Copeman>
__Subject:__ Re: CDs
Dear Jo,
I have not got time to have an email argument. If you are not happy, we need to have a meeting. Please call me to discuss.
Geoff

This was the usual piss-drenched drivel that I had become accustomed to receiving. No, I wasn't happy and we did arrange a meeting. As it turned out, I may as well have met up with Winnie-the-Pooh. It was a dull, midweek afternoon and I was already in a bad mood when I met up with smug Geoff. I seriously doubted that meeting with him would in any way improve my mood.

'Do you want a coffee?'

I nodded and sat down in Geoff's fancy-looking A&R office. He paced around a little looking for cups and I had a feeling that this office had seen a lot of talking and not much action.

'Jo you need to stop stressing about the timeframe on this project.' Geoff said casually whilst taking forever to actually come up with any coffee.

'Geoff, with all due respect [I had none], I am perfectly aware of my own age and I have taken your views on the 'demographic groups' on board but that doesn't mean that we should sit on our laurels. There is no harm in pushing things a little. I am merely a little dissatisfied with the length of time that it has taken to reach this point. My aim was to avoid the Christmas period bringing things to a halt.'

He sat down behind his desk and gave his best exaggerated sigh. 'I've explained the situation Jo and that some of the delay was at your end.'

I shifted uncomfortably in my chair as I could feel a disagreement approaching. He had made it clear that he had no time for an email argument and suggested that we meet so I presumed that he set some of his precious time aside for a good row in person.

'Geoff that's not strictly true. An artist changing their mind once over a particular picture shouldn't result in this kind of a delay and that's all I did.'

The office phone rang and he quickly told the caller that he was in a meeting and he would call them back. I had a feeling that it was probably only his wife.

'Look, the industry is a big machine and it has a timing all of it's own Jo. It will not be dictated to by you or I…'

I glared at him and said, 'We will have to agree to disagree then won't we? I imagine this could be the only thing that we're ever likely to agree on. I will just have to accept that feedback will now be next year and console myself with the fact that I'm not yet 45 and therefore time is of no great importance. I don't think that this meeting is really going to achieve much.'

He shrugged his shoulders and smiled. I picked up my bags and made my way to the door glancing at the cups on the big sideboard behind his desk as I passed.

'By the way Geoff, you forgot the coffee.' He looked slightly less smug, just for a second. 'I'm sure the coffee waits for you though and doesn't dream of going cold.' With that I left and took my uppity self home. The bloke was a tit. It was like banging one's bonce repeatedly against a brick wall. Why did he have no time for an email argument? The little puffy-faced shite wasn't busy sending any demos out was he?

Then it happened. My management company went bust, on its arse, down the pan, into liquidation, whatever you want to call it. They were in big debt and owed money everywhere. I don't even know if 'Old Puffy Face' ever sent my finished product anywhere. After all that hard work my little CD sat there unprompted. It really was a cruel business.

I must excuse myself from writing for a short period. Steph has just called and I have been summoned to her house to drink tea and give my opinion on her new wallpaper. I panicked for a second. I thought something sinister had happened to her winter cabbages.

**

As far as my personal life was concerned, it was around this time that Robbo and I had moved into a nice, modest, three-bedroom semi. We had become very adult and responsible. Prior to their collapse, some silly fool at Northern Rock had even decided to give us a mortgage. The house was situated in Burbage, around the corner from where Mum lived and only a mile away from my nan and grandpa. My grandpa was always very supportive of my singing and Nan was too but he was exceptionally passionate about it. He was my mum's father and therefore not the 'singing Grandpa' but he absolutely loved the whole idea. He was as enthusiastic as I was and he helped me in any way he could, whether it be emotional support (he used to say 'the world is a big place, dream big Joanne!') or walking the streets delivering posters to the little clubs. He really was dedicated.

Grandpa was originally from County Waterford, Southern Ireland, but moved to England as a teenager. He still retained a lovely soft lilt to his accent and was also blessed with a love of words, reading and poetry that stemmed from his motherland. He also had a wandering and adventurous spirit. When I wanted to go to Cyprus with Steph and everyone was saying it was crazy, he alone advised to, 'let her go and experience the world, life is an adventure'.

Unfortunately his father did a runner when he was very young. Being the eldest boy, he was left to look after his five siblings and help his mother in every way possible. He was a grafter. A lot of the original documents and birth certificates had been lost in Dublin in the uprisings and Grandpa, whose birth certificate said 1914, had convinced the parish priest to put his age on a year or so to enable him to get a job in the papermills and support the family. Strict Catholics they were, but a white lie compared to poverty could be confessed and absolved without too much trouble to the conscience.

We never really knew his correct birth date; in fact in those days in Southern Ireland a lot of people didn't even have a birth certificate. He wanted to see the world and his mother had brought the family over to England, so a few years before the Second World War broke out he 'took the King's shilling' and joined the army. He didn't leave the army until after the Second World War had finished and spent most of his service years in the Middle East. I loved to sit and listen to tales of his war years; it was fascinating.

Grandpa was, at this stage of my career, 87 years old and his health was failing quite rapidly. He had a previously undetected heart condition. As I understood it, a valve that hadn't been working properly, probably from birth, had remained undetected, even throughout his army career. His heart was weakening and he was taking as much medication as he could. He was too old for any sort of operation. His kidneys started to malfunction and basically there was nothing doctors could do. They took him into hospital and he asked them how long they thought he'd got. They said perhaps a few weeks. They asked him if he wanted to remain in hospital or be cared for at home. Nan said if the nurses could visit the house, she wanted him home. Grandpa said he wanted to die at home with Nan not in some hospital.

He and Nan had been married for 57 years. He remained 100% mentally alert right up to the day he died. The medical staff were accurate on the timeframe and he passed away within two weeks. I was devastated. I was exceptionally close to Grandpa and this was the first time that I had experienced proper grief. On the last day that I visited him, two days before he died, he was very frail and lay in the bed chatting to Mum about plans for the funeral. He had kept a journal that he had written in over a period of around 20 years. He didn't write in it every day but he would jot things down randomly, anything that interested or amused him. In this journal he had written a brief resume of his military life, his interesting and well-informed political opinions and various pages that were dedicated to his love of music. He was particularly keen on jazz, Count Bassie and Duke Ellington being firm favourites. Along with these entries, towards the back of the book, he had then written precise instructions on how things should proceed following his demise.

I cried and cried that afternoon because I knew it would be the last time that I saw him. I gave him a card and inside I had written what a great Grandpa he was, said how much I loved him and told him that I promised to get somewhere with the singing business. I wrote that without my chief PR man it may prove difficult but I would do it for him. Nan said that he read the card alone. She read it afterwards and it made her cry.

I was told that during his last few hours he seemed to have some sort of weird surge of physical strength. My mum and Aunt Bernadette had been by his bedside all day. My aunt was a nurse and had nursed the terminally ill for years so although this patient was her dad, she was still very practical. They nipped out to get some food and told Nan to call if there was any change. They said they would be straight back.

They left Nan's house and she said it was almost as if he knew they were gone. She said they had only been gone a few minutes and Grandpa suddenly got out of bed, which he had not had the strength to do for a week and physically forced her to move out of his way. She said he was talking and shouting at someone. He was even swearing, which he never did. He was fighting with somebody and it was not Nan. He was trying to get to the conservatory or the back door. We are not sure which. She couldn't stop him; she said it was strange because he seemed so strong. Nan panicked and phoned Mum. They came straight back and found him sitting, naked, in a chair in the little conservatory. Mum said he looked skeletal and was breathing heavily. Aunt Bernadette said his breathing was rattly and she knew it was only a matter of hours. She told him to let go, he didn't need to fight it anymore.

Berne said to Mum, 'We are going to have to carry him, can you do this?' She meant emotionally as well as physically.

Mum nodded.

'Right then we will have to lift him leg-and-a-wing style, after three…'

With Nan watching, Aunt Berne and Mum then physically carried their naked little father from the conservatory and put him back into the bed. He weighed next to nothing. As he would say himself, he entered this world naked and he would depart the same way. Mum said he gently passed away in bed a few hours later. She told me it was a privilege to be there with him during his last breaths. She said that it wasn't frightening or stressful; it was actually quite peaceful and seemed a natural process.

Although I knew it was coming, when Mum actually came and told me that Grandpa was dead, I cried and cried and cried. As must often be the case, there was a comedy moment during the sadness of that night that made me smile through my tears. Aunt Berne told Mum to keep Nan out of the way when the undertakers came to collect the body. She said that was often the time when people had a complete breakdown. Mum took Nan into the kitchen whilst Aunt Berne dealt with the undertakers.

They were just wheeling the trolley down the hall to the back door, with Grandpa on it, when one of the undertaker's mobile phones started to ring and his ringtone was the theme tune to *The A Team*.

Luckily it didn't register at all with Nan, but Mum and Aunt Berne laughed through their tears, and the offending young undertaker looked mortified. The look from the obviously senior undertaker to his young apprentice clearly said that he would be joining Grandpa on that trolley when he got him outside. Grandpa had a wicked sense of humour and would have loved that moment.

Grandpa told Nan that he wanted me to have all of his war memorabilia, all the books in his bedroom (which he used to call The Nerve Centre) and his special journal. I have read the journal many times and even now, if I get despondent about something, I still pick it up and read it again. Nan immediately wanted to join him, she didn't want to live without him and said she couldn't. It was hard to see her so grief-ridden and 57 years of marriage was such a long time. I could totally understand somebody wanting to die when the person that they have spent their entire life with is suddenly gone. The problem there was that he had told her just prior to his death that she must remember that she is a catholic. Suicide is therefore classed as a sin. He made it clear that she must not have those thoughts so she was pretty much stuck with it.

We all missed him immensely. He was a doting husband, a great father and an inspiring and much-loved Grandpa. Here are a few of his favourite sayings that he had jotted down in his journal. I don't know the original source but he liked them and so do I.

'We are all children our mothers would not let us play with.'
'It's hard to give up what you've got for what you want.'
'I cried because I had got no boots until I saw a man with no feet.'
'People know a lot more when you try to tell them something than when you ask them anything.'
'Failure is an orphan. Success has many fathers.'
'Size is not everything. The whale is endangered but the ant is doing fine.'
'The law is the only thing that separates us from animals.'
'What fears we endure from evils that never arrive.'
'Honesty can be socially inconvenient.'
'You have not had 30 years experience. You have had one year 30 times.'
'Life is something to do when you can't get to sleep.'
'Man is the only animal that blushes or needs to.'
'Life is a two-week holiday, forty starts the second week.'
'Always forget the past. No man ever backed into prosperity.'
'May you be in heaven an hour before the devil knows you're dead.'
'Old age is not a blessing. It's a reward for looking right and left before you cross the road.'

Written on the last page of his diary there is the following little poem. It's cute.

'Edward Mowatt is my name, Ireland is my nation.
England is my dwelling place, heaven my expectation.
When I'm old and in my grave and all my bones are rotten,
This little verse will tell a tale, when I'm almost forgotten.'

He will never be forgotten. Edward Mowatt, my Grandpa: 1914–2001.

With comedian Bernard Manning following one of my performances at Hastings Pier

Demo CD of original tracks, recorded at The Rock-IT Music Company studios

Hinckley Times, *1999*

Hinckley Times, *2002*

Nan!

Grandpa relaxing outside a country pub, in his retirement years (c 1995)

Grandpa (on the right) in the Middle East, during his service in World War II

CHAPTER FOUR

PAYING TRIBUTE TO A DAME

It was January 2003 and after eight years of hard work, and at 29 years of age, a cowboy management company and an A&R bloke with his head shoved firmly up his arse, had cut my career as a recording artiste brutally short. Over the following weeks I wondered what was to become of me.

I had a brief period of time to reflect but I spent most of that time picking up after Robbo. He was easy to live with and very funny but, Jesus, he was unbelievably lazy. If the kitchen bin was full and needed emptying, Robbo would get carrier bags out and hang them on all of the kitchen unit door handles. He would then fill up the individual bags instead of emptying the main bin. If we were going away on holiday and leaving for the airport at 4am, at around 3.45am, or whenever the car that was collecting us was honking the horn outside, Robbo would start 'packing'. His version of packing was opening the wardrobe doors and scooping everything that was immediately accessible straight into a case. It took literally two minutes. This is why he often ended up unpacking woolly jumpers in Benidorm, but as Robbo only did bars and not sun, that didn't matter too much.

It is difficult to describe his humour. He was as sharp as a tack and exceptionally witty. I don't think I have ever met anyone, young or old, who didn't fall about at Robbo's humour and daft antics. He did have a worrying side to his nature though. He had OCD tendencies, such as touching wood and throwing salt over his left shoulder. He ate the same food every night, whilst lying in the same position on the floor, watching the same films. Now I expect a lot of people will say what is wrong with that,

I do that? No, you don't understand, we had two years of *Titanic*, 18 months of *Auf Wiedersehen Pet* and two years of *Lock Stock and Two Smoking Barrels*. Please bear in mind that they were watched every night without fail and he didn't alternate them. When it came to the food, his first love was the Chinese takeaway he ordered *every* night from Little Lee on the Rugby Road. He ordered chicken curry extra, extra, *extra* hot with egg fried rice and chips. He ate this every single night and as one portion lasted two nights, he ordered four per week. If Robbo was out at night, on a gig say, Little Lee would leave the takeaway food on the doorstep and Robbo would pay him weekly.

When Little Lee told Robbo that he was moving to Birmingham, Robbo nearly had a breakdown. The takeaway was closed then re-opened under new management, renamed New Food Palace. I felt sorry for the new management as I knew it would take them months to get Robbo's curry right, if ever at all. He was a creature of routine and habit all right.

Anyway, time was now not on my side (no matter what that anus at Rock-IT Music had said about demographics) and a hateful thought was beginning to cross my mind. Would I have to get a normal job to make ends meet? I hoped not. Could I carry on just performing cabaret and make ends meet? It was possible.

Somewhat deflated après Rock-IT, at that time I hadn't got the heart to push the original material around record companies. I needed to make a decision and a disturbing alternative was available to me, but it was something that I swore I would never do. Although it would be a big earner in comparison to standard gigs, my alternative was the very thing that I had slated for years. It took a few days to sink in but during a rare moment of complete clarity, I resigned myself to the fact that I must sell out and become a TRIBUTE ACT. I knew exactly who I would be.

I was feeling fairly stoical over the next few weeks. I went to various tribute shows and researched the market well. Mum thought it was a good move. I think she was enticed by the thought of glitzy costumes. Robbo met my idea with an air of scepticism shall we say, although he didn't say too much at the time. Bazza didn't say much initially either. I think he was a little sad because he had previously enjoyed slagging tribute acts off along with me. We had spent many a journey on the way to and from gigs saying we didn't know what the fuss was about, whilst questioning why they got far more money than we did. I think we used the phrase 'boils on the arse of entertainment' to describe them. Once I told him what I was about to do I think he went through a period of mourning. He thought he'd lost me to 'the dark side'. It was now my job to eat my own words and convince him otherwise. In the meantime, he continued to do the odd solo gig but he didn't push for anything more. I think he was secretly keen to see how my new venture panned out.

The Welsh diva Dame Shirley Bassey, also known as The Tigress from Tiger Bay, was an international superstar. I have always adored her and I think she is one of the greatest performers in the world. I knew it would be hard to do her justice. She is the epitome of theatre and drama. I had seen her live and in my opinion her performances were simply mind blowing. Her voice is amazing and she is mesmerising without any need for backing vocalists, dancers and the pyrotechnics that are so relied upon by today's artistes. Fortunately she also has many 'Basseyisms' as everybody knows. I needed to study her demonstrative arms, long, spider-like fingers, flashing eyes, iconic sideways mouth, very straight back and slight tilting of her head. I would also require stunning replica gowns and fabulous stage capes.

I had made my decision. I was about to become Bassey.

I didn't consider myself to be a look-alike. I was not about to take a booking unless I was actually booked to perform. There were a few obvious differences in our looks, such as the age difference and our colouring but I didn't let that put me off. I was relying on fake tan to give me a touch of her exotic skin tone or at least make me look like I had a healthy Mediterranean glow. We were a similar height and build and we both had dark brown eyes and short dark hair, so that was a start. I would obviously have to study her vocal delivery and phrasing thoroughly and, as any tribute act knows, I would have to 'over-do' her mannerisms. The costumes would have to be spectacular; you can't get Bassey-style clobber off the peg you know. A fine quality dressmaker would be required, not to mention shares in St. Tropez fake tan and regular visits to Tantastic. It was a costly affair but I saw it as an investment and I was happy to spend every spare penny I had on my transformation. Mum threw some cash in too. It was hardly demanding for two women to be spending their time and money on glitzy frocks and make-up was it?

Despite my newly improved skin tone and sparkly wardrobe, I was not about to go off and do anything too radical. I didn't feel the need to get new teeth, a prosthetic nose and an ill-fitting, cheap wig. Some of the Las Vegas impersonators take things way too far. In the UK we are known as tribute acts but over in the States they call us 'celebrity impersonators'. I have been told that the Vegas Barbara Streisand actually had a nose job. Jesus! Off stage, when she's not being Barbara, she's just a woman with a big hooter. There is a Bassey tribute act (naming no names, you know who you are) in this country that flew off to Marbella and spent £13,000 on her face so that she could look more like Dame Shirley. She obviously would have been better off spending that on therapy. I have seen the 'before and after' pictures – she didn't look like Bassey before and she doesn't look like her now. There is only one Shirley Bassey and she is sitting sipping champagne and eating chocolates in Monte Carlo. Memo to surgery tributes: get a grip!

I had seen many tribute shows and I knew that one thing I needed was a good stage name. Before I go on, I must just tell you some of my favourite tribute act names. Some are clever, some are funny and some are both. My top ten are as follows:

The Red Hot Silli Feckers
Cher and Cher Alike
Elvis Shmelvis
Bon Jordi
The Bees Knees
Jon's Elton
The Rollin Clones
Gwen Stephoney
Y'Abba D'Abba
And an Indian Elvis called… wait for it… Elvis Patelvis

I was completely bored of:
Sounds of [original artist's name]
A Tribute 2 [original artist's name]
Bootleg [original artist's name]
[Original artist's name] by [act name]
Pure [original artist's name]
[Act name] as [original artist's name]
Or anything with 'review' on the end.

I could have gone for the very unimaginative Joanne Copeman as Shirley Bassey but I thought I would play on the name Shirley so I came up with Surely Bassey The Show. Professional tribute shows should be classy and credible but they can also be fun. I ask all artists to put some thought into the name. If nothing else, it may amuse fellow tribute acts.

I was studying Dame Shirley intently and enjoying the process. I had recorded a demo of *Diamonds Are Forever* and started to send it out and alert good agents. I expected a low profile, run-of-the-mill venue for my first outing as the Diamond Dame. I didn't want to feel too much pressure on the first Bassey gig.

It had only been six weeks since the depressing demise of Rock-IT when, during the first week of February, I received a call from one of my agents asking if I'd perform a 45-minute Shirley Bassey show for Ken Bates (at that time the renowned chairman of Chelsea FC London). They wanted me to sing in the chairman's restaurant at Chelsea Village for him and his friends on the evening of Valentine's Day. I was told he was a huge Bassey fan and his favourite song was Bassey's version of *Hey Jude*. I hadn't got *Hey Jude* at that stage but I was told in no uncertain terms to get it. That meant that I only had a few days to get hold of the backing track and learn it. Ken Bates was well known for being a rude, awkward, blunt, bastard. Even I had heard that about him and I didn't follow British premiership football. So there it was, the first gig was booked and it wasn't low profile. My first outing as Bassey was to be for a well-known, truculent, avid Bassey fan that spent most of his time bollocking people.

Robbo was very pleased because it was 'all things' football. He wandered around in his element looking at the pitch amongst other things. He got very excited when he saw Frank Lampard and the rest of the Chelsea team coming down the escalator in the hotel. I was a little apprehensive about the gig so I didn't give two shits about the pitch or Frank Lampard. At that point, I was having visions of the evening ahead. Ken Bates would be shouting, 'She's fuck all like Bassey, get her out!' whilst I was miserably cocking up the lyrics to the very late addition to my set *Hey Jude*. I would be wrestled to the floor by security and given a leg and a wing out the door. Somebody would find me outside the gates strung up by my boa, feathers scattered everywhere.

Thank the good lord above, none of that happened and it was a huge success. I miraculously pulled it off and didn't cock anything up. The audience were fabulous and old Batesy loved it. He got very drunk, which I'm sure helped, and sang *Hey Jude* at the top of his lungs. Everybody was swaying and singing like billy-o. I had got to the end of the 45-minute set when Batesy came skipping up, snatched the microphone from me and demanded more. I said I had no more. He gave me that don't-say-no-to-me look and said 'SING'. I told him I could sing *Hey Jude* again if that was OK with him. He nodded his approval, loosened his tie some more and we were all off again. Afterwards he came over and said some glowing things about me over the microphone and I got a nice ovation.

Chelsea village hotel was fully booked that evening but as I was now Ken's new best friend (that particular night anyway) he told one of his sidekicks to turf somebody out of their rooms and give the double room to me, free of charge. I was to stay over and have a drink. The events co-ordinator looked relieved that she had kept her job for another day and very pleased that old Kenneth was happy. Bless Mr Ken Bates, little did he know he was my first Bassey gig. I have performed at Chelsea a few times since but unfortunately the new owner and multi-millionaire, Roman Abramovich, is a tight dude. He made it clear that he would not provide free of charge accommodation for any act performing there or even offer us a small discount. He then shoved the room rates right up just to make sure we didn't stay over. Bring back Batesy, that's what I say. He was a great bloke.

***

I must digress for a few minutes. I paid Steph a visit last week. She has confirmed that she is in fact an alcoholic and has joined AA. She is also pregnant so she needs to begin the 12-step recovery plan sharpish. I was at her house for some time. I knew she had a problem with the drink but I had not realised that it was as serious as it was. It turned out that she had been hiding it for a while. She confessed to some pretty scary stuff. It was quite an emotional afternoon.

As far as alcoholism goes, Steph came from pretty good stock. Her dad had always had a definite drink dependency. I remember when I first became mates with her and we had arranged to meet at her house along with some other chums to go on a night out for her 18th birthday. The plan was to meet at Steph's early doors, have a few white wines and then hit the clubs. She had stocked the fridge up with a few bottles of vino blanc and left it to chill.

When the others and myself arrived at Steph's house later that evening, she seemed a little peeved. She said her dad had been at the vino and it was all gone. He'd guzzled the lot and not left us a drop. He was lying down in the centre of the living room, by the fire wrapped in what appeared to be a curtain mumbling something about us staying safe and being sensible. Steph just rolled her eyes as though she had seen him in far worse states. We awkwardly stepped over him a few times whilst moving around and agreed to go out early. As we were leaving, her dad slurred something along the lines of, 'be bloody careful and go steady'. Fat chance of us being unsteady, he'd necked all our bloody ale! She said she should have hidden the drink in her bedroom not the fridge, as he could not be trusted.

Anyway Steph's announcement about being a fully-fledged alcoholic had unsettled me. It must have affected me because I had a horrible dream that night. I dreamt that Steph and I were on holiday in Spain. Steph had got drunk because she had unwittingly eaten spaghetti bolognese that had been cooked in red wine. In my dream, I woke in the middle of the night and she was not in the room. I ran downstairs to the hotel bar and she was sitting drinking a bright blue drink. She was completely off her face. I asked her what it was and she said it was brake fluid. It contained pure alcohol and she was drunk. I rang AA and they told me it was my fault for not keeping an eye on her. It was a horrible dream.

Talking of Steph, the phone has just rang once more and she has asked me to go over to her house as she wants to put some shelves up. We have been attempting to do female DIY recently and I am fed up with big drills and uncooperative walls. Perhaps I could design a pink prototype drill and send it to Black+Decker for their consideration. They just need to make it pretty and very simple. It shouldn't be too noisy though as the noise scares us. The different parts should be explained as follows: 'small drill bit for smallish screw; medium drill bit for middly screw; large drill bit for biggie screw'. Perhaps it could have little picture symbols on it showing wood or brick. It could also have a little speaker that plays *Sisters Are Doin' It For Themselves* while we drill... oh and it should have an in-built vacuum system that sucks up the dust to save us cleaning up afterwards. It also needs a censor to let us know what we are drilling into (we don't want to have to go around tapping walls to see if they are solid), it should squeal at us if we are about to drill through a big electrical wire or something nasty. It would be really good if it could double up as a hairdryer, it seems stupid not to as they are both the same shape. It should also have a smaller handle designed specifically NOT to break our nails. Anyway enough of that nonsense, I better get back to Bassey.

***

Social clubs, whatever their size, were now a thing of the past. Thankfully their budgets did not tend to stretch to tribute acts. It was now late 2004 and it seemed that I had finally escaped. I now had really good agents and far nicer venues. That was the advantage to being a Bassey tribute; performing in some classy joints. The gigs were coming in nicely and things were going well. By this time I was earning decent money and averaging around £650 per gig.

The lower end of the monetary scale tended to be work via agents, the middle was private clients and the top end was corporate. Overseas event quotes were pretty bespoke and you could literally name your fee. It could easily cost the client a few thousand pounds plus flights and accommodation for two people. I could often tag a few days on as holiday, which was also paid for by the client. I never went on overseas gigs alone. There was an agent in Las Vegas who wanted me to go over there to the 'celebrity impersonators convention'. She said they had no Basseys out there and there would be some good work.

There was a well-known, long-running show in Vegas called *Legends* but the money was nowhere near as good as it was in the UK and acts were very restricted in what they could and couldn't do. The Vegas agent said I should come out and stay for a few days. Apparently there was going to be a big party that season because Shania Twain was marrying Arnold Schwarzenegger. Can you imagine them all in costume during the ceremony? I thought about it but I decided against it. I had a feeling that once I'd landed, they would have had me horizontal on a table and ready for surgery in a jiffy. I decided to stay on UK soil and get myself further established.

I was performing solely as Bassey now so I had forgotten what my natural voice sounded like. In the main my Bassey gigs tended to be cabaret nights in nice hotels, elegant corporate functions, private parties, James Bond themed events and casino evenings. I performed many of my shows in the heart of London and was often booked for events that were held at some of the city's finest hotels. I was certainly no stranger to The Park Lane Hilton and The Mayfair. Having said that, when I first started as Bassey, and for the first 18 months or so, I had to do what all young fledgling tribute artists had to do. Holiday camps.

The money was still good but unfortunately it was the 'tribute act' equivalent to social clubs. They were dreadful places unless you were partial to chips, under 7's dancing competitions, fruit machines and candyfloss. These places were full of over-enthusiastic, young entertainment staff that would sing, dance, organise competitions and double up as babysitters when the parents got pissed. The poor entertainment teams also had to dress up in giant rabbit suits and wander around the camp generally degrading themselves whilst trying to amuse the kids. The group of holiday camps that I had the misfortune of touring had two annoying rabbit mascots called Sparky and Narky. Sparky was pink and the kids loved him whilst Narky was black and slightly nasty. Narky actually made some of the younger kids cry. There was Sparky and Narky merchandise everywhere. Those six-foot rabbits and their annoying dance routines drove me insane for the entirety of two summers.

I did camp after camp all over the country. Most of them were situated on the coast. The weather tended to be typically English (predictably shite) and people looked totally fed up because it was always chucking it down. There is nothing quite as depressing as a bleak, rainy weekend at a holiday camp on the Isle of Sheppey. Kids wandered around in the rain with buckets and spades asking for more crisps. Dads looked like they wished they had never bothered booking the time off work and knew that they looked slightly ridiculous in their sandals and ill-fitting shorts when it was lashing it down. Mums were busy screaming 'no more crisps!' at the kids whilst fighting with collapsible pushchairs and the grandparents were sitting on a bench eagerly waiting for the bingo to commence. There were entire generations of unhappy campers.

Once you drove through the front gates the camps all looked identical. There was a bloody Sparky and Narky duo resident at every single one of them. For some reason I seemed quite popular in the Isle of Wight so I spent a lot of time on the Wight Link ferry from Portsmouth. I would hop over there and perform at a few of the camps on a regular basis. They used to put the acts up overnight in one of the caravans. Sometimes we were lucky and sometimes we were less fortunate. I remember that we were occasionally upgraded to one of the nice 'new' caravans but most of the time acts were directed to the dilapidated side of the park in one of the old caravans that had stood there since the 1960s. I used to call it the 'council estate'.

We had to stay in these caravans many times and most of them stunk to high heaven. They reeked of chip fat, hair spray and fag smoke. They contained fires that didn't work, televisions that didn't work and windows that didn't open. They didn't contain anything useful like toilet paper or bed linen. We had to ask at reception for these luxuries and make our own beds up on arrival (Mum was always chief bed-maker). Each campsite had its own little shop that sold various 'camp essentials' such as crisps, sweets, cooking oil, fags and lots of 'I LOVE THE ISLE OF WIGHT' t-shirts.

When cabaret night arrived, the entertainment team had to warm the audience up with an irritating singsong. Sparky and Narky came out on stage to say goodnight to the kids then do their nauseating dance routine (which everybody joined in with). They would then introduce a resident duo or singer. After their spot it was tribute time. We were classed as the star act because we were visiting cabaret, not resident. It was necessary training but I admit that I'm glad I will never have to see a holiday camp again. I had been offered seasons in Spain and Cyprus during that time but I was already booked in the camps so I had to stay put. They gave us block bookings because I think they knew that if we were not contracted and we just had one booking, we might never go back. The holiday camps were tedious but they did give me stage time to perfect my Bassey show and there was never any real pressure.

I remember meeting a gay drag act in a hotel once that lived and worked in Tenerife. He told me something that amused me although I couldn't laugh at the time because he was deadly serious. He told me I should get to Tenerife because they needed a new Bassey. According to him, the previous Bassey had won Tenerife's Star Impersonator of the Season award, which apparently had gone straight to her head. The word on the street was that she promptly started shoving coke up her hooter and staying out all night. He said that the last time he saw her on stage she had lost two stone in weight and all the sequins were falling off her frocks. She had literally become a victim of the Star Impersonator Award and nobody would book her anymore. A showbiz tragedy. It seemed that the great Shirley Bassey herself managed to stay on the rails and not embark on 24-hour coke binges but some tribute acts obviously found the pressure of celebrity and success just too much to handle.

I'd thought about cruise work around this time but a Dean Martin told me to avoid it at all costs, which put me off.

'Joanne, if you accept a long cruise you will get off the boat three stone heavier,' He said. 'Tributes perform one spot per night and the rest of the time the only thing to do is eat.'

Apparently there was food on the go constantly. He had just worked a seven-week cruise alongside a Cher and Mick Hucknall who happened to be married. He told me that he boarded the boat looking like Dean Martin and disembarked looking more like Johnny Vegas. Apparently it took him weeks to shift the excess weight. He also complained that he was deprived of sleep because the cabin walls were too thin. He'd spent the duration of the cruise having to listen to Mick Hucknall shagging Cher.

***

I moved on from the holiday camps and started to make room for the real corporate work. The only really gruelling part of the job was the travelling. By this time my mum (who I had re-named Ma Bassey) had left work and was now my full-time, fellow gigging partner. Robbo had been offered a promotion at work and came to the odd gig but Ma B had taken over duties such as driving, wardrobe and all of my accounts and paperwork. My income was now supporting us both.

A lot of the female tribute acts hand everything over to their husbands who then manage them and I can understand why. It's physically hard for women to be heaving bulky PA equipment up and down the country, planning routes and driving from one gig to the next. I completely understand why it makes perfect sense to let the men do it. What I can't relate to is why these women lose the ability to speak on the phone or take a simple booking from an agent without their husbands being present. Agents have moaned to me in the past that some of these women actually say things like, 'I don't know if I'm free on that date, I don't have access to the diary... I don't discuss booking fees; my husband looks after my affairs. You'll have to wait until he's finished his round of golf and I'll tell him to call you back.' That was just pretentious bollocks.

We seemed to spend most of our time in service stations or pounding up and down motorways. It seemed endless and I'm sure I have now frequented every single service station in the country, from Aberdeen to the Lizard peninsular. We ended up having no choice but to stop in service stations. Often hotel accommodation is free of charge and breakfast tends to be included but I always missed breakfast because I didn't finish the gig until late so I didn't get to sleep until about 2am. The woman on the hotel reception nearly always told me in an insipid speaking voice that breakfast was served from 7–9am. Great, why don't they serve it from 4–5am, that way they'll save a few quid because nobody will be able to eat it?

Service stations niggled me in general. Why oh why have these places not been shut down for daylight robbery? They rip us off on a daily basis and nobody stops them from blatantly taking the piss. Two cups of tea wouldn't see much change from a tenner. Something as simple as two jacket potatoes and two orange juices cost us about £20. To say I was slightly unhappy with the tariff within these establishments would be an understatement. The majority of staff are all underpaid, 19-year-old morons, apart from some woman in her 50s called Sue who is the moron supervisor. In the main we survived on Ginsters pasties and sandwiches.

I was thrilled when we pulled out of the car park at Knutsford service station one afternoon after doing something very cheeky. The reason for my elation was that we had just scoffed two plates of fish, chips and peas and not paid a penny. This was due to the fact that we had to stand in a queue with our food waiting for someone to come onto the till to take the money.

'This is ridiculous. The food is getting cold and it has already stood around for about three days anyway,' I stated to Ma B.

Now before you judge me, please bear in mind that I could have got this plate of fish and chips cheaper if I had ordered it at Gordon Ramsay's restaurant and I'm sure his would have been fresh. Value for money it was not. I was not prepared to pay £9 for a cold plate of food so, as nobody was at the till, I said we should sit down, eat it and I would go and pay afterwards. Whilst I was eating, I saw a sign saying if you were not totally satisfied with your food, you could go to the till and get a refund. I decided after I'd eaten it that if I was apprehended when trying to leave, I would say I had seen the sign and decided not to pay for it because I knew I wouldn't be satisfied so I was saving them the paperwork of a refund. Ma B is a Catholic and was struggling with the plan (although fast forward a few months and she became worse than me for service station shenanigans).

'I feel totally justified in my actions because they have been ripping me off for years,' I proclaimed.

'That doesn't matter. Wrong is wrong.' Ma B said. I think she was planning on going to confession.

'It does bloody matter and I'd do the bugger again at any given opportunity.'

Ma B was a good person, if not somewhat naive, and there were some things she just didn't get. At one gig for a bunch of media folk we were approached, whilst loading our car, by an audience member who shamelessly asked us if we knew where he could get a line. Ma B quickly produced her Nokia phone and said if he could get a signal, he was welcome to use it.

I thought if the food at Knutsford was always going to be free we should tell the other tribute acts. Perhaps we could meet up there for some sort of tribute act Christmas do. We could all arrive in costume. How funny would that look in the car park? It would be filled with 37 Elvis', 22 Abbas, 18 Tom Jones', 16 Kylies, 13 Robbies, 12 Franks, 10 Tinas and a Bassey (obviously I wouldn't invite any of the other Basseys). We could all eat our Christmas dinner and then do a runner, although running in our costumes could pose a problem. Ma B would be bringing up the rear with her Christmas hat on and chanting Three Hail Marys, clinging on to my boas and her rosary beads for dear life. As I said Ma B soon became a dab hand where service stations were concerned. I'll say no more other than guilt was soon a thing of the past for her.

There was tremendous rivalry between tribute acts that were performing as the same person. All the Tina Turners wanted to kill each other, the Dinos wanted to rough each other up at the bar and most of the Robbies fancied petrol bombing each other's houses. We constantly bitched about our competition. I think we were all a little guilty of it, me included. However, as with anything in this life, there were some people out there who took it to the extreme and I had two personal favourites. There was a particular rat pack tribute show that played a venue one night and a Frank and Dino from an alternative rat pack group had gone to see the show. I suspect they wanted to check out the competition.

The viewing Dino had gotten very 'into character' in terms of drinking way too much during the performance. After the show, he went straight up to the performing Dino and passionately criticised his portrayal of Dean Martin. The other Dino reacted violently to the criticism and a fight broke out. The two Dinos were literally wrestling and rolling about on the floor. The two Franks had to try and split them up. I'm not sure where Sammy Davis Jr was. He was perhaps tied up with the ladies. My other favourite (this one got a write up in *The Stage* newspaper) concerned two Elvis'. There are so many Elvis impersonators out there that they are now collectively known as Elvae. The first Elvis, I'll call him Elvis A, had actually informed the police that the other Elvis, I'll call him Elvis B, was harassing him and his family. Apparently Elvis B had started a website about Elvis impersonators. He had led people to believe that this site had nothing to do with him and was run independently by somebody else. He had some sort of voting poll on there, which listed him as being the most popular Elvis tribute act in the UK. People were totally unaware that it was his site and he had put himself at number one.

He had also completely slated Elvis A's portrayal of The King on the website. Elvis A saw this and publically announced that it was not an independent site at all. He also said he would take legal action; he said it could damage his career. Following Elvis A's comments, Elvis B allegedly started to call Elvis A at home and harass his wife and family. Apparently he got quite abusive. The authorities got involved and Elvis B got a good ticking off, followed by a caution. The last I heard was that Elvis B had publicly challenged Elvis A to a sing off. I don't know if it ever took place but I for one would have certainly attended.

***

'The minute you walked in the joint, bum bum, I could see you were a man
of distinction…'

Along with more corporate work, I was performing quite regularly in casinos. They liked the idea of a Bassey show because they immediately thought of *Big Spender* – they didn't really care what I did for the other 57 minutes of the set. Actually I tell a lie, they also found *Goldfinger* and *Diamonds Are Forever* appealing because of the sophisticated James Bond/casino link. After that, they *really* didn't give two small monkeys about the rest of the set.

Singing in casinos may sound a tad glamorous but I can assure you it was not. We had to keep the volume down because in the UK our casinos tended not to have a dedicated entertainment area so there was no sit-down audience as such – in fact there was no real audience at all. We couldn't have it too loud or we could have been in danger of offending the punters on the gaming tables and slot machines. Vegas it wasn't. I caused a dispute of some sort concerning a high roller in a London casino once because he said the croupier hadn't heard him place a bet during the last big note in *I am what I am* – whoops!

Casinos were also a pain because they seemed to always be located in busy city centres, on hateful one-way systems. There was never anywhere to park and unload the gear and they were often situated on upper levels so we had to get the PA equipment up endless flights of stairs or use awkward lifts. No matter how many times I performed at The Empire Casino in Leicester Square, I never managed to arrive at a time where we could access the building in the car and we always had to park somewhere stupid. It was a blessing that most casinos had in-house PA gear.

One Saturday evening in late 2004 I'd had the pleasure of working with Phil, a Frank Sinatra tribute act, at a cabaret event for a golf club in Nuneaton, Warwickshire. He had mentioned that he was putting a show together along with a Dean Martin and he thought Shirley Bassey would be a great addition to the line-up. He said the Vegas style show would be with a live band not backing tracks. I told him that I was interested in joining them but I had no sheet music so Phil kindly said he'd introduce me to his band leader, Matt. I was passed Matt's number and promptly got in touch with him. Matt's band was called The Matt Stacey Band and the idea of working with a live band really appealed to me.

During our first telephone conversation I found Matt to be very matter-of-fact and a little blunt, with no real time for pleasantries or chitchat. We discussed what we needed to and he suggested we meet early in the afternoon on the day of the show for a run through. I was a tad nervous to say the least and I thought that it was cutting things a little fine to leave it until the day, as it was to be my first time with a live band but I agreed. When I met up with Matt on the day, I felt like I gelled with him straight away and I didn't know why, I didn't expect to at all.

Matt was straight forward to work with and the run through with him was a doddle. He was talented, concise and took charge, which made me feel at ease. It felt exhilarating performing with a live band and I loved the experience from then on in. It became clear very quickly that Matt enjoyed a good cuppa, which I found rather endearing, and he also smoked. As was the case in any industry, a lot of bonding was done on fag breaks. Little did I know that I would be seeing a lot of Matt over the next six years and he would become invaluable.

Some of the corporate gigs were tedious but others were great. I was working with the band more and more as the big corporates tended to have larger budgets. The majority of these events were all about announcements, past and present directors publicly congratulating each other on being masters of the universe, a prize for 'wanker employee of the month', projections for the future, some woman called Jean from the accounts department being given a bunch of flowers for having no life and dedicating 25 years of her miserable existence to the company... oh and a bit of live entertainment.

During the afternoon on any given corporate gig, Corporate Knob Head (tends to be the director) always took around three hours in front of his podium to rehearse his mind-numbing speech. This was supposed to be the time when we were setting up and sound checking but no, he thought we turned up at 9pm on the night and just performed a full set with no sound check required. His 12-minute speech had to be thoroughly rehearsed for hours even though he had a script and a big screen, which prompted his drivel.

I remember one particular gig in York where I was performing with Matt and the band. We arrived at around 4pm to get the PA set up and do a sound check. We were still standing around at 6.30pm unable to do anything because Corporate Knob Head was on take 11 of his speech. He needed quiet you see and had his podium set up centre stage. People were due to arrive at around 7pm so we literally had no time to prepare for anything.

When the cheeky bastard had finally finished and before I had even sang a note, he came over to Matt and I and said, 'I don't want you lot banging around too loud up there tonight. Keep it down or you'll kill conversation on the tables'.

Banging around? Jesus Christ they paid good money just for us to let people have a chat. Some of those big clients booked a Shirley Bassey show as background music, which I always found a strange concept. The truth was, they didn't really think about the show in its entirety, we were simply an accessory to the Bond theme. That's what we were paid for so, as always, we smiled and nodded at our instruction. Actually the audiences tended to be enthusiastic and lively in the main and it was just Corporate Knob Head who needed his head pulling off.

Tales of my Bassey gigs amused Bazza. He was sceptical about the whole tribute thing at the beginning but once he realised the amount that we were being paid by the likes of Corporate Knob Head, he said he might become Kenny Rogers. His swift change of opinion didn't surprise me.

I think he quite fancied the idea of getting himself a Dolly Parton to compliment his act. He said he would consider all options but on a serious note, I think he was actually quite happy, not to mention very safe, in his role as a sales manger. I don't think he was prepared to leap into a Kenny Rogers suit and experience all of the uncertainty that went with giving up a full-time job at his age.

It was at this stage, whilst working with the band on the corporate events, that I was beginning to see what a character Matt actually was. He totally made up for his lack of social airs and graces, with his organisational skills and fine attention to detail. Everything had to be just so. He was a multitasker and often seen with a brew in one hand, sheet music in the other, a fag hanging out of his mouth and a flashlight on his head (which everybody laughed at until they found themselves faffing around in the dark at the end of the night whilst watching Matt neatly packing away in his blissfully convenient lit-up area).

He also made sure that one of us was equipped with a walkie-talkie. He would keep the other one so he could communicate with us wherever we were in the venue during the event. Ma B dreaded Matt giving the walkie-talkie to her because she always pressed the wrong buttons and got flustered. Matt's close attention to detail seemed to only apply to the band though. His personal possessions were a different kettle of fish. I noticed over the years that he was always losing his own MiniDiscs, car keys and, on one occasion in Scotland, his passport. He was always rummaging around looking for stuff. In his defence, I think this was due to the fact that he had so much shit to transport. Thankfully he had yet to misplace his teabags or milk.

Matt had a quirky sense of humour and, much to my and Ma B's horror, we found that one of his favourite things to do whilst sound checking on gigs was to play a completely out-of-tune rendition of *Goldfinger* on the sax at exactly the same time as the client/booker entered the room. He also did the same thing with *Diamonds Are Forever* on the piano and it sounded absolutely horrendous. Ma B and I would cringe whilst trying to get out of the way shouting, 'Oh Matt you are daft, stop playing things out of tune *on purpose!*' We could only hope that the client had heard and knew it was a joke. Matt did it regularly and his face would light up every time.

***

The most enjoyable and rewarding bookings performing as Dame Shirley were the occasions when the audience included true, dedicated Shirley Bassey fans. These events tended to be the cabaret style dinner dance scenarios and the audience members had seen Dame Shirley perform in concert many times. Unlike corporate audiences, they had paid for tickets and they were there solely to enjoy a meal and see the tribute show. They were studious crowds who really knew their stuff when it came down to the Welsh Tigress.

Although they had witnessed the real thing, I felt that as long as I put as much theatre and drama into my performance as possible and gave it my absolute all, they would make allowances. The part they really seemed to relish was the hour or so after the show when they came and chatted to me about when and where they had seen Dame Shirley in concert. They delighted in telling me how many of her concerts they had been to, the exact numbers she performed, the magnitude of her voice and which fabulous gowns she had worn. I really loved chatting with them.

They also enjoyed congratulating me on the parts I had got right and sometimes told me where I went wrong. They did it in such a lovely way and I didn't mind at all as they definitely had authority on the subject. It was all part of the experience for them and I loved it. We were like a little family, an excited group of Dame Shirley enthusiasts swapping tales.

I had seen Dame Shirley perform in arenas but at a later stage in my career I'd also had the privilege of seeing her during a rather more intimate performance at the Roundhouse in London in 2009. This performance quite literally blew me away. She looked stunning, sounded amazing and simply defied 72 years of age in every possible way. It was a small audience (around 1,900 standing) and I was right near the front of the stage. By then I had been performing as Bassey for seven years but that evening following her performance at the Roundhouse, I sat in the cab on the way back to the car and thought, 'Shit Jo, you could have chosen somebody easier!'

Performing at a 007 corporate event in Cheltenham with the band

Performing at a 007 corporate event in Cheltenham with the band

Performing at River Rooms, Puddle Dock, London

*Matt playing his sax set
at a private wedding*

Matt and the band backstage

Matt backstage with all of his 'relevant necessaries' such as tea, fag, walkie-talkie and torch

Matt carefully organising the band parts

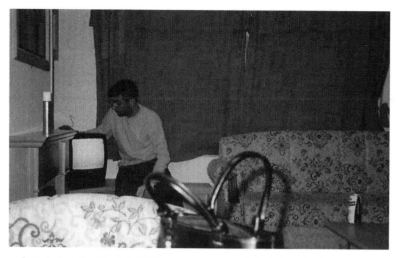

Robbo in front of another faulty TV, in a caravan, on a campsite in the depressing Isle Of Sheppey

Backstage with comedian Jimmy Cricket, following my performance at the Tameside Hippodrome

In the bar area of the Tameside Hippodrome, with actor Roy Barraclough

At Wolverhampton FC with the band, at a corporate event hosted by Susie Perry

Variety fun

A RUGBY dancer fresh from the bright lights of Broadway is among a talented cast appearing in a jam packed variety show at Rugby Theatre this Christmas.

Ricki Healey, 20, performed in Spirit of the Dance in Myrtle Beach, South Carolina, and Spirit on Broadway earlier this year.

Now he and his sister Siobhan, 18, perform as an Irish dance duo in the show on Sunday, December 12. Both siblings - former students of the Christine Anderson Theatre School in Rugby - are in the panto Sleeping Beauty at Coventry's Belgrade Theatre which runs until the end of January.

Headlining the variety show is renowned entertainer Joanne Copeman whose acclaimed cabaret tribute to Shirley Bassey entitled Surely Bassey was recently hailed by The Stage magazine in London as one of the best.

Self-taught pianist and singer songwriter Sean Rumsea, winner of this year's Rugby FM talent show held at Rugby Theatre in October, will perform songs by musical legend Stevie Wonder while The Gala Singers will be entertaining with songs from the Broadway shows.

Young singers and dancers from pop school FAP, theatre regulars and well known comedian Peter Cook are among a host of other stars of the night which will be compered by Margaret Dulcamara and Vicki Davis and is directed by Mike Allen.

The show starts at 7pm. For ticket prices and more information telephone Rugby Theatre box office on 01788 541234 .

● A tribute to Shirley Bassey can be enjoyed at Rugby Theatre's Christmas Variety Showtime. (s)

Rugby Observer

Reader Offer

Rugby Observer, *2004*

Feeling the heat in a hot tub at a promotional event in Milton Keynes

77

CHAPTER FIVE

WHERE THE FUCK IS THE TRAVELODGE?

Since becoming a tribute act and after years of driving around getting hopelessly lost, Ma B and I decided that it was time to get the increasingly popular satellite navigation system. We were fed up of map reading, setting off three hours before we needed to and screaming, 'Where the fuck are we?!' when travelling to gigs. We were females with no sense of direction and appalling map reading skills so a sat nav was welcomed with open arms.

Nevertheless, as we all know, they don't always do the job and our sat nav had weekends where he was particularly badly behaved. I did warn him on many occasions that if I heard him say, 'Perform a u-turn where possible' one more time then he would be gone. Ma B said I should show Nan how it worked so I said I would programme her address in and she could sit in the car whilst I took her home and she could listen to the computer directing us to her house.

When the voice started she said, 'How does he know where I live Joanne and where is he speaking from?'

I tried to explain that it is information that is pre-programmed into a computer but she was having none of it.

'Can he see us now?'

She told me that the man who was directing us must have a woman working with him too because her friend's grandson has a woman's voice in his car.

'They must be very busy with all the traffic on the road today.'

Bless her. I did laugh. She actually thought that a man and woman were sitting in an office somewhere high up, looking down on the roads directing all the traffic.

Talking of driving, I must quickly mention a newspaper article that made me smile. There was a very well known Frank Sinatra tribute on the circuit working at some top venues and earning an impressive amount of money. According to reliable sources, this Sinatra had been pulled over for drink driving following a prestigious gig in central London. The beauty of this little tale and the reason it made the papers was that the copper that pulled the Frank Sinatra tribute over was called Dean Martin. What a beauty!

Sometimes I swear certain gigs were plain jinxed. Everything seemed to be against us. It was a Friday night in winter, the weather was atrocious and the Friday afternoon traffic was so heavy that no matter how early we set off, we arrived in the dark amongst rush hour mayhem. The journey to this event was during a cold, wet January in 2005 and was particularly fraught as Ma B was severely jet lagged having just returned from a holiday in Vegas. We had been on a gig the night before in Leeds performing with our Frank Sinatra mate Phil.

We had bought Phil's Peugeot people carrier from him as our new gigging vehicle and, not being geezers, we didn't simply jump in, locate everything and spin off, enjoying the new driving experience. It was only a seven-seater but you would have thought from the fuss we made that it was a London double-decker bus. We had no manual. We had driven back from Leeds the previous day, stopping off at home to collect PA gear. All the way down the M1 we were flicking all of the wrong switches and generally frightening ourselves to death. Things got considerably worse as Ma B pulled onto our drive and promptly gouged two side panels on the gate post. We had been the proud owners of this vehicle for possibly two hours. We were not at all happy when we set off for Monkey Island, which was our second in a run of three gigs.

Monkey Island Hotel is in Bray on Thames in Maidenhead. Exhausted, we crunched on to a gravel car park and bumped our way across a lot of rain-filled potholes. It had been hammering it down all the way and visibility was poor. All of a sudden, we stalled to a jerky halt.

'Where the fuck is the bastard handbrake?' Ma B shouted desperately.

In her defence, the handbrake was in a particularly stupid place on the right side of the dashboard, or was it the column? I still can't remember. Handbrakes are quite important though; we had learned this as we had been forced to park on the flat when we couldn't find the bloody elusive thing. After another few frustrating minutes flicking the wrong switches, we were eventually able to switch off the lights.

'Thank Christ for that,' said Ma B clambering down from what she thought was a great height, and straight into a puddle. We peered through the dark, relentless rain looking for any signs of life. A shape started to form in the gloom.

'Is that a hotel, on an island, in the middle of the river?' I asked.

We stood in the rain for a few minutes hoping that our eyes were in fact deceiving us. Another shape then loomed into view and was coming towards us – a tall, thin, elderly Indian man. Ah, a car park attendant, I thought optimistically. Help was here and all was not lost. Ma B was getting herself thoroughly drenched trying to open the back doors to the confounded vehicle.

'Hi, I am the act for this evening. I seem to have got myself on the wrong side of the river, if you can just direct me to the road that will get me to the hotel I will get my PA equipment unloaded,' I said to the exceptionally tall Indian car park attendant.

'No wrong side of river. You go across that,' he replied, pointing to a rickety, narrow, wooden slatted bridge. I looked in the direction he was pointing and thought, 'hell no!'

'I can't possibly carry my whole PA equipment across that old wet bridge!' I gasped, trying to keep control of my mounting panic.

Meanwhile, Ma B had still not managed to open the back doors and the language coming from the back of the car was not good. I was sure I heard the word 'cocksucker' being hissed from the rear of the vehicle but I must have been mistaken. The Indian man shook his head from side to side, in that way that they have, and smiled a gap-toothed smile. 'Ah, no problem, for you we have this.'

He pointed with satisfaction to the bridge and leaning up against the side was an ancient looking trolley that had a tiller for steering. It was one of those moments suspended in time. We couldn't swim or erect a raft so it was decision time. We either chose to get back in the vehicle and go home or summon our best siege mentality and get on with what we were given. We started to load our gear onto the trolley.

'I hope our insurance covers us for this insanity,' Ma B said as we wrestled with the medieval tiller, which every few yards went its own way.

I had visions of the bridge collapsing and the whole lot, us included, landing in the dark, swirling Thames beneath us where we would promptly drown. That scenario was preferable to the task that lay ahead. We made our way slowly and painfully across the wet slippery bridge. I was trying to steer the tiller whilst Ma B, with her arse in the air, was going backwards trying to pull and guide. I had to give it to Ma B's warrior attitude in these situations, or possibly on this occasion it was jet lag that had crossed over into delirium.

'You know they have a trolley just like this sod in Tesco, either each one is like it or I pick up the only one every time, but I am used to these awkward bastards. You don't pussyfoot around with them, oh no, a bit like horses.' I was thinking she'd finally lost it as we thankfully pushed the trolley onto *terra firma*.

We had to make another couple of painful trips to get all of the gear over the bridge. I would like to say it got easier but I actually think it got worse as the bridge got more and more slippery and we got weaker. Our Indian car park attendant friend had decided that he must watch over our vehicle, the equipment and the car park whilst we did the graft. Perhaps this was the way of things in India or perhaps he had seen it all before and was no fool.

Now. I know. You know. Monkey Island Hotel knows. The agent who put us in there knows. Even the Indian man knows, that some other act will have done this gig before me. They will have got through it and then phoned the agent afterwards and said something along the lines of, 'Never put me in there again.' It was above and beyond the call of duty just to get the gear in the place. Had I known it was going be some sort of bush-tucker trial, I would have stuck an extra £200 on the gig. Would the agent take any notice of the act that complained? Nope. Monkey Island would phone the same agent the very next time they needed an act and the agent would say, 'No problem, I have just the person'. The agent would wait until the act was officially contracted and standing in situ in the pouring rain at the gig, faced with Monkey Island Bridge, safe in the knowledge that he had once more got away with it. He would have his commission safely tucked away in his arse pocket and he knew very few performers would piss off and let an audience down.

How we got the equipment in, I don't know. I think we actually mentally blocked it out, a bit like when women block out any recollection of painful childbirth. Inside at last, we quickly got the gear set up and sound checked. My radio microphone was kicking off so I decided to play it safe and use my lead microphone. I'd had enough of this gig already and it hadn't got started yet. They had some sort of generator because they often had trouble with the power supply. Not surprising really as it was an eighteenth-century building sat in the middle of the River Thames.

'Well at least they have a generator, I expect that will be some sort of backup if all the power goes off,' I said to Ma B as we had a drink in the bar.

I then merrily went off to get ready. Ma B and I must have some sort of genetic psychological disorder that keeps us ploughing on optimistically, when more cautious, realistic folk would stop and think. Although I have to say without this insanity gene of ours, we would not have been in this crazy business. I had 45 minutes to transform myself from a stressed woman from the Midlands into the glamorous Dame from the Welsh valleys.

And that's exactly when the power went off and the generator failed.

Staff frantically ran around placing candles in the bar, restaurants and toilet areas. I had a changing room upstairs so I sat there in the dark, unable to see my make-up mirror let alone apply make-up. I sent Ma B stumbling around the place in search of a candle. I got one and did the best I could.

'You look more like Alice Cooper than Shirley Bassey, but you'll do,' Ma B said when I had finished putting my make up on.

With a due sense of dread, we waited around for the power to come back on whilst the worried event organiser got slowly paralytic. As soon as the power came back I was straight on. They were a good audience, although the event organiser wouldn't have known. I spoke to her a week later and she said she couldn't remember a single thing after the power cut. She'd had the right idea.

We left Monkey Island straight after the gig. We were completely deprived of sleep and staying in a local Travelodge. We knew that finding the hotel would not be a barrel of laughs so we asked if we could come back the following morning to collect the PA equipment. We were very aware that packing it all down and getting it back over the bridge in the rain at 1am was not going to happen. Ma B was seriously flagging and I think the hotel owner saw the sheer desperation on my face and told us it wasn't a problem, of course we could collect it the morning. We were performing in Aldeburgh the following night and really needed to find the Travelodge.

Life on the road trudging from gig to gig was not for the faint hearted. Sometimes we were given sumptuous accommodation at the venue or hotel we were performing in. We could go to our room and have a cuppa before wandering down to the ballroom to do our sound check. After the show we had the luxury of having a few drinks whilst chewing over the gig we had just done. We had some hairy moments finding our way from our bedroom/changing room to the stage in some of the big city hotels and as we would often have to be a surprise, we could be lead through kitchens, back stairs and all sorts or rat runs, always with minutes to spare and desperately praying to get to the stage before the intro finished. However, we were always grateful to be given overnight accommodation at the venue because, as all singers will know, the packing down of the gear, battling through the dance floor carrying heavy speakers, loading the car and driving home was the real hard part of the job, especially in the winter. When accommodation could not be provided at the venue and depending on how far from home we were or where the gig the following night was, we would have to pre-book or find ourselves a Travelodge. Oh how simple that sounds.

'OK put the postcode in sat nav, the Travelodge didn't look far from here.'

Travelodges or Premier Inns (the real ones not the ones that Lenny Henry stays in) could, on occasion, actually work. However, nine times out of ten, the experience was an absolute nightmare. Often we had just got everything loaded into the car, which for two women was sometimes a Herculean task in itself, and desperately needed to find the place as we needed to sleep. Sometimes we would be going up and down the Commercial Road in the city and we could actually see the Travelodge or Premier Inn over the vast dual carriageway, but could we bloody get to it? No we could not.

The feminists will no doubt be up in arms when I say this but my God I believe it is a female shortcoming. Whenever we were with the band or had a man driving they seemed to find these places relatively easily. Alas, mostly it was just Ma B and I with barely half a brain between us direction-wise so we had no chance. Sometimes in winter we could be on one of those endless roads like the A14 or the A34 and seriously, in our defence, it actually seemed like they hid these places just off roundabouts, down what appeared to be dead-end roads, without any helpful signs. We would just keep driving round and round the same island, trying different exits with the sat nav saying, 'You have reached your destination'. I kid you not, the air in that car would be blue.

There have been occasions when we were so tired and it was so late that we have abandoned hope of ever finding the Travelodge that we pre-booked before leaving home, which seemed a lifetime ago, and checked into the first place we saw that was in the right direction for the next gig. We were never under any illusion that we could just call one of these soulless places and say, 'Oh hi, we are very near to you, we're just on the island, can you help direct us please?' In return if, and it was a big 'if', the call was answered, we would be greeted by someone who did not 'speaka de Eenglish'. I confess that I have been both rude and abusive around 2am to some of these 'receptionists'.

My only saving grace was that they generally could not understand a word I was ranting about. Assuming we got through all of that and eventually pulled onto the car park, we were literally crying for our beds. These are purely functional and comfortless places. Within minutes of our heads hitting the way-too-firm pillow, the noise would start. There were lunatics racing up and down the corridors and fire doors banging loudly. These places seemed noisy whatever time of year, but December plumbed new depths. Drunks would return at all hours from their office Christmas parties, stumbling down the corridors. In December there should be a sign at the entrance saying, 'For mad men only'.

Travelodge, Premier, Ibis, you know who you are. You were not fit for purpose and you remain unchanged. You were one unholy trio. You could not be found, you would not be found, you would not use any form of communication and your staff could not or would not speak. I have considered that learning the various languages of your foreign receptionists may have been quicker than them actually answering my telephone call. Also, one of you three offenders had something described as a 'family room' on offer. A family room gave the impression of space and perhaps more than one bed. We have stayed in many of these rooms and what you actually got was the same small size room as any other, one double bed and one sort of cot bed affair. This tiny bed was always shoved up against the wall next to a dodgy heater that didn't work, underneath a window that had thin green and blue curtains hanging up that never met and would let in all of the light.

Most people exchanged a 'good night' before going to sleep but Ma B and I would simply say 'good luck'. During the desperate wee hours when all hope of sleeping was lost, we would sometimes stumble down to the cold, unwelcoming, empty 'reception' area with its little blue supposed-to-be soft seats in search of a savoury morsel or sugar fix. The only thing that we were ever met with was a huge vending machine with hardly anything in it but a bag of beef flavour Hula Hoops, a tube of miniature Colgate whitening toothpaste and a box of Coco Pops, all to be washed down with a small carton of concentrated orange juice (often without a straw).

When dawn had broken and the crazies were all sleeping it off, we regularly had another 200-mile drive to attempt. After slamming the fire doors as loudly as we possibly could, we would take their Do Not Disturb signs off their doors. Revenge on the crazies was indeed sweet in the morning. We would then heave open the weighted, prison style, exit doors to gaze in wonderment at our daylight surroundings and see how tantalising and torturously close we were to the Travelodge the night before when we were driving round and round the island. Then we'd see it – oh deep joy! We were attached to a Hungry Horse. We tried to wrench open the door to the pub only to see in sheer horror that the sign said, 'Open at 12pm' and it was only 10am – *bastardo*!

Ma B would shout, 'Get in the car. Let's get to the nearest garage for a Ginsters and a pot noodle'.

Our experience of Travelodges was far from 'travelogical'.

***

Ma B and I decided that it would be nice to branch out into another area of the industry so we decided to put together a theatre show, which could also work in other venues. In addition to the gigs that Matt and the band did with me, Matt also did a similar amount with Phil as Frank Sinatra. We decided that as Matt already arranged all the songs, it would be a good idea to put the two together. We threw ourselves into creating posters and flyers for a new Vegas style theatre show. Our line-up was Bazza as compère, Vegas dancers, myself as Bassey, Phil as Sinatra, along with The Matt Stacey Band and Ma B covering all administrational and promotional duties. We only performed our Vegas show for five or six theatres but they were all successful.

The great thing about theatres was that they were very structured and ran like clockwork. We could always rely on a stage, proper changing rooms and, in most cases, a decent lighting and sound set-up. They started on time and finished on time. We were so accustomed to chaos, fire fighting the unexpected and thinking on our feet that theatres almost became boring. The audience were so well behaved and of a certain age, due to it being a Sinatra and Bassey show, that there was a danger of us going into auto pilot. We had to create our own amusement and Bazza came in very handy for that. Whatever the situation, he turned it into comedy. For me, working with Bazza made the regimented theatre shows enjoyable. The more regimented the show, the sillier he became. There was one occasion where Bazza and Phil were deciding in compère terms who should 'bring the other one off' at the interval, as Phil liked to put it.

Bazza said, 'Look Phil, I'm only used to getting an orange at half-time but if you want to bring me off, go for it.'

Bazza told Phil that he himself did not need 'bringing off'. He said he was quite capable of bringing himself off.

When the theatres were empty, whilst running through a rehearsal or sound check Bazza would randomly walk past us across the front of the stage with a sweeping brush whilst wearing a stupid hat, pretending to be a stagehand. He always found silly props from backstage. He used to do it in the social clubs too. It was all old school stuff but it still made me laugh. He did have a habit of bursting into the dressing rooms where he was quite obviously and persistently trying to cop the dancers in their underwear but they seemed to make allowances.

I put it down to Phil being laid back but on one occasion during one of the theatre shows, Bazza introduced 'Old Blue Eyes' on stage but there was a no show. We didn't know at the time but Phil was actually two storeys up above the theatre having a wander round the car park. After a few minutes of no Frank, an uncomfortable silence and following a second, somewhat louder, introduction from Bazza, a flustered Sinatra suddenly appeared. Phil said, in his defence, that he thought there were another two songs before he was due on. Bazza said next time he would give him a 'Kick in the Head'.

***

'This area gives me the creeps,' Ma B said as we inched around Whitechapel trying to get to the particular pier we were to leave from. Tall old buildings lined the dark, narrow cobbled streets.

'This is just the area where Jack slashed the throat of, and genitally mutilated, Mary Ann Nichols and chums,' I said, munching happily on a bag of spicy onion rings.

'For fuck's sake Jo, this place is spooky enough without a running commentary on Jack the Ripper's brutal slayings. I am trying to concentrate; we are beyond late as it is. As we know, they are pedantic on these river cruises, when they say the boat leaves at 6.45pm they don't mean 6.46pm!'

It was November 2005 and the start of the corporate London Christmas party scene, we were booked to perform on a Thames river cruiser. I glanced at the time on my phone and panic began to build. The boat was leaving at 6.45pm prompt and would then go to collect the clients from the next pier. It was gone 6pm and we hadn't even parked.

'Ah, here we are, this will do,' Ma B said. As she pulled up to the kerbside a loud bang came from the back.

'Oh shit, what have I ran over?'

It was a deep gutter and I don't know what we had hit but whatever it was must have been sharp as we had a flat. I jumped out and we both stared at the tyre as if we could will it to mend itself. We now had less than 40 minutes to change a tyre, unload the equipment onto the boat, set it all up and be in costume before the boat sailed.

'Where is the spare kept?' asked Ma B.

I started to laugh hysterically. 'Like you are going to get out the tools and change the wheel – does it fucking matter where the bastard tyre is?!'

We looked at each other. 'Right, you ring the AA and I will go down those steps to find someone from the boat. We seriously need a man, if not two.'

Off I went in the direction of some ancient old stone steps. They looked like they were probably the same ones King Charles I went down before they took him up river to lop his head off. Charlie could have saved them the bother as those steps were lethal in the rain and I doubt his state of mind would have been much better than mine, as although I wasn't facing the block, I was seriously starting to panic with time ebbing away like the blood of one of Jack's victims onto the Whitechapel cobbles. The rain continued to come down and a cold mist rose from the dark, swirling River Thames. The dank, dirty smell from the river was so strong that I could almost taste it. Other than the sound of the raindrops hitting the street, it was eerily quiet.

I returned to the vehicle with a Polish waiter in tow who had agreed to help. Ma B had got hold of the AA who unsurprisingly could not get to us for at least an hour, at which time we should have been cruising up the Thames. We both hated the thought of leaving the problem until we got back, which would be late. The Polish waiter, whilst unloading the gear out of the back, had located the spare and the necessary tool, but that was as much as he could do.

Now, I don't believe in guardian angels or fairy godmothers but on that cold wintry November evening, without so much as a wave of a wand or a 'bibbity bobbity boo', a man pulled up behind our vehicle. He should, by rights, have been on a white charger, but he was just in a regular white transit van. I went straight into damsel-in-distress mode and told him of our predicament and he changed that wheel for us in record time. Sometimes the kindness of mere strangers astounds you. He was an expert at it and, I must confess, Ma B and myself, and I also think the Polish waiter on the sly, fell ever so slightly in love with White Van Man as he jumped onto that big handle-type-thingy that they use for wheel nuts. He then just walked off into the night. I didn't even get his name. If his van hadn't remained behind ours, I think I might have wondered if I had imagined the whole thing. Ma B rang the AA back and told them we were sorted, we shouted thank you again to the disappearing back of our knight of the road and rushed off after our Polish waiter to board the boat. It was 6.43pm – we were going to make it.

Our changing area was the staff's coat cupboard and, being winter, it was full of long coats, bags and boots. I thought of the demure Dame sitting in her plush apartment in Monte Carlo, sipping her glass of Bollinger and nibbling on caviar. When I pictured Dame Shirley in my head, never was she in a coat cupboard. Some of the river cruise boats we worked on were quite big with outside decking, which catered to my addiction to Marlboro Lights. However, this one was the runt of the litter and was just glass windows and no deck. My 'stage' was a corner of the tiny reception room where Ma B squatted behind the mixing desk and I butted up, literally, arse touching and virtually sitting on the desk.

I faced another problem as we got underway and the boat began to move. The whole area went 'on the piss' – I mean microphone stand sliding and me with it. Now, had I had my usual two pre-performance glasses of chardonnay, I could have merrily gone on the piss with everything else, but I had been met with a horrid and alien concept as soon as I boarded. I was told in no uncertain terms that this was a dry boat. *I'm sorry! Excuse me! WTF!* I was confused.

'What sort of Christmas fun is that for everyone?' I asked the manager.

He laughed. 'Oh no, the clients have every drink conceivable for their party. It is just the crew and staff who are dry and you are a member of staff whilst on this boat.'

I wanted to protest loudly that I had been press-ganged, I was a singer and not about to hoist the main brace, or whatever it was they did. However, I had the ability to know when I was beaten and had absolutely no chance so I quickly changed tack so he wouldn't realise my desperation.

'Oh of course, silly me, I fully understand,' I replied, whilst grabbing hold of Ma B's combat trousers as she bustled passed like the roadie version of Alice in Wonderland's White Rabbit.

'Sneak whatever you can get your hands on when they start serving reception drinks,' I hissed. 'I am not getting changed in a cupboard, hanging on to my mic stand, standing toe-to-toe with corporate Johnny Foreigner, so close as to be indecent, and be stone cold sober.'

Ma B snaffled what she could and I faced my audience more sober than I would have chosen, but as they were all men and well bevvied before they even boarded, they were a breeze and we all had a great time. At one point we were in the middle part of the river where there must be some strong currents because when swaying and singing to *Hey Jude*, we were swaying more than has ever been swayed before or shall ever be swayed again. Never before in the history of short river cruises has so much swaying been done, by so few, for so long!

***

As the old saying goes, hell hath three gates: anger, lust and greed. In my job greed presented itself in the form of 'the double-up'. The term 'the double-up' was used when an enquiry came in for two separate gigs, on the same day/evening, in different areas of the country. In the majority of cases, the double-up was simply not physically possible. However, if the double-ups were within an hour or two away from each other and we were booked for an early spot at one and a later spot in the evening at the other, there was a small chance that it could actually be done. Even if it was achievable, apart from the odd one, I always found the double-up a highly stressful experience but once both contracts had been signed, there was no going back.

There was definitely an element of luck involved if the double-up was to be successful. We were at the mercy of the traffic and any accident or congestion could be a total finisher. We also had to pray that set up and sound check times ran to schedule. If the first event ran over in any way, we were in serious trouble making it to the next one on time and, as we were always painfully aware, events rarely ran to schedule. It was not really protocol to tell a client that their event had to run to plan timings wise, because we had another booking somewhere else on the same night. Clients always assumed that they were paying good money for me to perform and I should pretty much be present all evening.

To make it to just one gig on time, considering the state of our British roads, (particularly the M6, M1 and M25) was an accomplishment, but to make it to two gigs, sticking to the timings on both bookings, was indeed a challenge. Having said all of that, if a do-able double-up raised its ugly head, the temptation to take both bookings was often too great.

The most stressful double-up I recall was when I took a booking for a gig in London and another booking for a gig in Farnham, Surrey, for the same evening. It was in the early days before Ma B and I became completely 'match fit'. It appeared quite possible when we looked at the map because the distance between the two gigs was only around 50 miles. The first gig in Farnham was a 9pm start and I was booked to perform for 45 minutes in a marquee within in the grounds of Farnham Castle. On that booking a sound company supplied the PA equipment so I didn't need my own, which was indeed a bonus.

The second gig was an odd one. I had been booked to perform *Big Spender* at a hen party in Shoreditch, London. The party was to be held in a one-bedroom flat situated in Brick Lane. I was informed that I would be singing to only seven women in total. The bride-to-be's mother had made the booking and she was paying me £650 to sing one song. This was not uncommon. I had once been paid a small fortune just to sing *I Who Have Nothing* at a mansion in Sandbanks. It was for a Persian couple to mark their wedding anniversary. (The irony of that song title chosen by these millionaires in Sandbanks!)

Anyway, I digress, the bride-to-be's mother said her daughter's name was Anya and her favourite song was *Big Spender*. Anya was a TV scriptwriter and her husband-to-be was a film director. I knew I would need my PA equipment for that booking but I was slightly concerned about how we were going to physically fit it in a tiny flat. The thing with this double-up was that I had been booked for the hen party as a total surprise for Anya. For that reason, they needed me to bring scaled down PA equipment into the flat at lunchtime when she would be out and we had about 45 minutes before she was due to return.

They didn't want me to perform the song until 11.30pm that night. The problem was, I couldn't arrive and sound check at the first gig until 5.30pm because the sound company were not setting up the equipment until that time. That meant that we would have to drive to the flat on Brick Lane first. Our plan was to set up the equipment in the small flat in London at lunchtime for a quick sound check then drive to Farnham Castle, relax for an hour or two, sound check at 6pm before the show at 9pm, then leave at around 10.15pm to return to London for 11.15pm. We agreed that I would stay in my Bassey attire for the journey between the two gigs to save time changing. Following the gig in Brick Lane, we would need to take our PA equipment down, reload the car and drive back to Hinckley in Leicestershire so we estimated that we would get home around 2.30–3am. It all sounded do-able.

The weather that particular week had been unusually hot. Little did we know that we were about to wake up to the hottest day recorded for the month of July for the past seven years. As soon as we climbed into the black Peugeot Euro bus on the morning of the gig we knew it was going to be a scorcher.

'God, I wish this vehicle had aircon, it's already stifling. What a day for a double-up,' Ma B groaned as we set off for London at about 9am.

At that time, sat navs were not yet commonplace. It was simply Ma B, the map, a printed route sheet and me. Just like on any other London gig, the journey to London was fine until we actually arrived in London. The intense heat in the car was starting to get to us and opening the windows made no difference; there was no air inside the car or out. I called my fellow Frank Sinatra tribute act and mate, Phil, on the way.

'Hi Phil, just thought I'd let you know that we are wilting away in this vehicle we bought from you. We are on the way to London, where are you working tonight?'

'Birmingham,' Phil replied cheerily. 'I'm on the way there from Leeds now. Just heard on the radio it's going to be an absolute killer down south.

It's cooler up north but it wouldn't matter because I've got good air-con in this new people carrier, have a good one girls.'

'Thanks, I really needed to know that you are as cool as a cucumber, that makes me feel so much better. Got to go, I might have to take over as Ma B has just collapsed at the wheel from heat exhaustion. Go and fly yourself to the moon.' I ended the call.

Anyway, apart from some rude honking of horns, a couple of unconvincing lane changes, for which we were cruelly berated by the London cab drivers, and the odd unauthorised u-turn, the auto route had led us near where we needed to be, pretty much unscathed. That's where the fun started. We were on time and only a couple of miles away from Brick lane. We needed to make a left down Old Street. Unfortunately Old Street was surrounded by sheer chaos due to a burst water pipe and was consequently closed. That was the end of the route. Getting diverted in central London was never a hoot, especially when we were so close.

London was a very cruel city, waiting until you were less than a mile away from your destination before showing no mercy and fucking you right up. After around 45 minutes of getting hopelessly lost, panting like a pair of Labradors due to the freaky weather, we finally got to Brick Lane. Ma B had adopted the erratic driving technique and hostile attitude of the locals, and was hanging out the window giving the middle finger to a fellow road user accompanied by some choice language. I laughed out loud because she had rivulets of sweat running down her face and an attractive four-inch ring of sweat around the neck of her black vest top.

'I don't know about you but my combats are ringing wet and what is left of me has stuck to the seat. Sweet Jesus, what now?' She said.

There was a row of traffic cones placed across the entry to Brick Lane; we were going nowhere. We were really pushed for time and needed to get a shift on in order to get the gear set up in the flat before Anya returned. The guy guarding the cones, blocking our way, looked like he could not wait to tell us the reason why we were not allowed to pass. He had been waiting all of his life to be trusted with a job of this importance and as long as he had a breath in his Hi-Vis-jacketed, council jobsworth's body, he would not fail. A heat haze sort of framed him and his cones and the delicious smells of various curries drifted up from the forbidden land that was Brick Lane. Ma B stopped the vehicle and slumped her forehead onto the steering wheel with a groan.

I peeled myself out of the vehicle. 'Not today, of all days, please. I don't want to have to kill you, it is too hot,' I muttered to myself, putting on my most pleasant smile. I would try being nice first; if that didn't work then I would have to kill him.

'You can't drive down here miss, you see there is a street party this afternoon and this road is now closed. If you had come an hour ago it was still open, but now it is closed.'

The bubble reply in my head was dripping with sarcasm but that was not going to get us down Brick Lane. God it was hot and I wanted to just punch him in the throat.

'I have a parking space reserved by a rate paying resident on this street who is putting on some expensive entertainment for her wealthy daughter. I have to unload some equipment and then I will be out of your way, but unload it I must.'

We had some argy bargy and I considered offering him £20 but I didn't want to get banged up for trying to bribe a council official. Anyway the upshot was that it was just too damned hot for arguments and when I suggested he could go down and tell my client that her party entertainment must be cancelled, he reluctantly moved aside the cones.

'Make it snappy, you have 30 minutes,' he said, as I went back to the vehicle.

I let him have the last word. Thirty minutes? He could kiss my Bassey ass! We slowly drove down Brick Lane looking up at the house/flat numbers. 'Here it is,' Ma B said as we pulled up in the middle of the street. We both looked at the small space left for us to park and then looked at each other – Ma B and I were famous for our inability to park. We always needed the length of two spaces. There were cars parked on both sides of the road in true, cramped, London style and this was the only parking space available as far as the eye could see. Ma B took one look at it and shouted, 'Too fucking small!' A couple of minutes passed and the space had not grown.

'I'll have a go but it won't be pretty,' she growled.

We tried to go in frontwards, we tried to go in backwards, I even think we tried to go in sort of sideways. We were getting hotter and either the space was getting smaller or the vehicle was getting bigger. We could have been there until Nelson got his eye back but that vehicle was not getting parked in that space, not by us anyway. There we were in the middle of a double-parked street. A guy had driven up behind us and he was obviously a resident on that street and clearly wanted to drive out of Brick Lane. A woman was sitting in his passenger seat, presumably his girlfriend, and we were blocking his way. He waited for a few minutes then honked his horn impatiently.

'This just gets better,' I groaned.

Ma B got out. 'She is going to lose it,' I thought, getting out of the vehicle, mentally cursing our inability to park. We looked such planks. Now, this may not work every time, and I suspect it does have to be a genuine situation.

'I'm sorry, you have obviously seen the mess I am getting into trying to park this vehicle into that space. God knows I've tried but I just can't do it. The only way I can see you getting passed this vehicle is if you were able to park it for me.' She had cleverly slipped in 'able', such a lovely little word. I watched his expression change from annoyance and disbelief to one of determined challenge. I never loved the male ego more than on that blistering hot day in Brick Lane. He got out of his car and took our keys out of Ma B's outstretched hand. Without a word he got into our Euro bus, carefully adjusted the seat and mirrors and we watched delightedly as he performed the perfect parallel parking manoeuvre, slotting nicely into the tight space. He wordlessly handed the keys back to Ma B, got in his car and drove off!

A couple of giggly young London 'it' girls, who were Anya's friends, let us in and we quickly set up in a tiny corner whilst they titivated and blew up balloons. We rehydrated ourselves, told the girls we would be back at 11.15pm and climbed back in the vehicle, heading off for the next leg of the double-up, Farnham Castle in Surrey. The traffic was hell and the car was a sauna but we arrived safely about 3.30pm. Claire, the events woman, a posh middle-aged lady who bore an uncanny resemblance to Hyacinth Bucket, was there to meet us and I expected her to take a call from Sheridan at any moment. She had allocated us a room in the castle to change. It was the least practical room in the whole place, if not, the whole world. We had to drag our suitcase up three, long, winding, stone staircases that were so narrow we could hardly move the suitcase up each step.

We deposited our suitcase in the room (just a room – no bed) and made our way outside to find a shady tree. It was a glorious lazy summer afternoon. The old castle grounds were straight out of a period drama. The late afternoon had a quiet almost heavy stillness to it and with just the sounds of bees buzzing we found a big old oak tree a little way away from the marquee where we dozed for probably half an hour. We woke to find the sound guys arriving outside the marquee with the PA equipment. They were ready for me at 6.30pm as guests were arriving at 7pm. Claire beckoned me over and said she wanted a word with me about my start time. With a sense of dread I put on my best accommodating smile. If I started any later than 9pm, I wouldn't make it to my next gig on time.

Usually I stipulated in my contracts that I didn't perform during dinner, as my set was not a background one.

I always told bookers that I would start the performance during coffees but not when the audience were still eating. Claire said the dinner was likely to run a little late and as she was completely aware that I did not perform until people were on the coffees, which she said she totally understood, she would be happy to have me start at 9.30pm instead. Had it not been a double-up situation that would have been the perfect case scenario, but in this instance I had to switch tactics. I told her that she didn't have to worry about that at all. I said in this case, as I could see they had a packed agenda for the evening, I would be happy to help by starting when people were finishing their main course or on the desserts. I said I didn't want her to have to alter anything on my part. I almost believed my new altruistic self. She thanked me for being so flexible and helpful.

Little did she know that flexibility had nothing to do with it. Usually I complained like buggery if anyone asked me to perform when punters were still shovelling food into their mouths, but on this occasion, I would have happily burst out singing *Goldfinger* before they had even glanced at their starters. While I was getting ready and applying my make-up I had my two customary glasses of Chardonnay to give me a bit of a lift for the night ahead. I was ready and waiting at the back entrance of the marquee at 8.55pm. Ma B was in place next to the soundman and we were ready to go. At 9pm, instead of my intro, I heard a man announcing that over the course of the evening they were having some kind of fundraiser. This person went on to explain what they were raising funds for and how much they were hoping to raise.

At 9.10 pm, I was still waiting and the bloke was still talking. At 9.15pm I wanted to kill myself. The only plus was the weather had cooled down and I was no longer hyperventilating. I had on my thick white fur cloak but as there was now a breeze, at least I was no longer sweating like a farmyard animal. I was silently contemplating how to take my own life when I heard my intro. At last, I was on. The 45-minute show flew by. I said my goodnights and left the stage at 10.10pm. We got back in the car and began leg three of the mission as we headed back to London. I hid outside of the little flat door while Ma B went in to check all was well. She beckoned me in and pressed play straight away. *Big Spender* started as I entered the room with my big gold boa. Anya was very surprised and she squealed with delight. Those women were an absolute joy.

We got back in the car at around 12.45am and bid London goodnight. Our timing was impeccable because Brick Lane was heaving with people coming out of bars and eateries. We crawled along with people quite literally falling into the car on either side. It took at least 15 minutes just to make it to the bottom of the road. What was it with that road? We arrived back in Leicestershire at 3.15am. Poor Ma B had done more hours on the road than was physically comfortable and her knee was hurting. I was also completely finished. Similar to when you are nursing the mother of all hangovers and you vow to never drink again, we went to bed that night and swore that we would never ever accept a double-up again. We had been lucky. We had made it to the gigs on time with no casualties, the clients were happy and we got paid, but what price can one put on one's bloody health? However, as with a hangover, the effects wear off and you forget how bad it was. It was the same with the double-up. They came again and we did them!

Bazza as compère during the Vegas-style theatre shows

Performing at a wedding where I was scooped up in a fireman's lift mid-song. This was not uncommon!

Backstage with TV personality Jeremy Beadle following my performance at River Rooms, London

Joanne's career takes off - and pays tribute to Shirley Bassey

SURELY it's not Shirley... Well, OK, no it's not - but it will take you a while to establish that for certain - because she's that good.

Atherstone girl Joanne Copeman is a woman with a career that has sky-rocketed in two years and she's set to return to her home fans at the The Concordia Theatre in Hinkley this September - as the one and only Shirley Bassey.

Having played the Assembly Rooms in Tamworth earlier this year Joanne has been enjoying great success and rave reviews. She was recently booked to perform at a James Bond Annual Ball in Rochester, Missouri USA for next year where organisers will fly in a

15-piece big band from New Orleans to back her show, and she is still wowing the home crowds.

"I can hardly believe it. My shows are going down a storm. I am performing, then having hours of photo shoots taken with various members of the audience! It's fantastic - a bit like a photo shoot for *Hello!* I'm really enjoying it."

Hailed by London's Stage newspaper as 'the best at being Bassey,' this month Joanne sang at the 'People's Day' Lewishams Gay Pride Festival in London to an audience of 13,000 and she also topped the bill at The Royal Ashton Variety Show at the Tameside Hippodrome in April after performing 'Surely

Bassey - The Show' in a five-star star hotel in The Kingdom of Bahrain from March.

Joanne started out when she won a deal with management company Rockit Music, but was left high and dry when it went into liquidation two years ago.

"Time was ticking away and in my late twenties with bills to be paid, I decided to drastically change course and do something I said I would never do - become a tribute artist," she said.

"The places this has taken me in only two years are unbelievable," she said.

Call The Concordia for more information.

Leicester Mercury, *2005*

Ma B grabbing 40 winks backstage, wearing her trademark black combats, at a band gig for the military

100

Surely Bassey

CHAPTER SIX

00' HEAVEN

Unlike Matt who was possibly the world's biggest Bond fan, I was one of the rare few people who had never watched a James Bond film in my entire life, so I found it slightly ironic that, due to the job I was doing, my life and the world of Ian Fleming's 007 character had become so closely entwined. At least 70% of my gigs were Bond themed events. Dame Shirley had recorded three Bond hits so when a Bond event was organised, a Bassey tribute act was always a popular choice.

If I counted how many 007 functions I have performed at over the years the number would probably be staggering. I've seen it all; from fancy James Bond events held at Stoke Park Golf and Country Club, where the actual golf scene in *Goldfinger* was filmed, and official events staged at Pinewood Studios, where many of the Bond movies were filmed, to humble, private Bond parties held in a marquee in somebody's garden. On the bigger events, each table was often named after a Bond film and they usually had a 007 quiz, asking questions about different Bond movies. One of the Sean Connery look-alikes usually had to appear as Bond and deliver some sort of 007 speech, incorporating links to the client's specific company or industry. He'd then fire his replica gun, adopt the James bond stance, fireworks would go off and the DJ would then play the Bond theme music. Once that happened, the evening was usually under way.

Due to the amount of Bond gigs I performed at, I was very often working with the 007 look-alikes. Different agents booked us so sometimes we knew who was going to be on the gig but quite often we would just run into each other when we arrived. Bond gigs were long, drawn out affairs so it was always nice to work with the look-alikes. We were like one big family. They amused me and it helped pass the time for all of us. There were quite a few old Sean Connery look-alikes, one young Connery, a couple of Daniel Craigs, a brilliant Oddjob, a great, although very temperamental, Jaws and an arrogant, irritating, Pierce Brosnan whom nobody liked. They earned similar money to tribute acts and their job was to meet, greet and mingle with guests from the reception drinks onwards. They usually did around 2–3 hours in total and posed for pictures with punters throughout the night. Sometimes there was extra work for them and they had to get involved in scripted speeches or re-enact some of the Bond fight scenes using stunts and props.

Quite often one of the Sean Connerys introduced me on stage and Oddjob escorted me, holding the train of my fur cloak until I was safely in position. Wherever we were performing, we were always given a communal sort of a room (the green room) to hang around in, enabling us to keep out of the way of the guests when we were not required so we spent a lot of time together. There was only one Oddjob and one Jaws look-alike and they were both great at what they did.

Just like when they were in character, when out of character they were two completely different personalities. My favourite was Oddjob because he didn't take anything too seriously, including what he did for a living. Don't get me wrong, when he was working he did the business but he always came across like he knew it was a strange and very lucrative job, one that could disappear at any time and he should enjoy it while it lasted. He had been doing the job a long time so he would spend his time taking the piss by criticising new, up and coming Bond look-alikes or giving a bit of a dig to the existing ones. He was always on some sort of weird diet but as I told him on many occasions, as long as he could do his jacket up and get that bowler hat on his chubby Chinese head, he didn't need to diet.

The Jaws look-alike was indeed a fantastic character. He stood at 7 feet 3 inches and weighed 25 stones. He honestly did look like the real Jaws and he also had the huge metal teeth. He was pretty frightening stuff. His hands were the size of Dunlop tyres. Our Jaws had lots of little tricks that he played on guests when he was working. He did the routine meet and greets business but he then added a little something of his own to the proceedings. Guests were always amazed and startled when they first saw Jaws. Visually he was quite alarming but he always made a huge impact on Bond events. He stood by the door of the entrance area and as guests arrived for reception drinks he would offer to take the gentlemen's jacket, then he would get the guy by the neck and physically lift him up in the air by his jacket. I don't know how he managed to do this without damaging their jackets or their necks but he did. The photos always came out great.

If guests were gathered around a bar area or relaxing on casual chairs and sofas, Jaws would saunter over and pretend he was about to plump out the cushions. When he got close to one of the sofas he would pretend to stumble as if he had lost his footing and would end up looking like he was about to fall and flatten the guests and the sofa beneath them. He was so good at it and it always frightened them to death. Even the men would let out a little involuntary squeal.

Jaws took no prisoners. He had certain stipulations listed on his contract when clients booked him and they had to be adhered to. Certain expenses had to be paid for by the client on top of his fee; we all did this but his requests were a little different. If he had to travel by train, extra legroom had to be organised. When he needed overnight accommodation arranging, he had to have a king size bed. Don't get me wrong, these were all fairly reasonable requests for a guy of 7 feet 3 inches. He would work his contracted 2–3 hours no problem but after that he wanted to sit and drink his red wine undisturbed. I'm telling you, once the metal teeth came out and the red wine went in, that was him finished. He was not to be messed with. Needless to say, he was excellent at his job and no real 007 event was complete without him.

Due to the fact that the Bond look-alikes spent so much time together in a working environment, sometimes tempers would fray. We were like one little 007 unit so it was inevitable that we should occasionally get on one another's nerves. Gigs could be tiresome but sometimes they could also be intense and what could quite easily be deemed a trivial matter from somebody on the outside, seemed very irritating to the people on the inside.

I remember a 007 gig we were all booked for that was being held in a Manchester hotel over a Christmas period. I know it must have been in the month of December because I distinctly remember that the hotel and Manchester city centre looked very festive indeed. I also recall that we were all completely knackered as December is a killer of a month. Everybody in our little clan got sick to death of James Bond during December even though we knew that we couldn't afford to be. We were all tired and everybody started to get up everybody else's nose. The smallest thing could wind us up.

I knew that during December Jaws was to be watched very carefully and this particular gig was no different to any other. We were performing in a big function room with the usual Bond backdrops, 007 props, star cloths, plasma screens and casino tables. It was a corporate event for British Aerospace and I had already done my sound check. It was around 6.30pm and we all needed to be out of the way before the guests arrived at 7pm. It was all pretty standard stuff. The only thing left to do was for Oddjob, Jaws and Sean Connery to quickly run through their fight scene. During the course of the evening, after the guests had eaten their meal, Jaws and Oddjob were supposed to kidnap the Managing Director of British Aerospace and James Bond was supposed to rescue him. Sean Connery was already complaining that the client had given him a script that was far too long.

'I'll never remember it all. I need to run through it in full.'

Jaws glared. 'You can bollocks. I'm not hanging around. I want to get back to my room and eat,' he mumbled in his heavy Geordie accent.

An atmosphere quickly began to form and Oddjob casually said to Connery, 'Chill out and just wing it.' Jaws was getting fidgety and Ma B and I were thinking of making ourselves scarce.

'It's alright for you two, you don't have to read out a full script and remember the fight scene,' Connery replied. 'I have the most to do and I'm not winging anything.'

'Just fucking get on with it then,' Jaws snapped.

After a few minutes of Connery flicking over the pages and pacing up and down the room, Oddjob said, 'Look I'm happy to wing the whole scene tonight to be honest.'

Sean Connery looked absolutely horrified and said, 'No! We better run through it and you better take note of where the screens are hanging. The last time we did it you slung your bowler hat straight at a £7,000 plasma screen!'

Oddjob simply shrugged and smiled, he then turned towards me and said, 'It's the metal trim around the bowler hat that caused the damage, anyway they were insured.'

'Right, we run through it once. Then that's it,' Jaws barked.

They did what they needed to do but as they got towards the end of the fight scene, right at the part where James Bond has to hold his gun towards Jaws' face, Jaws stopped, stared directly at Sean Connery and shouted, 'If you put that gun that close to my face again, I'm gonna pull your fucking head off, you stupid c**t!'

That was the end of that little rehearsal. The three of them stomped up the corridor in total silence and didn't utter a word to each other. Their hotel rooms were next to each other and they each banged their own door shut. They were like sulky, teenage girls who had fallen out at a sleepover. As Ma B and I walked behind them to our room we had to smile because we knew that within a few hours they would have to meet back up again and do their job. We also knew that they would do it well and everything would be fine. They did just that and as we suspected, it was faultless. By the end of the evening, when we were all off duty and having our après Bond drinks they were best chums once more. That's how things went sometimes during the month of December. At least the Pierce Brosnan look-alike was not on that gig. Nobody required it to be the month of December in order to slap the Pierce. Not one of us needed an excuse to give him a good right hook. He had a face that one would never tire of slapping. He was truly the spy who loved himself.

Oddjob delighted in telling everyone how he once found a pair of Pierce Brosnan's shoes in a dressing room that they were sharing. Everybody was aware that he was a little on the short side to be a Pierce Brosnan look-alike. Oddjob told us that the shoes he had found had some sort of blocks inserted inside them that were designed to make him appear taller. He said they were not visible on the outside of the shoe. The heel appeared normal; they were inserted into the shoe and raised Brosnan by about three inches. That tickled Oddjob and from that day forward we knew that Pierce Brosnan as Built-up Bond (BUB).

I remember a gig in Aberdeen with Matt and the rest of the band for an American company called Chevron. We were flown to the event and booked to play for an hour from 9–10pm. About an hour after we arrived at our hotel I spotted Oddjob at reception. He informed me that he was booked to do an afternoon slot with Jaws and BUB. They were due to do a fight scene at around 2pm involving BUB and a motorbike stunt. Apparently Jaws had the impression that it was an evening event so he'd booked his train at the wrong time and hadn't turned up. He later proved that this was his agent's error and not his own. Ma B, the band and I went to eat in the bar area at around 5pm and BUB was already in there. He said he and Oddjob had performed the Bond scene and it had gone rather well. He then proceeded to bore the pants off us with his bad joke telling. Not only did BUB fancy himself to be a bit of a ladies man, he also fancied himself as some sort of comedian off stage. He wasn't but he loved the sound of his own voice. He appeared to have had a few alcoholic beverages and after around 45 minutes of listening to his drivel, we were all painfully aware that he was about to launch into another one of his poor comedy sets, so we made our excuses and left.

Three hours later and well into our one-hour long set, a drunk BUB appeared at the side of the stage and made his way up the stairs, towards the centre where I was singing. He seemed to be acting out something impromptu and un-rehearsed that none of us knew anything about. He adopted the Bond stance and stood right next to me while I was singing *Goldeneye*. He then proceeded to start feeling my arse – while I was bloody well singing! I turned around and looked at Matt, who looked like he was about stop playing the keyboards, and was ready to give BUB an ear-pull. I also glanced nervously at the rest of the band who were all wearing a what-the-fuck-does-this-bloke-think-he's-doing expression on their faces. Luckily, a few of the event organisers spotted that BUB had obviously consumed a bit too much liquid refreshment, saw the bewilderment and general discomfort on our faces and removed him from the room. We didn't see BUB again on that particular gig.

***

During 2005 I was pretty much covering the whole of the UK. We were travelling up and down the motorways endlessly. It was a good job Ma B had everything under control. She was perfection in her role and had endless responsibilities. To be honest, the only thing she didn't do was the singing and that was the easy bit. She dealt with all of the email enquiries, quotes, contracts, riders, flights for us and the band, payments, autoroutes, costumes, driving, packed lunches and sometimes she operated the sound. Everything she did was copied, documented and stored in date order.

Ma B was an absolute trooper and without her there would have been no show. She literally ran the whole shebang and that's probably why she fell over so much. You see, Ma B was known to 'go down' on the odd occasion. At one Bond event when we were with the band, we were all walking in a line up a hotel corridor, just about to go on stage when there was an almighty thud. We turned around to see Ma B behind us, in a huddle on the floor, poking out from underneath my big furry black cloak. She had tripped up a step again. I shouted, 'Ma B down!' It was quickly established that she was OK but Paul the drummer wasn't. He was laughing so much that I was worried he was unfit to play.

Ma B simply said, 'It's no wonder I fall over so often with all the shit I have to carry. I've got your cloak, boas, music stand, lyric book and at Christmas I've got that bag of bloody Santa hats and boas. It's a wonder I ever stay upright!'

***

One of the things about my job that really got up my nose was the charity gig. These were large events designed to raise money for various charity organisations. I would like to think that I am not an uncharitable person but, to be brutally honest, many of these events were indulgent bullshit. Not all of them, but most. It always seemed to be certain sorts of women that ran these events and they drove me insane. It would begin with the irritating phone call where they started the conversation by stating their registered charity. They then told me that they had looked around my website and wanted to enquire about booking the show. Everything would go swimmingly until I gave them the price.

Once the quote was given, I was always met with something like, 'Oh dear, that's expensive. We are a charity you see. The event is going to raise money for blah blah blah and we have a tight budget. As it's for charity can you reduce your fee?'

I always wanted to reply by asking them how much Schweppes had reduced the price of their tonic water for the event, or how much the Hilton Hotel had knocked off the hire fee for the function room. I knew none of the big service providers knocked anything off the price for charity functions. I however, one small self-employed individual, was expected to halve my fee. I had to explain that I give to charity when I choose but it cannot be incorporated into the way I earn a living. The staff at the hotel got their hourly rate and my fee was my fee, it was not up for negotiation just because they were putting on a charity event. If that were the case I would have been performing for half price at charity gigs every week. Once I had explained myself in the nicest way possible, the women adopted a slightly more abrasive attitude but they often then agreed to the fee and that's when the real nonsense started.

Most of these charity gigs were James Bond themed events. For saying the whole idea was to raise money for charity, I was always amazed at how much money these people spent. They held a lot of the events in flashy marquees. There would be Bond shootout games, casino tables, props and backdrops, girls that were sprayed gold standing around serving drinks and canapés, chocolate fountains, outside caterers, red carpets, Bassey, a DJ, 007 look-alikes and a few Aston Martins parked outside. All of the guests were decked up in their finery, the ladies in their long gowns and the gents sporting their best dickie bows. These gigs always seemed to last for an eternity because they needed to raise a certain amount of money, which didn't surprise me due to the gross amount that they spent. They had quizzes, auctions and various prizes.

Charity gigs were truly tedious events. At the end of the evening everybody had to stand around thanking the female organisers for all of their hard work when in reality all they did was run around flapping all night and open the casino tables at the same time as they told the act to start, even though we told them that it never worked very well. They were a royal pain in the backside.

I didn't really like working for female event organisers. A few stand out in my memory as being reasonable but they were the exceptions, in the main they were all the same. They always came across as bossy, like they had something to prove. It didn't matter that we, the entertainers, performed at those sorts of events three times a week, they knew best. Men were far more laid back and would often tell us the general running order. They would then say something along the lines of, 'You do these events all the time, what do you think? Tell me what usually works best.'

Not the women, oh no, they wanted to remind us all night that we were working for them. Normally they would be totally impractical. They showed us the area where they wanted us to perform and were adamant that it was the best place, until we pointed out that there were no plug points. They often told us that we were to go on stage directly after the auction even though the guests had just sat still for two hours and this was the exact point to let them get up and have a ciggie and a wee before the next thing began.

The female event organisers could easily spend 30 minutes fiddling with one flower display but at 8pm they still had no idea where to tell the act to get changed. These thoroughly annoying females always managed to make the running orders as illogical as possible. Acts usually ask for a hot meal when on a gig and these women always arranged for our food to be served just before the performance was due to start.

The scene was always the same; feather boas and costumes filled the changing room, there were makeup mirrors littered everywhere, fake tan spray being applied and dancers limbering up. Then they would arrive – the two young hotel youths delivering the food. We would inhale the wonderful aroma of roast chicken, potatoes, broccoli and rich gravy. The problem was, I was busy trying to turn myself into a glamorous diva from Tiger Bay, the dancers had feather head gear on that was so big they could hardly fit through the door let alone eat, there was no room to put the food down and we all had to be on stage in five minutes. We never complained because in the main we were all happy to actually have a changing area.

I had been given some truly bizarre changing areas in the past. I was once told that I was to get changed on a grassy area behind a marquee that had been cordoned off with a bit of yellow tarpaulin. There was no light, no mirror and my heels kept digging into the grass. Ma B found a mirror and we managed to pull a little lamp in from the back of the marquee. The lead just about reached. When I was half way through applying my makeup, the light went out. Upon investigation, Ma B returned to inform me that one of the catering staff had plugged in a dodgy kettle lead somewhere; apparently they were running everything, including the PA equipment and lighting, from one 13-amp plug. In the end we had to locate a torch.

One of the most inappropriate changing areas that I was ever given however, was when I was performing for some very wealthy people in Dorset.

They had a huge house and I was booked to perform for 30 minutes in a marquee in their back garden.

Upon my arrival, the lady who owned the house said, 'I have a house completely full of people and unfortunately my husband is setting up a projector screen in the marquee with his friend. You are a surprise for his birthday so he must not see you. I have nowhere for you to change. Can you use the garden shed?' I swear she was deadly serious. I had to squeeze into a shed surrounded by lawn mowers, pitchforks, compost and shite. There was no real light so we were lucky that it was summer. She had two young kids who were playing football in the garden. They kept kicking the ball up against the shed whilst I was trying to change and remove bits of grass from my fur cloak. They kicked one ball too many so I shot out the door and gave them a look, which I know showed them that I would actually hurt them both if they did it again. I may have been impersonating a diva but some of the changing areas I was given proved that was where any similarities truly ended.

***

'Hey Mr DJ put a record on, I wanna dance with my baby…'

I worked with DJ's on most of my events and it always baffled me why some of them didn't seem to understand that they were not the main attraction for the evening. I think some of them disliked tribute acts immensely. It didn't matter whether the gig was in a marquee, a hotel, a casino, on a boat, indoor, outdoor, home or abroad, the scenario was always the same. The DJ always seemed to turn up late telling me how manically busy he was whilst heaving in enough equipment to blow Wembley stadium away. If we didn't get to the venue before them they'd set their gear up smack bang in the middle of the stage, leaving us absolutely no room.

When I arrived they said things like, 'Hello love, I take it you're the Bassey cabaret act. I presume you will be working the floor.' I wanted to reply with something along the lines of, 'Hello mate. I take it you're the egotistical DJ and no I am not working the bloody floor,' but I kept my mouth shut every time.

We then fought for space. On most occasions they were there to finish the night and take the crowd through to around 2am. Most punters were pissed by midnight so why the DJ had to be centre stage, I don't know. I have worked with a few whose sound checks were far longer than mine or any live band. I didn't get it. The tracks had already been mixed and mastered to within an inch of their lives by a major record label for Christ's sake. Tina Turner's vocals sat perfectly with the music so there wasn't too much to do was there? All they had to do was stand there and play one record after another with cheesy chatter in between.

If we got hostile towards the particularly awkward ones, they had a tendency to deliberately play the real Shirley Bassey just before I went on. We both fought for plug sockets and tried to nick each other's extension leads and XLR cables. It really was every man for himself at the end of the night and the tedious part was always trying to ferret around on the floor in the dark trying to find the cables. In fact as soon as I had performed the encore and said goodnight, before I had even fully left the stage the DJs were at it. Poor Ma B had not even had a chance to scoop up my cloak and wrench my microphone from the stand before Mr DJ banged on the Scissor Sisters full throttle and the dance floor filled. She was then plunged into immediate darkness. Whilst I scurried off back to the room to get changed, Ma B was always scratting around some DJ's legs whilst he played the 20-minute version of *Valerie* trying to work out whose leads were whose. She was always concerned that if she unplugged the wrong extension lead *Valerie* would be cut abruptly short and there would be carnage.

***

By this time, Steph was two years into, and well under way with, her 12-step, AA recovery programme and had thus far remained sober from the time she found out that she was pregnant. She had since given birth to a beautiful baby boy whom she named Harvey and she had everything to live for. Having said that, she knew the power alcohol had over her and she was taking no chances. She was attending AA meetings three times a week and clinging to the Serenity Prayer for dear life. I was supporting her as much as I could and I willed her not to crack on a daily basis. I looked after Harvey for her whilst she attended her Wednesday evening meetings and consumed as much tea as I possibly could.

There were AA references all over her house and although I was under no illusions regarding the serious nature of her illness and the force of the addiction, I also noticed the sheer power of AA. She had handed herself over to it 100%. It was almost as if AA had formed a protective barrier around her, shielding her from alcohol and as long as she followed the steps and believed in the programme, it would not allow the demon drink to penetrate that barrier. The Serenity Prayer took pride of place on the kitchen fridge and on the inside door of the upstairs loo.

> *God grant me the serenity to accept the things I cannot change;*
> *Courage to change the things I can;*
> *And the wisdom to know the difference.*

Steph had a few rocky patches along the way and there were times when she wouldn't draw back the curtains, get out of bed or answer the phone but she didn't drink. She was prescribed anti-depressants, which she welcomed and as the time passed, she got busy. She booked herself in to as many self-help groups as possible, in my opinion far too many but that was Steph.

To help with the fact that she was a single parent, she went to Thrifty Shoppers on Mondays, Fasta Pasta on Tuesdays, to add to her cooking skills as a busy mum on the move, Wednesdays was AA, Thursdays was 'NA' because she had smoked a couple of joints when she first stopped drinking and thought it could be a slippery slope, Fridays was a business administration class just in case she fancied going back to 'real work' at a later date and Saturdays and Sundays were both AA meetings. To be honest she didn't really have time for a drink or a breakdown. Steph had her moments but she was doing well and remained on the wagon. I had my fingers firmly crossed that she would never again touch a drop of the devil's urine.

Matt's green Maestro outside Stoke Park where two 007 movies, Goldfinger *and* Tomorrow Never Dies, *were filmed*

At Talk Of The Town with the eight-piece band (one member is missing, he'd nipped off for a ciggie)

At a 007 event in Birmingham with Oddjob and Jaws

*On stage with the band
in Aberdeen*

With my Bond girls at Tatton Park, Cheshire

In the bar area following a 007 event in Birmingham with Oddjob and Jaws

CHAPTER SEVEN

GOING GLOBAL

I was happily meandering around the house one morning in the spring of 2005 when I noticed another website enquiry had come through. It immediately got my attention as it was from the Bahrain Welsh Society. They were holding their annual expat ball at the very plush Gulf Hotel in Bahrain and wanted to fly me over to perform. They had chosen a Shirley Bassey act for obvious reasons. Now this posed a huge problem for me and I'll tell you why.

I had a serious flight phobia. I had flown many times when I was a kid and seen many faraway lands. I had no fear of flying until I reached about 22 years of age. My fear developed quickly and I had been petrified of flying since around 1996 after a particularly turbulent flight to Madrid. From then on I seemed to focus all of my fears and anxieties on flying. Although I knew it was irrational, I could do nothing about it. I only flew when absolutely necessary and I would rather not go on holiday at all than have to fly. Even a two-hour 30-minute flight from England to Portugal saw me curled up in my seat in tears. I would start to worry about it days before the flight and once I made it to the airport I rarely spoke.

I think there were various elements that contributed to me being scared of flying. For starters, I simply didn't trust a metal tube 35,000 feet up in the air. I had no control – that was a biggy – I couldn't stop it or get off. There was a definite element of claustrophobia. If something did go wrong mid-flight, passengers did not merely come out with a few cuts and bruises, all mumbling, 'Shit that was a close one'. In my mind, people didn't survive plane crashes. Everybody died. There were no stretchers carrying the wounded to hospital. People didn't suffer the odd compound fracture or prolapsed disc. Oh no, when these beauties came down, passengers were identified by their teeth. The only way of knowing what happened was to wait weeks and investigate the little black box.

That's why I never saw what difference 'adopting the emergency landing position' would make. If the plane crashed everybody would be dead anyway. Whenever the cabin crew were doing the 'in case of an emergency situation, please do the following…' sequence, I used to feel like bursting into hysterical laughter and screaming:

'What fucking difference is that going to make you stupid cow! Our limbs are going to be scattered all over the ground and the aircraft will be in a ball of flames. How is that stupid little yellow plastic bag and a small tube going to save us? Well? Come to think about it, a little seatbelt is not going to be a huge lifesaver either is it? And I'm sure that little whistle will attract great attention when we are drowning in the Atlantic. Who are we whistling to, each other? You are welcome to serve us all a suicide pill because that would be helpful but please fuck off with the oxygen mask routine. Emergency exits my arse. We will be tangled up amongst a heap of burning metal. There are no real exits so sit down and stop lying to everybody!'

That was another thing that puzzled me. Why did they not issue everybody with parachutes? Surely that's like being on a boat without a life jacket. At some point before the plane hits the ground, it must be flying at an altitude where people could jump out. Now that's an emergency procedure I could understand may be of some use.

The pilots could run out into the aisle and shout, 'OK folks we need to jump erm… about nowish. Everybody get your shit on and do one.'

Surely that's the only way you'd stand a chance in a doomed plane, the rest of it seemed like bollocks to me. Not many things in life scared me but I was petrified of flying. I would only have to see a stewardess whisper something to a colleague and in my head she had said, 'Brace yourselves we're going down'. She was probably just warning her co-worker that they were nearly out of orange juice in business class, but not in my head.

When I encountered turbulence, I was horrendous. They tell you that turbulence is nothing to worry about and it's not dangerous. Well excuse me but being bounced around in a metal tin thousands of feet up in the air is not my idea of safe. I always pictured the pilots fighting with the controls, trying to keep the plane straight, fighting every bump. In my mind, things would be flashing in the cockpit and all of the lights would go out. Squeals would come from the stewardesses and glasses would smash as the pilots lost control and the plane spiralled down in the sky.

Even if there was no turbulence, I was anticipating the pilot being physically unfit and suffering a fatal heart attack. I envisaged faulty hydraulic and electrical systems, air cabin pressure mal-functioning and engines failing. I was ecstatic whenever we landed. While the other passengers were calmly unfastening their seatbelts and collecting their hand luggage I always felt like jumping up and down clapping my hands and shouting, 'We made it, we're alive! Thank the good lord above, we're alive!' I always had the urge to run up the aisle, break into the cockpit and kiss the pilots, screaming that they were the best pilots ever. When the stewardesses lined up at the exit of the aircraft saying things like, 'I hope you enjoyed your flight' I would pass them with a big beaming smile and enthusiastically say, 'thank you very much!' I felt like moonwalking off the plane. It was a totally different 'me' to the one that had boarded only hours before. Once I'd got over the fact that I was happy to be alive, I got tired very quickly. Flying exhausted me and the sense of relief was relatively short, as I then had to prepare for the trip back!

That was my relationship with planes. We really didn't get on. I didn't like seeing them in the sky; I didn't even like pictures of planes. I hated hearing them take off even if I was not due to board one. To me planes represented imminent death on a grand scale! How in God's name was I going to complete a 6-hour 30-minute flight to Bahrain on a Wednesday, do the gig on Thursday and complete a 7-hour 30-minute flight back on the Friday? I told myself I couldn't possibly do it, gig or no gig.

Ma B really wanted us to do it. I said I couldn't and I'd have to tell them that I was already booked or price myself out of the gig. Ma B asked me if I'd do it if we were able to extend the stay but I said I didn't think that I could. She replied to the enquiry asking for a lot of money, an extra three days stay free of charge, all flights, transfers, meals, accommodation for two people to be paid for by the client, two separate rooms and half the fee cleared in my bank account up front. I went off to bed that night and prayed that they thought we were cheeky bitches and refused.

They came back to us the following morning and had agreed to the lot. Ma B was now applying the pressure and it was horrible because I knew it would be a great gig and good for my career. Had it not been a gig, it would have been an easy decision. I went to the doctors and asked if they could give me something to take to calm my nerves during the flight but my doctor said no because passengers are supposed to remain alert in case of an emergency situation. Oh the irony of that response. I would have died of fright by that point. That would be the precise moment that somebody like me didn't want to be alert. I was getting desperate so I scoured the internet, searching for anything helpful. There were various forums where 'flight phobes' chatted and exchanged stories. Many of them had managed to get their hands on two sorts of drugs to help lessen their anxiety.

I noted the names of the pills and was about to try and get hold of some when a website address caught my eye. I had seen various websites but most of them were ran by the major airlines and offered fear of flying courses amongst other things. I hadn't seen this website before and it looked slightly different. For fearful flyers everywhere, I suggest you check out www.fearofflyinghelp.com. I would personally like to say a huge thank you to Captain Stacey Chance (it's an unfortunate surname for a pilot but the bloke really does know what he's doing) and I am eternally grateful to him. As a result of the captain's help, I was about to attempt a 6-hour flight to the Kingdom of Bahrain.

The plane landed and we didn't crash, which for me was a great result. I admit I spent most of the flight hiding under my jacket with my headphones turned up to the max, but I didn't cry or try and burst into the cockpit and demand that they land the plane. As far as my phobia was concerned, the flight to Bahrain was definite progress and I think Ma B was pleasantly surprised. As soon as we landed I vowed not to think about the return flight until I was on the way to the airport for the journey home. As the cabin crew stood near the open exit of the plane, bid us all farewell and wished everybody a pleasant stay, I resisted the desire to pop my head into the cock pit and slip the pilots £20 each for not killing us. I considered their probable annual salary and decided that not killing us was surely incorporated into their modest wage.

I skipped enthusiastically past the Gulf Air cabin crew and said my thank yous and goodbyes. I was now ready to check out Bahrain. It was the beginning of March and we landed at around 7.30pm. I remember that the air felt warm but not stifling, it was that pleasant, late evening, gentle heat. We quickly spotted a guy in the arrivals area holding a board with my name plastered across it and made our way to his car.

On the journey from the airport to the hotel I recall thinking that the area seemed serenely quiet. I didn't know too much about Bahrain, only that it was situated in the Persian Gulf and it was under the rule of the Al Khalifa royal family. I also knew that it was known for its oil and pearls and it was the place where the popular Bahrain F1 Grand Prix took place, but other than that I knew very little about the country. We arrived at the

Gulf Hotel at around 9pm and it looked quite stunning. It really was a picture of gleaming opulence and for some reason it looked exactly as I had imagined it to.

It was a 5-star hotel and very ornate in its décor. The floors were marble, so shiny that I swear I could have used them as a mirror to apply my makeup. The huge, crystal chandeliers that hung from the ceilings sparkled like finely cut diamonds. Soft music played in the vast lobby area and I quickly clocked the BMW Formula 1 racing car that they had placed on show as it had attracted a small gathering near reception. I also noticed a huge display board positioned near the lifts advertising my show. It was a picture, in a glass encasement, surrounded by a gold frame. I don't know how big it was but it was far bigger than any promotional material I had been used to.

Our hotel rooms were also very grand. I had never been to the Middle East before and I was quite fascinated by the Arabs wandering around the hotel. I thought that the men appeared very regal in their whiter than white, flowing clobber. They seemed to have excellent posture and walked bolt upright with their heads held high. We had been booked in the restaurant that evening and whilst we were having a drink and perusing the menu, I noticed that a young Arab couple with a small child were moving behind a screened area. I asked one of the waiting staff in the restaurant why the couple were moving to a special enclosure. I was informed that the female, who was dressed in a black burka from head to toe and whose face was completely covered, was about to eat. She would need to remove the cover from her face to put the food in her mouth and it was customary that no other male saw her face other than her husband. For that reason, she could never eat in public. If the women ate out in restaurants, they had to go behind a screen. I didn't really know what to make of that at the time.

The first evening meal in the Gulf Hotel was a relaxing one. We were not due to meet the chairman of the Bahrain Welsh Society until the following lunchtime and the sound check had been arranged for the following afternoon. That evening we decided to have a couple of drinks in one of the bars within the hotel. There really was nowhere else to go out and have a drink in Bahrain other than hotel bars because it was still very much a dry state. We heard music coming from within a bar near the reception area in the hotel so we went to investigate. It was called The Sherlock Holmes and the hotel had obviously gone for ye-olde-English-public-house vibe when they designed the bar. I remember there was an old style red telephone box near the entrance.

The place was busy and quite rowdy compared to the general feel of the rest of the hotel. Young Arab men dressed in westernised gear were merrily drinking beer and smoking. Some of the older women looked like they had knocked back a few too many Pinot Grigios and a few of the guys hogging the bar area were clearly betting on the result of some sporting event on the TV in the corner. None of that behaviour was accepted on the streets in Bahrain so I was not surprised that the atmosphere in the hotel bar was so rowdy, I supposed it had to go on behind closed doors. We ordered our first drink and quickly realised that around 70% of the people in that bar were aviation industry folk.

Bahrain was a stopover point for pilots and cabin crew. Through the haze of smoke and the sound of Angels by Robbie Williams playing on the juke box, we could just about see and hear the inebriated air hostesses and worse-for-wear pilots talking and laughing. I sincerely hoped that they were not taking to the cockpit the following day. Judging by their level of intoxication, their airline needed to be renamed Keep-Your-Fingers-Crossed Airways. There was one particular airline pilot who resembled a slightly dishevelled, well-oiled Richard Branson, who started to strike up conversation by asking us the nature of our business in Bahrain. I explained that I was booked to perform a Shirley Bassey tribute show for the Bahrain Welsh Society the following evening. He became wildly animated and threw his hands in the air, declaring how much he adored Shirley Bassey. I'm sure his enthusiasm was helped along by the fact that he had probably necked 12 vodka and Cokes, which appeared to be his tipple of choice.

He swiftly began a sort of brief Q & A session with me, asking me the positives and negatives that were attached to my job. While I was answering his questions to the best of my ability, a ropey, plump, blonde woman approached the table, carrying another round of drinks. She was well into her forties and many years of sunshine had done her skin no favours at all. She was wearing lots of gold jewellery and a short black dress that displayed way too much cleavage. Our new friend looked very pleased to see her, along with the tray of drinks that she was wobbling along carrying. She sat down and he put his hand firmly on her thigh, announcing that she was his girlfriend. He introduced himself as John and said her name was Karen. Once the formal introductions were out of the way, he informed us that he was a commercial airline pilot currently flying for Gulf Air. I very nearly told him that his airline company had indeed paid for our flights and were sponsoring the show but I didn't want to over excite him.

He declared that he and Karen had been together for six years, although only two years officially. That information came as no surprise as within two minutes of meeting them it was clear that things had been happening between them unofficially for a while. Karen didn't volunteer what she did for a living and she was, in fact, finding it increasingly difficult to say anything at all, due to the obvious alcohol consumption. She just kept grinning at him inanely and shoving her sun-damaged chest out. I imagine that's exactly what she did for a living and had been doing it a long time. I sensed that he had probably experienced a privileged upbringing and, in some circles, I imagined his job was considered somewhat glamorous. For that reason I was pretty sure he behaved badly when drunk. You know, the sort who loudly hold court, try to control who's drinking what and when and relentlessly keep topping up glasses, even if you don't want another drink, because they want everybody to be as pissed as they are. They are the individuals who throw their money around and casually invite complete strangers to join them at their table because they love a big audience.

'Jo has a flight phobia you know,' Ma B suddenly announced to the slurry pair. 'She has done really well during the flight over here.'

I think she was quite proud of me. I briefly told John about Captain Stacy Chance and how he had helped me.

He looked amused but interested and said, 'So what sort of things help somebody with a fear of flying?'

I rattled off as many things as I could think of and I admit that I was keen to talk to him about this subject because, drunk or not, he was in fact a pilot. He listened to, and generally agreed with, my list of technical reasons why I had been told planes were so safe and pondered for a few seconds. He then laughed and said, 'Yeah but the fuckers will still come down occasionally.' He quickly adopted a slightly smug expression.

'What? Why?' I replied.

He chuckled again and slurred, 'Most plane crashes are caused by pilot error. No-one can control or account for pilot error Jo.'

I shot him an annoyed look and he said, 'What? I'm only being honest. Anyway, what does everybody want to drink?'

He was getting naughty. I was tired from my flying experience and I think Ma B was starting to sense a little hostility from my end so before he'd had a chance to turn me back into a quivering flight phobe and before I'd had the chance to empty my white wine all over his head and kick him in his hydraulics, we made our excuses and went off to bed. On the way up to our room Ma B said she was not about to let some pissed-up pilot undo all of Captain Stacy Chance's good work.

The following morning we relaxed by the pool and soaked up a bit of sun, then went back to our rooms to change. Next on the agenda was to make our way down to the hotel bar and meet Mr Garfield Jones, the chairman of the Welsh Society. Garfield was a pleasant little man and his accent was a funny one. You could tell that he was Welsh but he had been living and working in Bahrain for many years. He was managing director for various 5-star hotels in Bahrain but Garfield had also been elected for the role of chairman of the Bahrain Welsh Society. Alongside his general responsibilities within that role came the most important job of all and that was to arrange their annual piss up – that's where I came in.

The PA spec had been emailed across weeks prior to leaving for Bahrain and it had been agreed to by all parties so everything was supposed to be in place ready for the sound check. As always, that's where the fun began. It was a Wednesday afternoon and the restaurant gig was really an 'add-on' to the main show for the Welsh Society, which was being held in the ballroom the following evening. Garfield had decided that as they were paying to fly me over there anyway, it would make sense to have me sing in the hotel restaurant the night before the main event.

When we entered the restaurant, I was given the name of the duty manager so I could find out the timings for the show. The duty manager didn't speak English very well so it was a little difficult to establish much at all. I looked around and noticed that there was no PA equipment in view. I asked the guy where the sound equipment was.

Johnny Foreigner casually replied, 'You have CD, we have microphone and you sing. No?'

I adopted my usual practice when dealing with Johnny Foreigner, which was to say the same thing slower and louder whilst including non-descript hand gestures and as always it failed. I explained as best as I could that whilst his suggestion was a lovely thought, it was not the case and I would actually need a MiniDisc player, a set of speakers, a small mixer and the corresponding cables. He had a look on his face that told me he had no idea what I was talking about. I would soon learn that no matter where in the world the gig was, one thing could always be relied upon – everybody would agree to the PA spec, and then completely ignore it.

I left Johnny Foreigner in the restaurant with a bewildered look on his face while we hot-footed it to reception and put a call out for Garfield Jones and he appeared within minutes. Once I had politely informed him that there was a definite lack of PA equipment in the restaurant, Garfield explained that the tech spec had been dealt with for the evening performance in the main ballroom but somebody at the hotel must have overlooked the fact that it was also required for the show in the restaurant.

A sound company was installing the proper PA equipment in the main ballroom the following day. It was 1pm by that time but Garfield assured me that he would sort something out within the following two hours and I could 'pop' back for my sound check around 3pm. We returned to the restaurant a few hours later to find Johnny Foreigner looking very pleased with himself. He had obviously been told to go off and source some equipment and was proudly standing next to a big old mixing desk. I had never heard of the manufacturer of this particular desk before but it appeared to have done a few rounds on some sort of a circuit and looked like it had been bashed to buggery. There were two speakers, a minidisc player, a lead microphone and stand. I didn't dare push my luck and ask Johnny Foreigner for a radio microphone.

Ma B soon found out only three channels out of 12 worked on the mixing desk. We were fortunate that we only needed three. We sound checked and apart from the fact that one of the speakers kept cutting out, the desk had hardly any vocal reverb and the three working channels could quite possibly turn into two at any given moment because the sliders were playing up, everything was fine and dandy. Before we knew it evening was upon us and it was showtime. By 10pm all of the restaurant diners were seated and finishing their desserts. I was hiding outside the restaurant entrance, where mainly only staff were milling around, tentatively listening out for my intro. Two members of the waiting staff were at the ready to open the double doors, enabling me to attempt a grand entrance or at least and entrance of sorts.

A minute or so before I heard my intro a little Japanese man appeared out of nowhere and started shouting, 'Shirley Bassey! Shirley Bassey!' He had a big camera and it repeatedly flashed in my face. I'm not sure what advertising or promotional material he had seen but he was obviously confused and thought I was the real Dame. I knew the show had been advertised well because I had heard it on Gulf Radio, but that had clearly promoted it as a tribute show. I tried to hurriedly explain to the little Japanese man that I was only a tribute act but he didn't understand and he was absolutely not listening. He was jumping around, taking pictures and shouting, making it very difficult for me to hear my intro music.

I did hear the music but only just. The doors were opened and I left the little Japanese man at the entrance, squealing with excitement. The performance went down well and with my outro music playing I made my way out of the restaurant, waving and blowing kisses to the diners in a diva-like fashion. As soon as I opened the door to make my exit, the little Japanese man and his camera met me once more. This time there were two of them. He must have gone and fetched his mate then waited outside. They were shouting, 'Miss Bassey picture! Please picture!' I remember thinking, 'Jo, you tried to explain that you were not the real one and they were having none of it so you may as well lap it up'. I didn't let it go to my head though, I know what the Japanese are like when it comes to taking pictures of anything, they are truly camera obsessed. The Bahrain Welsh Society's annual bash was obviously a popular event and they had sold out. It was not restricted to Welsh expats, it was open to all of the UK.

Before we knew it, the next day had gone and it was the evening once more. Showtime had quickly approached again and I was all decked up in my Bassey gown, ready to do the business. Ma B had, as always, escorted me through the hotel to where I needed to be, holding the train of my big white stage cloak then making her way into the room to supervise the sound man. As I sashayed down the staircase that lead to the Awal Ballroom entrance, I spotted him. The little Japanese man was waiting for me. I had been wearing a black gown with splits up both sides the previous night but that evening I was dressed in baby pink. I don't know if it was the pink sequins that hit the spot but he seemed more excited than he was the night before. He began frenziedly snapping away with his camera. I tried to explain that his little photo session would have to take place after the show, as I had to be on stage in around 30 seconds. The camera flashed relentlessly until the intro started and the doors were opened.

The audience were a joy that evening. They were banging, whooping, whistling, the full works. Towards the end of my set, lighters were being held up in the air and arms were swaying. I had been asked to stay in costume after the show to have some photographs taken with the British Ambassador of Bahrain and his wife. I also had to pose for pictures with the Gulf Air sponsors for a magazine article in the area outside of the main ballroom. That's where my little Japanese fan was situated. I was a little concerned that he may become jealous but it appeared to make him even more excited. I made sure he got his pictures, after all he was the only real fan that I was ever likely to get and that was only because he thought I was somebody else. I seriously considered moving to Japan, maybe I could have fooled the whole country.

Following the official picture session, I had a glass of wine and mingled with the guests for an hour or so. It was getting late and we were thinking of heading back to our room when one of the Scottish ex-pats came over and asked for a picture. He was the managing director of some oil company in Bahrain. The guy was amusingly drunk, however he did look very smart in his Scottish attire and I told him that his kilt looked just the part. He responded by swiftly lifting up his kilt and flashing me, Ma B and anybody else who happened to be standing in the vicinity. I quickly looked around to see if the British Ambassador's wife had witnessed the knob flash but I couldn't see her. A couple of the other ladies who were sipping champagne near the bar looked horrified but old Jock McKnobflash thought it was very funny indeed.

It didn't shock me too much as I had done many gigs in Scotland. The gigs I'd done in Edinburgh and St Andrews were always divine but I'd also performed in Glasgow enough times to know that the knob-flashing incident was nothing. Those jocks were crazy folk. If that had happened after a show at the Glasgow Hilton, it would have been followed by another round of whisky and a quick punch up. Although I have to give credit where credit is due, the haggis served with breakfast at the Glasgow Hilton is second to none and I would forgive the place playing host to cock exposing sessions, top shelf drinking contests and late night brawls for a portion of their finest haggis.

Well, the Welsh Society gig had been a successful one and we happily made our way back to our rooms for a good night's kip. We had another two nights' stay left in the Gulf Hotel so, with our work there pretty much done, we planned to take a look around Bahrain the following day. We were up bright and early the next morning, which was around lunchtime for me, and we decided to visit one of the local markets.

Garfield said we should have a look around the Manama Souq. The shops ranged from tiny open-air market stalls to leading department stores and they were packed with everything from clothes to electronics, tobacco to incense and antiques to gold. Labyrinthine lanes and alleys took us from one area to another. There was no way anybody was getting a car down those narrow streets. There were lots of stalls selling herbs and spices and having sampled the food for the brief time we'd been there, I already knew that the Arabic cuisine was truly peachy with its heavenly taste and subtle aromas. At each stall people were greeted with mounds of colourful, fragrant spices of every possible variety. I also noticed that these folk were partial to a carpet or two. Everybody seemed to be buying carpets but I only purchased two marble wine glasses and a pair of flip-flops.

On the way back to the hotel, Ma B and I amused ourselves by silently mocking the interior of our taxi. All of the taxis outside of the souq looked 100 years old. This one was falling to bits on the outside and the interior was sky blue furry fabric, which was slowly turning a nasty shade of brown. There were rips, tears and shit hanging off of every part of that car. We were laughing about the general decay of the interior when Ma B suddenly pointed out of the car window.

'Jo that's you!' she shrieked.

We were just approaching the main Manama roundabout and on the left-hand side of the road, set way back, was a gigantic billboard with nothing but my name and face plastered all over it. When I say gigantic, I mean gigantic. I squealed and shouted, 'Shit that's huge!' We made the taxi driver go around the island again while I ferreted around looking for the camera. This billboard was the same sort of size that you see Vodafone or Nike using in any given city centre. The taxi driver clearly thought that we were insane but he went around the island again whilst I tried to hang out of the window and take a picture. It was dusk and the billboard had a big light positioned at the top, which was overhanging so the whole thing was lit up, which made it appear all the more imposing.

I didn't think that I would ever see my face on something that big again so Ma B and I vowed to wait until it got darker then walk down to where the sign was situated with our camcorder. We got back to the hotel, had a drink and rested our feet then, with camcorder in hand, we trotted off down to the Manama roundabout. I wanted to record Ma B standing underneath the billboard so we could show how big it was. I remember thinking that Bazza would have loved to see it. Ma B looked like a tiny dot underneath the sign and you couldn't even tell that she was a person or see her at all. Now I know that size isn't everything but I'm afraid it is when you're a tribute act and it comes to one's face on a billboard.

I was trying to instruct Ma B where to stand but it was very noisy due to some pretty loud praying. All we could hear was what sounded like loud chanting coming through a monster PA system. I had learned whilst in Bahrain that 'adhān' is the Islamic call to prayer recited by the muezzin Adhān is called out by the muezzin in the mosque five times a day, summoning Muslims for mandatory prayers. Loudspeakers are used for the purpose, and it was loud.

The following night we relaxed and got ready for the return journey home the following day. The plane landed and nobody died. We safely arrived back home and I had enjoyed my first gig in the Middle East. I had been home only a week and already Bahrain seemed like a distant memory. *EastEnders* was playing away on the TV but I was not really watching it. Robbo and I only had it on if there was absolutely nothing else and that was usually because we enjoyed mocking the cast who constantly screamed and yauped in their over-done cockney accents. Every episode was the same. I was lost in thought when I over-heard Robbo's outraged voice coming from the kitchen.

'Terry I ain't being funny mate but can you sort this chow mein thing out? It's happened twice now. The first time was last week when you were away but it happened again on Tuesday night when you were here... I know Terry but seriously mate, BEAN SPROUTS! I've been using you for a long time now and you know I'm allergic to veg. What next, water bastard chestnuts? Terry, please tell me again exactly what goes into my chow mein. Yes, noodles, meat and sauce, extra, extra, *extra* hot... That's right... Thank you Terrence and be sure to keep your eyes on them... What? Oh sorry yes, onions are still fine. I won't change my mind on onions. Yep, see ya in a bit mate.'

Robbo entered the living room shaking his head. 'Honestly Jo you've got to watch the fuckers. They all start off OK for the first year then they take me for granted and start to slide.' He sat down and positioned his can of Carling next to him along with a copy of *The Sun*.

'Robbo you really are a heathen,' I said disapprovingly.

He opened up his newspaper. 'Look if you want me to be more refined Jo, I'll start drinking bottled lager instead of cans and I'll tell Terry to leave a few shrimps in my Singapore chow mein,' he replied dryly without looking up from his paper.

'How do water 'bastard' chestnuts differ from standard water chestnuts anyway?' I asked.

'They don't. They only become water bastard chestnuts if I'm expected to eat them.'

I smiled and switched the TV volume down slightly as there were big things kicking off in Albert Square.

***

Airports were places I usually associated with flying not singing. However on one particular occasion I was booked to perform at John Lennon airport in Liverpool. I was not booked to give the folks in arrivals a blast of Bassey, I was in fact booked to sing for another big corporate 007 event that was being held in one of the airport hangars. The hangar was a fair size as it had to cater for 800 people and they all had to be seated. There was a huge PA system installed and various sound operatives wandered around the area. There were also massive projector screens, which were strategically situated around the hangar so I, along with everybody else, could see my performance on the big screens. I never got used to seeing that, I always found it a little off putting so in the end, I stopped looking.

Due to my unique ability to falsely predict, or rather imagine, a catastrophic plane crash at the drop of a hat, I was slightly concerned about the frequencies of the radio microphones interfering with the air traffic control and pilots' communication systems. I assure you that this fear however, had some basis. I did a gig for a police club in Sutton Coldfield many years before where the DJ's radio microphone was picking up the local cop shop and mine was intermittently cutting into Sutton Coldfield's busy taxi service.

Every so often I would hear, 'Cab 12, cab 12, first on the rank now. A 7pm pick up in Erdington for Mrs Beadle. Thanks Chris.'

I certainly didn't want to cross frequencies with a BMI Boeing 757. Instead of getting guided in by air traffic control, the poor, unsuspecting pilots would end up with an earful of *Goldfinger* whilst I would have to land my first commercial jet, containing 216 passengers fresh in from Lanzarote. I imagined saying something like:

'Listen lads, I'm in the middle of a gig here. I can't see you from inside this hangar so you can either just circle around until you hear the end of *I Am What I Am* and I'll pop outside, or you could have a peek and see if you can spot a very long road with some lights on it. If you see it and there's nothing on it, land. Try and make sure it's a runway though because if you fuck up and land on the M62 there will be casualties. Roger Roger. Over and out.'

My fear was, on this occasion, unfounded and the gig went without a hitch let alone a full aviation disaster. It just goes to show that one can never really predict the eventualities of a flight or indeed a gig.

Whenever there was an overseas gig to be done with the band, there was never anybody whose behaviour was more bizarre and amusing than our Matt's. He was fully prepared I'll give him that but the amount of zipping/unzipping of bags and general rummaging he did was inconceivable. He organised the band well in advance, making sure they all had the relevant necessaries for the trip and he always ensured that everybody understood the general timings and logistics of the event.

Musicians obviously departed from different airports depending on where they lived but Matt made sure he took full responsibility for all of the boys, leaving no room for errors. He would travel to the airport in his little green Maestro that reeked of milk due to his tea addiction and was always packed to the hilt with tackle such as PA equipment, sleeping bags, camping equipment, comedy wigs, fold-up chairs and blankets.

Matt always had a large, squidgy bag that he kept in his car, but this was no ordinary bag. It was a cheap, blue, nylon bag that had busted zips and was sort of tied together. It wouldn't have looked out of place sitting on the floor next to a vagrant selling the *Big Issue* in Birmingham city centre. The bag was always heaving with typical 'Matt essentials'. There was always a collapsible chair that he had great pleasure in telling anybody who cared to listen that he had found for £1 and it folded up as small as a fag packet. He informed us that it was a crucial addition to his equipment and came into its own when there was a long wait in a big crowd with no available seating.

He would then unpack his miniature travel size Connect Four, which was handy for relieving boredom during long, waiting periods. The bag always contained various fizzy sweets to keep his blood sugar up and packets of fizzy Cola bottles and Tangfastics were particular favourites. In this delightful holdall he also carried the musician's sheet music, which he kept in a big, ripped, scruffy looking folder along with the odd spare dickie bow for the fuckwit band member who happened to lose one just before the gig. Then, whilst nibbling on a half-eaten sandwich or an old apple and after lots of rummaging around inside the bag, Matt finally unleashed the most important items: his huge I LOVE TEA mug, a small box of teabags, two flasks, a white, plastic kettle and some odd smelling, long life milk. He even managed to squeeze his dinner suit into that magical blue bag. This meant he could bypass waiting for his luggage in arrivals and simply jet out of the airport for a ciggie before anyone else. If Matt ever lost that bag he would truly have been a broken man.

My first airport experience with Matt was slightly watered down as it was a duo gig and therefore he didn't have the rest of the band to organise. We had been booked to perform a James Bond set at the Ritz Carlton Hotel in Cannes. It was a big event and Matt was accompanying me on piano. We were flying to Nice so Matt collected me from my house at around 3am and I was then subjected to a rather lengthy spell in the green Maestro before arriving at Heathrow. Once at the airport I was quickly introduced to the blue bag, offered a Tangfastic and challenged to a game of miniature Connect Four. I knew from that point on that Matt was indeed unique.

I tried to sleep for the short duration of the flight (my fear of flying was much improved thanks to Captain Chance) whilst Matt worked on some musical arrangements. He was always busy, even in flight. The Carlton was a posh gaff and to avoid my imminent embarrassment when faced with Matt getting his tea making paraphernalia out of the blue bag in the hotel reception area, I decided I should purchase one pot of tea. My efforts proved futile. The pot of tea cost me €16 and Matt's face was a picture. I tried to justify the ridiculous price by pointing out that it was presented beautifully and the little biscuit that came with it was a lovely touch along with being very tasty. Matt shook his head and promptly got his kettle out. He did make sure he polished off one cup of the 'posh tea' before drinking around nine mugs of his own. He was obviously unimpressed with the fancy tea and thought it was decidedly average. One thing that I would never argue with Matt about was the quality of a good brew.

Fancy establishments and the stench of money never overwhelmed him. What you saw with him was exactly what you got. He dealt with people and occasions in exactly the same way, regardless of whether it was a 5-star hotel in Dubai or a social club in Leeds. His behaviour never changed due to his surroundings and I admired him for that. He was a down-to-earth, reliable, no-nonsense bloke who respected the elderly, loved animals and was devoted to his wife Andrea and their beloved dog Scruffy. Matt could not be superficial or false even if his blue bag depended on it and as far as people in the entertainment industry went, Matt was a breath of fresh air.

He would never pay to stay in a hotel on overnighters. If the client didn't cover the cost, Matt would stay at a nearby campsite for £4. If there were no local campsites available, he would kip in the Maestro. He wouldn't even buy a bacon sandwich at the campsite if he didn't have to. He once tried to heat up a can of all-day breakfast using his kettle. He informed me, somewhat disappointedly, that it got a bit gooey when he tried to boil it up and it burned the elements out in his kettle.

Whenever we finished a gig in central London, whilst Ma B and I were driving around getting hopelessly lost trying to find our hotel, we would get a text from Matt saying he had already arrived safely at his 'outer London residence', which meant he'd got to his campsite before we had found our hotel. He had no sat nav, just the maestro, his finely tuned brain and a map. The only time I had known Matt to book a hotel was when the Travelodge offered special deals that were only available if you booked well in advance. He checked his gigging diary and booked the Early Bird Saver rooms for £19 per night, around six months in advance of a gig.

He did one gig where he had nowhere to stay so he pulled into a lay-by and slept in the car. The following day he received an email from the Travelodge asking if he had enjoyed his stay. He then realised that he had booked a room so far in advance that even he had forgotten he had booked it. He had slept in the car that night, when the Travelodge he'd booked was only two miles away from the lay-by where he had parked up. I told him the moral of that tale was that one could be too organised when booking that far in advance.

Matt and I expected the gig in Cannes to be the typical, hoity toity corporate nonsense whereby we were pretty much ignored for a lot of money. We chatted on the sound check and agreed that the general rule of thumb was: the fancier the gig, the more ignorant the audience. On this occasion we were pleasantly surprised. The audience were a mixed European bunch and they were a great crowd. The gig was perfect in every way. We still maintain today that Cannes was one of our favourite duo gigs. Matt's only complaint was that whilst the Halle Berry look-alike may have been easy on the eye, the Pierce Brosnan they had booked on that Cannes gig stank. He reckoned that the nose was totally wrong and his hair was far too grey. In his opinion, and it pained him to say it, he felt that visually, Built-up Bond would have done a better job.

***

It was an uneventful, chilly morning during the beginning of March 2006 and I was at Ma B's house as we had just walked the dogs. I noticed the inbox on the laptop was showing a new message. The email was from a well-known UK agent who wanted to book the show for a gig in Dubai. My initial thought was 'Oh no not another long-haul flight'. I had, however, enjoyed my time in Bahrain so I pushed the negative thought of a lengthy flight out of my head. If I could face the flying issue again then perhaps another little trip to the Middle East was in order. It didn't really matter what I was thinking because whilst I was contemplating the situation, Ma B had already fired off a response to the agent on email. The agent had then replied in record time, telling us that the gig was on and we would be flying out on 20th March. The event was to be sponsored by Qatar Airways and flights would be booked that very day. I do remember thinking that the entire enquiry through to confirmation had all happened rather quickly but I put that down to Ma B giving me no option to wriggle out of a flight.

Before flying to Dubai a few weeks later I watched my fear of flying DVD again prior to my departure and printed key information from the website, which I took with me. I also visited the pilots in the cockpit just before we departed, just as Captain Stacey Chance had suggested, which really helped. I sat down in the middle of the two pilots who were wearing their crisp, white pilot shirts and I was sporting a bright pink, velour, 'Katie Price' style tracksuit. We must have resembled a jam sandwich. They both smiled at my printed information.

The pilot on my right turned to me and said, 'What's your name?'

I was bewildered by the cockpit and a little distracted by all of the technology. 'Err... Joanne,' I replied a little nervously.

'Well Joanne, I can honestly tell you the only time we have had to divert a plane was due to the toilets blocking up. Flying over water is nothing to worry about either. We are never very far from land.'

I gave him a very serious look and said, 'According to my DVD you should be exactly 180 minutes away from being able to land at an approved airport at all times.'

They both laughed. 'I can assure you that we are. That is indeed the case and you are very well informed,' the pilot on my right replied. He was very nice looking.

I was really surprised by how small the cockpit was but all the gadgets, buttons and dials fascinated me. Once I had checked that their hydraulic and electrical backup systems were in fine working order, I was off back to my seat. Just before I left them to it, I said, 'Track the land and don't take any short cuts over water. I am in no rush and safety comes first.' The pilot on the left laughed again whilst the nice looking pilot on my right gave me his best twinkly grin. Oh yes, I was in there all right.

Ma B had been a little hasty in organising the Dubai gig and in doing so she had overlooked one tiny detail – our flights were indirect. We had to make a stop in Doha airport before catching the final flight to Dubai. To the non-fearful flyer, I'm sure an indirect flight is merely an inconvenience but to a flight-phobe like me it was a nightmare. It meant two take-offs, two landings and the bit in between was far from relaxing. Doha airport, in my humble opinion, was a grade A shithole, a royal dosshouse. It was supposed to be a relatively modern facility but the people employed there were not exactly a joy to deal with. I was completely shocked by their bad attitudes, surliness and general all-round rudeness. Comfortable it was not. The toilets were un-presentable, the seating capacity needed to be increased and the food facilities were in dire need of improvement. People sat around on the floor trying to get comfortable on their coats and blankets. I vowed to never again travel via Doha airport, unless it had been knocked-down, rebuilt and put under competent management.

Ma B and I were separated on the connecting flight from Doha to Dubai, which is probably just as well as I would have constantly reminded her of the indirect flight faux pas she had made. The plane was jam-packed full and I was seated next to a fellow wearing a bright yellow shirt. He seemed very engrossed in a book that he was reading as we taxied to the runway. I couldn't see the title of the book but he appeared to be making notes. In my totally irrational pre-take-off state of mind, I imagined the title to be something like *How to Achieve Ultimate Success as a Suicide Bomber in 10 Easy Steps*. The book was probably on loan from a training camp in Pakistan, although I was sure if the trainee was successful in their new role, the loaned books were never likely to be returned.

I decided that if he intended to take the pilots hostage and divert the plane and passengers towards certain death, he should have chosen a far more discreet shirt. I didn't really expect a blinding yellow shirt to be the uniform of a suicide bomber but times change, as do fashions and etiquette. Anyway, the flight was only 60 minutes long so he really needed to pull his finger out and get to the end of that chapter. I'd convinced myself that there were probably quite a few of them dotted around the plane so I had a quick glance around to see if I could spot anymore. If the chappy to my right was anything to go by they would probably have vibrant shirts on, their heads buried in a book and their ears would keenly be awaiting a loud and dramatic signal.

Old Canary Shirt didn't move for the entire duration of the flight but just as the seat belt signs went on for landing, he got up from his seat. He'd left things a little late in my opinion but I braced myself regardless. A female member of the cabin crew approached him and asked if he could take his seat. He began by explaining that he realised he had left it a little late (I thought it was a bizarrely polite response given what he was about to put us through) but could he possibly use the toilet, very quickly before landing. The lady said that unfortunately once the seat belt signs had been put on he must remain in his seat. He simply nodded and sat back down. So that was it. Well Allah would be most disappointed. He'd left it too late and should have executed his real plan far earlier.

The plane landed in Dubai and I had escaped death once more. My relationship with the aviation industry had remained untarnished and I was delighted. I really didn't want us to fall out. My contact in Dubai was a porky drummer called Alan. My UK agent had informed me that Alan was from Manchester but he and his wife Donna had been living in Dubai for around 10 years. My agent and Alan worked as a team flying UK tribute acts to Dubai. The agent would book them in the UK, Alan would meet them when they landed and they would split the commission. Alan was a bit of a chancer in my opinion but many in the music industry were. He knew a lot about Dubai and I got the impression that he was very pleased with how far his money stretched whilst living out there. He said the people would do virtually anything for a pittance. He made reference to the fags being cheap and his cleaners even cheaper.

Alan showed us around briefly, introduced us to the restaurant owner who I was due to work for the next evening then took us to our hotel. Ma B and I were certainly in need of our beds. The hotel that we had been booked into was called The York and we soon found out that it was a noisy joint. During our sleepless first night, Ma B said she had never experienced such uncooperative pillows in her entire existence. The *Boom! Shake the Room* racket that was coming from somewhere downstairs was horrendous and our room literally vibrated. As dawn approached, the building site that was situated directly outside of our room, complete with industrial diggers and scaffolding rigs, got very busy. The workmen kicked off dead on 6am. Ma B said she was in no way, shape or form staying another night in that hotel and I said I was going to have strong words with Alan. We couldn't get hold of him for a few hours and I imagined he was all tucked up in bed blissfully asleep. Once he finally answered the phone, I summoned him to The York. He arrived quickly, listened to our sorry tale, looked a little sheepish and said he would transfer us to another hotel later.

It was the day of the gig so with the nasty night behind us and on absolutely no sleep we went off to do the sound check. The restaurant was called The Alamo and it was quite small but atmospheric. The owner was a pleasant man called Phil. He seemed to notice that I appeared to be somewhat bleary-eyed and asked if everything was all right. Whilst Alan was busy talking to somebody on the phone, I explained to Phil that we had experienced a less than peaceful night in our noisy hotel and we really hadn't slept.

He asked which hotel we had stayed in and when I said The York he looked horrified. 'You are fucking joking? He didn't book you into that place did he? That hotel is the cheapest shithole in the area. It's where all of the hookers stay. There is a club downstairs that is part of the hotel where they pick up their punters and they basically all do their 'work' in The York. I know Alan is a tight arse but he should never put anybody in there.' No wonder Mr Fat Belly looked a bit sheepish.

Ma B simply retorted, 'Well even hookers shouldn't have to suffer those pillows. They were clearly made of brick.'

We had made it known that we were never setting foot in The York again and left it at that. That evening, in my changing area within The Alamo, I prepared to get into my Bassey ensemble for the show. I smiled at all of the posters of tribute acts who had performed there before me. The walls were adorned with pictures of Madonna, Cher, Tina, Rod, Cliff and the rest of my UK tribute gang. The gig went according to plan and everyone enjoyed the night. The second hotel we stayed in was dreamy in comparison to The York and we slept like babies. Our sound night sleep was very much needed as the following night we were due to seriously party underground style.

The following day we wandered around Dubai with Alan at our leisure. That evening Alan's friend, Guy, pulled up in a very expensive Mercedes to collect us. He was a tall, techy-looking man whom Alan had told me was quite big in advertising over there. He did reek of money. The Blue Bay Bar was a big, underground bar situated within a hotel, as indeed they all were. You wouldn't really know that any of these bars existed unless somebody pointed them out as they tended to be hidden underneath hotels in the basements. Once you stepped out of a taxi or somebody's flashy car, you didn't really know where you were being taken until the lift doors opened. Once ushered inside by Alan, Donna and Guy, Ma B and I noticed the heady atmosphere of the place almost immediately. Alan guided us to a table whilst Guy fetched the exotic blue cocktails.

The room was very busy and dimly lit with a stage that appeared to be so long that it seemed to stretch forever and I would soon see why. After a few drinks and an alarming number of Marlboro Lights (around 35p a packet out there) some young Filipinos appeared on stage with their various instruments. They looked like teenagers and there were at least 12 of them. I commented that it was a big band and asked Alan how much they got paid. He told me that they get around £25 between 12 of them to perform for five hours and they send a portion of that money home to their families. I could not believe it and he said if I found that shocking, he was keen to see my reaction once they started playing.

They began to play and I couldn't believe my ears. I had never heard such talented singers and musicians in my life. These Filipino kids were unbelievable. They were tiny but every single one of them was an absolute showstopper. The young guys could play guitar like Hendrix and the girls sang like Whitney and Aretha. They almost mimicked the original artists but they were amazing and I'd never heard vocals like it from so many young people in one room. Their vocal range and ability was stunning and Ma B and I were utterly amazed. We stayed in the Blue Bay for hours listening to that band, drinking blue cocktails and smoking. People seemed to lose all sense of time and I could see why. The musical experience we'd had that night was truly amazing and it was to be the absolute highlight of my first Dubai trip.

Dubai is the most cosmopolitan Emirate in The UAE. Expats and foreigners make up about 85% of the population so locals are greatly outnumbered. With its tax-free living and extreme wealth, temptation and decadence bubbles under the surface. However, all that glitters is not gold and to me Dubai seemed as fake as the handbags sold on the market stalls. It was also heady and intoxicating and it felt dangerous.

Whilst there, I had heard stories about people who had fallen foul of Dubai laws and paid a hefty price. If you steal they chop off your hands. Public displays of affection are met with jail sentences. Even if you appear slightly wobbly on your way home from a bar, they will lock you up.

The hookers have to dress a certain way in public but go underground and anything goes. You could fill your boots with all sorts as long as you did it in the right place. Our second hotel was based in the corporate end of Dubai and the hookers came into the hotel bar wearing trouser suits. They would sit sipping a glass of red wine for around an hour and if nobody approached them, they would glance at their watch then quietly leave. Visually, they resembled corporate businesswomen and looked nothing like your typical hooker. Occasionally, they were lucky and a group of military men would come in for a drink during a stopover on their way to Kabul. If that happened they seemed to be in for a lucrative evening. As long as these women looked the part, they were welcome to do their trade in any corporate hotel bar or lobby. It seemed to be a lethal cocktail of 'do everything but be seen to do nothing'. Dubai is a hypocritical place where people lived in hedonistic excess. It's supposedly a place of infrastructure, opportunity and stability but in my humble opinion it didn't have a very stable feel, even the houses were built on sand. I felt like one big shift and the lot could move. I preferred Bahrain. I admired the country's authenticity as a society in which a far greater proportion of the population are nationals. I felt Bahrain was an honourable and genuine place in comparison with Dubai.

Somebody actually said to me, 'The thing you have to understand about Dubai is nothing is what it seems. This isn't a city but a con-job. They lure you in telling you it's one thing – a modern kind of place – but beneath the surface it's a medieval dictatorship.'

On the day that we were due to leave I had a call from a Dubai-based sound company who I had been speaking to in the UK. Mario, who ran the company, told me there was a large corporate event going to be held at the Grand Hyatt Hotel in three weeks and the hotel director, Paul, was interested in booking my Bassey show. He asked if I could meet with Paul before I returned to the UK and I agreed. It sounded like it was going to be a rather lavish affair so I agreed to give Paul a firm quote when I had returned back to the UK. I said I would speak to my Sinatra tribute act that I worked with regularly and quote him for our Vegas show.

I then thought 'why wait?' and called Phil straight away. He swiftly told me that he was available and up for it. We came up with a quote over the phone there and then, along with the usual requirements, a lengthy stay at The Grand Hyatt and a large fee. I decided there was no time like the present, got back in touch with Paul at the Hyatt and quoted the gig. The deal was done. Paul said he only wanted a 20-minute set in total, as we would be performing for around 500 European delegates but it would be mid-week so for them it was a school night. He made it clear that he wanted them tucked up in bed early and we were not to over excite them. Consequently Ma B, Phil and I could have a delightful one-week stay in the Grand Hyatt with all the trimmings and we would literally only be singing around four songs each, what a doddle.

Ma B and I considered not getting the flight back to the UK that day and staying for an extra couple of weeks, as I had nothing important to return to the UK for. It seemed a good idea, we could catch some more rays and Phil could fly out and meet us. I called Robbo to discuss my plan and pretty much worded it that way.

He sounded deflated. 'No I don't suppose you have anything important to come back here for...'

I tried to explain that I was talking in terms of gigs but he was having none of it. We changed our plan and decided to return to the UK, although in hindsight I doubt it made any difference to Robbo at that point. He had taken that comment very personally. As far as our relationship went, it was probably a nail in the coffin. We left for the airport and another flight loomed ahead.

Ma B had lost her Gucci sunglasses and was unimpressed with the situation. She blamed Alan and insinuated that he had taken them when she unwittingly left them in his car.

'You can't be sure that's the case,' I said.

'That shifty Mancunian has got them all right. They're probably the only pair of genuine Gucci sunglasses in Dubai!'

'Well we'll be back in a matter of weeks so you can accuse Alan then. In the meantime you should shut up about the missing glasses as I have an impending flight to panic about.'

The plane landed in the UK and I had to admit that the whole 'plane landing without major incident' plan was going surprisingly well. Once back home, Robbo and I just got on with things as usual. We got on just fine but there were some changes. We had become more distant and were doing most things separately. He put this down to my job, amongst other things, and he had a point. Was I selfish? I suppose I was. I was spending more time overseas, performing. Even when I was home, I spent a huge amount of time at Ma B's organising our bookings and had been for a while.

As a result, Robbo was spending more time in the pub. He was, in fact, spending most of his time in the pub. He was a must at all parties and a very sociable person. You could put Robbo in any setting with people from all walks of life, even the hoity toity, and everyone loved him. Recently he was starting to isolate himself in just one pub, with the same few people. I felt like he was slipping. He was hedonistic, indulgent and very 'of the moment'. I had those tendencies too, but nothing compared to him. Things had also started to spiral downwards as he'd started a management job and at that time he was so not cut out for accountability and responsibility. I'd noticed that his drinking had gone from evenings to lunchtimes and I had a horrible feeling that the slippery slope into full-blown alcoholism had begun. I couldn't believe it, first Steph then Robbo and little did I know that worse was to come. We had been together for over 10 years and I thought I knew him well but at that point, I was unaware of the seedy depths to which Robbo would fall.

We flew out to Dubai a few weeks later and the Vegas event was perfect. Phil, Ma B and I had a fabulous time a lovely week of relaxation before the show. The performance actually fell on the last night. I had a booking the following night in Prague so as soon as we had performed our encore, Ma B and I literally had to leave. We didn't even have time to have a drink with Phil after the show; it was straight into our jeans and off to the airport. We had packed beforehand so we said our goodbyes to Sinatra and Dubai then left for my favourite place – the airport.

The booking in Prague was held at Spearmint Casino, which was situated on the Vltava River and it was an event for Sony and MGM. I had been booked by a Los Angeles agent, who I have to say couldn't do enough for us. The event had been organised to celebrate the last day of filming for the Bond movie *Casino Royale* in the Prague location. It was a fantastic evening and the audience was made up of Sony/MGM executives, along with some members of the movies cast and crew. I mingled like a goodun and networked my backside off. I was, however, very disappointed that Daniel Craig did not attend. Apparently he was very tired from filming. Did he not consider how a picture with him could have enhanced my career? I bet Sean Connery wouldn't have been too tired in his day. Honestly, Bond too tired for a Martini in a swanky casino?

I arrived back on Blighty's soil to be met by a very sombre and somewhat depressed Robbo. It was a Saturday evening and as he stood in the kitchen doorway of our pretty but modest little semi-detached home, I noticed how sad he looked. Once he had asked how the Dubai and Prague gigs had gone, as he always did, he said, 'Jo I can't do this anymore'. I just nodded and I knew that we had pretty much arrived at the same place at the same time.

'You are not bothered either way and you haven't been for a long time so I'm finally done too,' he said.

I told him that I felt the same and we should part ways but remain friends. At that point it was mutual and although I had become mentally detached some time ago, I still felt very sad. We both did. There was no arguing, no lengthy crisis talks, just a very sad realisation on both parts that our relationship had ran its course. For over a decade Robbo and I were more than just partners, we were best friends and we both felt like we were losing a soulmate. I knew I had neglected the relationship and that hadn't been fair. After around half an hour of heavy silence, I said I was tired and I should go to bed. I said I would look into putting the house up for sale.

'This will be the last night you stay here won't it?' Robbo said. He was tearful.

'Yes, I will stay at Mums from tomorrow and we'll sort everything out with the house,' I replied.

We were both emotional because we knew it was really the end. We both hugged and cried a little and then I went to bed.

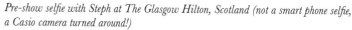

Pre-show selfie with Steph at The Glasgow Hilton, Scotland (not a smart phone selfie, a Casio camera turned around!)

TRIBUTE ACT: Lookalike performer set to bring Shirley show to local stage

They call me best at Bassey ... and this is my life

STEPPING into the star-studded shoes of Shirley Bassey has taken lookalike performer Joanne Copeman all over the world.

She's worked with the likes of Frank Carson, Jimmy Cricket and Roy Baraclough, performed with Steve Davis and taken part in charity fundraising with Heartbeat's Bill Maynard.

She has been touring with her Shirley Bassey tribute show. Surely Bassey, and this year performed in Bahrain and sang for British ambassador Robin Lamb.

Joanne said: "The places this has taken me in only two years is unbelievable. I am now performing my Bassey show for the likes of ex-Chelsea chairman Ken Bates and big corporate clients in London.

"I sing at many glitzy James Bond theme parties. The Stage newspaper in London said I was 'best at being Bassey'."

The performer, who currently lives

■ STAR-SPANGLED... Joanne with Jimmy Cricket and (above) the real Bassey

By Marion McMullen

in Crick, near Rugby, with her father, is currently starring in a Vegas-style tribute to Frank Sinatra and Shirley Bassey with a live band and dancers.

She is bringing The Frank & Shirley Show to Rugby's Benn Hall on Sunday, following dates in Oman.

Meanwhile, next year is already

looking busy for Joanne.

She said: "I have been booked to perform my Bassey show at a James Bond annual ball in Rochester, Missouri, USA. They are flying in a 15-piece band from New Orleans to meet me and back my show next May.

"I can't believe it."

Tickets for the Rugby show on Sunday are available on 01788 541516.

■ GLAMOUR... Joanne Copeman, who lives at Crick, near Rugby, with Roy Baraclough and (right) with British ambassador in Bahrain, Robin Lamb, for whom she sang. She will be performing at the Benn Hall in Rugby after dates in Oman

Coventry Telegraph, *2005*

Desert song - Joanne has just returned from Bahrain, where she performed two sell-out concerts and to advertise them, her face was featured on a huge billboard.

Diamonds are forever - Joanne Copeman is enjoying a double life as the glamorous Shirley Bassey. Pictures: Jens Tomlinson

Tribute to a legend

By Steve Shaw

FROM Burbage to Bahrain, Joanne Copeman has stars in her eyes, thanks to the biggest diva of them all.

Little in stature, but big in voice, the Burbage woman, 30, makes her living by impersonating the one and only Shirley Bassey.

Using the stage name, 'Surely Bassey', Joanne is enjoying success as the show-stopping Welsh Dragon, and has just performed two sell-

Fittingly, she performed for Bahrain's Welsh Society, at its St David's Day annual ball.

A distinguished audience included the British Ambassador to Bahrain, Robin Lamb.

Joanne said: "It came about from my website, when somebody made an enquiry.

"It was a brilliant experience. Over there

"I had to pose for photographs and held a press conference.

"There was even a big billboard with my face on, which my mum noticed as we were driving by.

"Luckily I saw it after the performances as I would have felt even more nervous."

In the business for nine years, Joanne wasn't always a tribute act, and in a

Manning and Frank Carson.

She appeared in The Hinckley Times a couple of years ago, after signing to a management company, but the dream turned sour, when it went into liquidation.

Disillusioned

because I wasn't getting any younger, as I was heading for 30.

"Becoming a tribute act, I did feel a bit fake - a bit like I was selling out.

"But you have to put a lot of work in, getting the voice and all the costumes right.

"It can be difficult because you rely on giving your

Joanne is now reaping the rewards, earning between ██ and ██ for each performance.

China now beckons, as Joanne is hoping to tour the country, to further her international following ever more.

Closer to home, she'll be performing at the Concorde Theatre, with a Frank Sinatra

Hinckley Times, *2005*

Bahrain best – Joanne Copeman as Surely Bassey

Joanne Copeman, who presents one of the best tribute acts under the title Surely Bassey, is delighted at the success she has achieved in the two years since she started the act.

She recently presented her show for a week in Bahrain, and has now resumed an impressive list of top corporate events. On April 23 she is appearing at the Tameside Hippodrome, Ashton-under-Lyne, backed by a 15-piece big band.

Another string to her bow is as half of the Frank and Shirley Show, which is booking for theatre dates in the UK and abroad. In this she is partnered by Phil Fryer – who has had similar success on the corporate circuit, including Bahrain – and backed by a live band and female dancers.

The Stage, *London 2005*

CHAPTER EIGHT

PLANES, YACHTS AND AUTOMOBILES

Whilst sitting in the kitchen on a sunny Monday morning in 2005, an enquiry came in from Rochester Hills MI, USA.

'What state in the USA is MI?' I asked Ma B.

'I don't know – is it Missouri?' she replied.

It was the usual vague email enquiry from someone or something called OPC for a Bond event in May 2006.

'Oh bloody hell, another long-haul flight and this time across the Atlantic. The jet lag will be horrid. I will bang in a big price. They won't go for it anyway. Oh and if we are going that distance we'll make it a one-week stay plus, plus, plus…' I rambled on.

They had gone for it. They wanted me with a 15-piece band from New Orleans and accepted every bit of the rider. It was actually the state of Michigan not Missouri and we were in fact Detroit-bound. We only found out that MI was actually Michigan after a few months of telling Nan and everyone else that we were off to Missouri. I knew little about Detroit other than it was the automotive capital of the world and the home of Henry Ford's Ford Motor Company. We were actually off to Motor City. It was also the place where Berry Gordy, Jr. founded Motown Records. I had a job on my hands getting the sheet music written up for a 15-piece band but, as always, Matt got stuck in and organised the parts. I was introduced via email to the gentleman who was to be my band leader for the event. He was a great guy from New Orleans called Jimmy Maxwell. Matt worked on the arrangements for Jimmy whilst he and I kept in touch via email.

Everything was going well until the TV news blasted an absolute tragedy into our living rooms. It was 29th August 2005 and Hurricane Katrina had struck New Orleans in a catastrophic way. The OPC organisers and myself were frantically worrying about Jimmy and the band. As the extent of the horror unfolded over the following weeks nobody heard anything from Jimmy. When we eventually heard from him, we learned that everything he had was gone – everything he owned! His house, computer, contacts, his world had been totally devastated. It was so sad. He was also an absolute professional and although we feared that Jimmy would be unable to fulfil his engagement for the OPC, he proved us wrong. Somehow from all that devastation, like a phoenix from the ashes, he got his band back on track and carried on. I was looking forward to meeting him. Matt sent all of my arrangements to Jimmy and the gig remained very much on. We marched on through the winter gigs and, with engagements in Dubai and Prague behind us, we soon reached May 2006 when we left for Detroit.

The area where we were staying in Rochester Hills turned out to be a sleepy, affluent, retirement sort of a place. OPC stood for Older Persons' Commission and the event I was performing at was their big annual bash. These retired folk in Rochester Hills had got life sorted and it was a very relaxing place. I'd had some trouble with my ear on the flight over but due to the ridiculous state I got myself into when flying anywhere, I dismissed it as just another symptom amongst the general sweating and shaking mess I stumbled off the plane in.

'Oh just check out these cosy white dressing gowns, this is pretty luxurious!' I shouted from the bathroom as Ma B was unpacking the Bassey case.

'Yeah they have done us proud, I am looking forward to relaxing for a week here,' she said.

'What did you say? I still can't hear anything from this ear!' I came out of the bathroom poking my finger in the offending blocked ear.

When we had settled ourselves we went downstairs to meet up with our partners in crime for the event, Jimmy Maxwell and the Sean Connery lookalike, or 'impersonator' as the Americans like to call them. We sat down with our drinks and looked around the bar.

'That guy over there is a dead ringer for Kenny Rogers,' I nudged Ma B just as she was about to take a sip of her gin and tonic.

'Bloody hell Jo,' she cursed, dabbing at her silk trousers, 'I've only brought a couple of outfits. Oh yeah, I think it could be Kenny! If not he should definitely be at the Vegas Impersonators Convention as Kenny. That is spooky, I am going to ask him.'

Ma B was a big Kenny Rogers fan and loved nothing more than a rendition of *The Gambler*. Off she went, tripping over drink in hand, just about to bother the bejaysus out of Kenny when he turned towards me, bypassing Ma B completely and said, 'The name's Bond, James Bond'. The bewildered look on Ma B's face was comedy gold. It is a good job she didn't get over to him before he came over to us because our Kenny had promptly introduced himself as the Sean Connery lookalike. In Ma B's defence, it has to be said that at some brief point during Sean Connery's life, he did resemble Kenny Rogers. Ma B maintained he probably did a bit of Kenny on the side. Our Kenny/Sean was a very funny man and he and I got on like a house on fire. We both shared a passion for serial killers and suffered cheese intolerance. It was a match made in heaven. Jimmy Maxwell had just arrived in the bar area and Kenny/Sean introduced us. Jimmy was absolutely delightful, as I knew he would be. We all had a few drinks and retired to our rooms pretty early as everyone had had a long day of travelling.

'I'm going to put some of these eardrops in tonight,' I grumbled, getting into my pjs. 'This thing is getting worse.'

'It will be just the flight and tiredness, it will be OK in the morning,' said Ma B.

'What did you say?'

I woke in the morning, completely deaf in one ear. The sound check was due to go ahead in the afternoon and I couldn't hear a thing on one side. This is not ideal for a singer. OK, OK, I know, there will be some famous singer who is deaf but I just wanted two working ears for the gig and I started to panic. Ma B, it has to be said, is not the most sympathetic in these situations and, having listened to my usual moaning on the long flight over, she was pretty much ignoring me and getting stuck into her costume duties. She started checking my dresses, sewing on a few sequins and basically told me to shut up and get a grip.

'There are 15 musicians flying in today from hurricane-torn New Orleans, put more drops in!'

I think that's what she said. It didn't matter what she said really, as I loudly pointed out that I couldn't bloody well hear her.

A few hours later we met with the organisers. As usual before the gig, they cannot do enough for us, so I asked if they had a medical centre or hospital nearby where I could quickly get my ear syringed. The tribute Gods were smiling down on me, or so I thought, as one of the main sponsors for the event was a local hospital. The OPC had serious influence at the hospital, not surprising really as I am sure a town full of oldies are great business, and they arranged for their minibus to take us straight there. It was lunchtime and before leaving for the hospital I popped into the ballroom where Jimmy and his band were starting to set up.

'See you in an hour or so Jimmy, I've just got to get this ear unblocked.'

'No probs honey,' Jimmy replied. 'I will just about be set up and ready for you then.'

Ma B and I spent the little journey to the hospital in silence. Well I thought we did. She may have been talking for the duration but I couldn't hear a bloody thing. The hospital was only five minutes away so I was hopeful that we would be back with the band in record time. We arrived at the hospital reception a few minutes later. There was a blonde lady who was obviously the receptionist sitting behind a large maple coloured desk. She wore way too much makeup and I imagined her to be far more attractive with a little less slap. Visually she reminded me of Sue Ellen from Dallas but blonde.

'Can I help you?' she asked, smiling enthusiastically.

'Yes hello, my name is Joanne. I am here to get my ear syringed as arranged with OPC,' I replied.

'I am sorry ma'am, could you repeat that?'

This went on for what seemed an age, as the Sue Ellen look-alike could not understand my accent. I could understand her clear enough because all she kept saying was, 'Could I have your passport and credit card please ma'am?' I had been told we were not to pay for this treatment as OPC would be picking up any bill and I was not about to put a big hole in my gig money, as these show-me-the-money Yank medical types really know how to charge. The time was ticking on, Ma B was going into panic-mode and I could not get passed the heavily made up, coiffured harridan that was Sue Ellen on reception.

The commotion at reception was getting louder and our accents were causing some interest when, thank the lord, a doctor appeared. He had heard all the noise and knew about the OPC phone call and the situation.

'Hi Joanne, sure is nice to meet you. Just come into this cubicle, lie down and let's have a look, I'm sure we will soon have this sorted for you.'

Fast forward about an hour and I was still on the bed, a whole lot wetter from the syringing. Doc had reluctantly admitted defeat and gone off to get someone else, Ma B was pacing up and down cursing and giving me an accusatory time check every 15 minutes, it was lucky no one understood the accent. She was getting more and more agitated, we both were, as our sound check/rehearsal time was ebbing away. A lady doctor then appeared, new syringe in hand.

'Well now Shirl, I'm going to the ball for OPC tonight and I am so looking forward to hearing you sing. Yes, I can see it and it's a big piece – hold still Shirl, I'm going in.' I was feeling wet, frustrated and anxious and was just about to snap, 'Don't call me Shirl!' when out came a piece of wax the size of Kim Kardashian's arse.

'Look at this, I told you, no wonder I couldn't bloody hear!' I shouted to Ma B's back as she frantically collected our things and headed out the door. I caught up with her in the hospital car park on the phone to the hotel.

'Have you seen the time? Christ we are going to have trouble getting any rehearsal in,' she said.

'Alright, alright no need to shout.' I now had completely the opposite problem as every sound was loud and crystal clear.

'Wonder how long that piece of wax has been building up to that size'? I said, feeling relieved that I could hear properly.

Ma B gave me one of those looks that said she had really had enough of ear conversations. After about 45 minutes we were still waiting on the hospital car park for the hotel's driver. I called the hotel again. 'Oh, sorry Joanne, he has been so busy ferrying people in for tonight's celebration. We are having our annual ball tonight you know?' Give me bastard strength, I thought!

It was about 5pm when we ran into the ballroom. Jimmy was running through his swing numbers, the sound guy was messing around at the mixing desk and the organisers were already in evening dress, gaily titivating their table decorations. They all looked pretty chilled. I looked like I had just put my head in a bucket and Ma B looked like one wrong word and she would take out the lot of them.

Now, I could devote a whole chapter on bands. I have worked with quite a few from a three-piece up to a 17-piece and the orchestral strings and horns of the Bassey/Bond music is tricky. I have huge respect for all the musos I worked with but I'd had some disasters with bands in the past. Jimmy's New Orleans band sounded fabulous on his jazz and swing stuff but for the Bassey numbers we could have done with a few days to really sort it out. But hey, we had 30 minutes because it was already 5.30pm and they wanted us out of there at 6pm. I hadn't been around to fight for space so Jimmy's band had taken up the whole stage. I was going to have to be on the dance floor. I had no time to argue and the last thing we wanted was for the organisers to think everything was less than totally splendid. Jimmy and I were professionals so we quickly made a decision to just wing it. Now that I could actually hear I thought I had better belt out a few lines just to get the sound on the vocals right.

'Could you give me some reverb now please?' I called over to the sleepy sound man sat at the mixing desk. He nudged up his baseball cap peak and scratched at his head, looking confused.

'You know? Vocal effects? Celine and Mariah use them sometimes,' I snarled, making my way over to him. I could write yet another whole chapter on soundmen alone but his reply surpassed all others.

'Don't got no reverb ma'am, I kinda wasn't planning on using any.'

It had been a very long day. I knew I was facing a challenging night with the unrehearsed band, no stage and now a flat microphone.

Oh, and guess what, my hearing was now super charged so I was going to hear everything! I had two choices, kill the sound man with my bare hands in front of the oldies and finish up in the state penitentiary where I could end my days engrossed in conversation with serial killers, or work with what I had. It really was a tough choice given my fascination with serial killers. I glanced across at Jimmy and his band, who had just survived unbelievable hardship at the hands of Hurricane Katrina and summoning up as much control as I could, trying not to frighten the elderly ladies in their gowns who were merrily titivating tables, I hissed, 'Well I kinda was so please go and get a reverb unit NOW.'

Showtime arrived and, as gigs went, it was a testy one. I had to be escorted from an Aston Martin by Sean Connery to make my entrance. The reverb was not up to much and I would have been better on backing tracks as far as the swing band went, though they were great at swing. We all got through it unscathed. The audience seemed, as usual, to be oblivious to any problems and thoroughly enjoyed the show.

One of the organisers ran up to me after the show and said, 'You were fabulous our talented little friend!' I was unaware that I was little. Ma B said that as nobody could actually see me, due to me performing on the on the dance floor, amongst a pile of sashaying oldies, I would indeed appear 'little'. Jimmy, Sean, Ma B and I all had a bit of a party in the hotel bar after the event and we had a great time.

We had added a week on to this gig and were looking forward to relaxing in the Rochester Hills hotel. The hotel had the loveliest Egyptian cotton dressing gowns and Ma B and I spent most of the time watching TV and reading magazines on our beds in the delicious robes. The downside, however, was that you could not get a decent cup of tea for love nor money anywhere. The brew was very suspect in the USA. It was bizarre. When we first ordered a pot of Earl Grey tea in the hotel, we were impressed and somewhat hopeful. The waitress appeared with a fancy box of speciality teas and we chose ourselves a nice Earl Grey brew bag.

What came next beggared belief. She appeared with these two tall latte style glasses with handles, out of which stuck a stick with sugar on the end and, get this for a kicker, a jug of cream! The water was not completely boiling either. I couldn't cope with the tea. Matt would have gone straight back to the airport had he sampled the Yankee brews. We quickly found ourselves an Irish bar up the road where we could get an 'acceptable' brew and the staff kindly told us about a little place called Sheila's Tea Rooms. Sheila was Welsh and she served up a piping hot brew. We spent most of the week between the Irish bar and Welsh Sheila's.

We didn't venture out much at night. The robes were too comfy and besides, it was the week of the *American Idol* final and we were avid fans.

We were excited for the final on the Wednesday night and frantically cheering on Taylor Hicks to win. We did go to a couple of American bars and tried to get into a baseball game, or was it American football? I don't know. That's how interested we were. Although I was in the US, I was busy making phone calls to the UK, trying to sort things out back at home. I had decided to buy Robbo out of our house and rent it out whilst staying at Ma B's. Robbo was happy with that and I needed time to decide what I wanted to do. I was a little worried about Robbo's mental state because I had been reliably informed by his work colleagues on numerous occasions that he was out of control and constantly drunk. I did receive a text message a few weeks after our split saying, 'I miss you. We've made a mistake. P.S I am sober', sent at 10.30am. I presumed he should have been at work so being sober at that time in the morning should not have needed clarifying, unless one was usually drunk of course.

Eventually, after a pleasant and relaxing week, we said goodbye to Rochester Hills. On the drive back to the airport our taxi driver started to tell us all about Detroit, Motown and Henry Ford. Actually Henry sounded like my kinda guy. The taxi driver told me that Henry reportedly ripped up the railway tracks around the area so everybody had to buy a car. How true this was, I don't know. He also told us that we could actually see Canada from the car window. It struck me that I always learnt far more interesting facts from chatting to taxi drivers than ever I did in a class room. We also realised, once again far too late, that we should have done much more than hang around Welsh Sheila's and the Irish Bar during our Detroit visit.

Around six months after arriving home from Detroit, a bill dropped through the letterbox from the Rochester Hills Medical Centre for $400. What did I tell you about those Yank medical bods? Well, they could kiss my Bassey ass! I never did pay it.

***

We had performed in some beautiful places overseas but one of the most scenic was the bay of Naples. The band and I had been booked to perform on a fabulous yacht that was sailing around the Amalfi Coast. It was a 007 event and part of the wedding celebrations of a wealthy Danish couple. Paul the drummer couldn't make it on the gig because he was promoting something in Los Angeles so we had another young drummer on board called Jack.

'Jack seems young, I hope he will be OK,' Ma B said to me out of earshot of the others as we were boarding.

'Matt says he is good so I'm sure he will be fine,' I replied reassuringly.

I knew what she meant; the drummer is a pretty crucial part of the band. Paul had often remarked, when we were having an after-gig inquest on who had made what mistake where, 'You will all know who it is when I drop a clanger!' As it transpired we need not have worried; Jack was a diamond.

We were collected from the airport and driven through the tiny streets of Naples. We all stared out at the tall, old buildings that edged the narrow streets, washing hanging from the windows and balconies. These houses were somehow made more handsome by their varying states of decay. With the windows down we could hear the old Italian women, all dressed in black with head scarves on, shouting greetings across the street and the men sat at pavement tables drinking their coffees. It was a beautiful day and the coastal views were breathtaking but my heart was in my mouth swinging around those ridiculously narrow streets and hairpin bends, our driver just merrily honking his horn to let any oncoming vehicle know we were actually on their side of the road. We were dropped off at our little hotel just a few streets away from a marina and told we would be collected in the morning to be taken to the yacht.

Our rooms were pretty basic and all in a row next to one another. When we were out on our little balconies we could chat to each other and pass over various necessities like a cigarette lighter or an iron. Needless to say we had a few drinks in the bar that night and Matt entertained us all with some rather bizarre magic tricks he had just perfected. Matt did not drink alcohol, however if he did have a couple of beers, which was rare indeed, strange things would happen. I remember one trick was a little disconcerting for Ma B as she too was not much of a drinker. You needed to have had a few bevvies for this one because it involved Matt plunging his hands down his trousers and rummaging around a lot. The 'climax', or should I say aim, of the performance seemed to be to produce his underpants without taking his trousers off. A huge cheer went up in relief when Matt succeeded in pulling this trick off, so to speak, as the alternative would not be welcome and the Italian barman was looking slightly disturbed.

As arranged, we were collected the next morning to be taken to the yacht. We all climbed aboard a small boat with our instruments and suit holders. I had splashed out on a new black gown for this gig, with a thigh high split. It had beads and crystals around the strapless off the shoulder bodice. It was very glamorous but it had to be really tight to keep the top in place. Once I inhaled and was zipped into it, the bones in the bodice came into play. From an engineering point of view all was secure. From a breathing aspect, I felt like an extra from *Pride and Prejudice* and was slightly concerned about singing because the diaphragm and breath is quite important. The scenery on this coast was stunning and we looked out across the sparkling sea to where the yacht was moored. We were all pretty quiet, we were just taking in the whole adventure.

I had no experience of luxury yachts but even I knew this looked super luxurious. Once aboard, everything, every single inch of that yacht, gleamed and shone as if an army of cleaners worked all through the night. It was all shining brass, highly polished wood, gleaming glass and white leather. You could see your reflection in every surface. It was all so beautiful. It was also, apart from crew, pretty empty, as the guests had been taken ashore into Naples for the day. As we sat on the white leather suites, on one of the upper decks, in the glorious sunshine, a waiter brought us drinks and we gazed out over the dazzling still waters, at a view of a coastline that artists have been painting for centuries. This was the life. We could all only imagine for a few precious hours how the mega rich lived.

Once we were reasonably happy with our sound check, we were taken back up on deck for lunch. I think perhaps the crew thought we were guests because our tables were all crisp, blindingly white, cotton tablecloths with crystal glasses and shiny silver cutlery. I don't think they knew we were just hired hands like themselves. We tucked into some delicious grub that we were told had been flown in from top chef Gordon Ramsay and ordered drinks as if we were 'to the manor born'. Sir Elton John's florist had arranged the flowers on the tables.

Once again we were based in the library, which was to be our changing room, and after a very pleasant few hours up top we set up home there. We soon littered the place with dresses, suits, feather boas, bow ties, instruments and all sorts of band paraphernalia. There is always an inordinate amount of time when gigging that is spent just hanging around waiting, but unable to leave your post. Sometimes this time is spent in comfortable and lovely places, sometimes pretty bleak. Due to the simple fact that set up and sound checking always has to be done before any guests arrive, there were always hours to kill. We played hangman and the band would argue about all sorts of facts regarding films and the degrees of separation between actors and their connections to specific films. Matt often challenged other members of the band with his geography questions. He was well qualified because he admitted that he tended to read an atlas whilst on the bog.

'Right I'm going stir crazy,' I announced. 'It's time to play the 'replace the word in a movie' game. I'll start. We must replace one word in the movie title with the word... mmm... PENIS!' I declared. I had the band's attention.

'It's a Wonderful... Penis,' I said quite amused with myself.

'The Man with the Golden Penis,' Matt quickly replied.

There was a brief pause then Jack the drummer said, 'Thunder Penis'. Matt quickly pointed out that he couldn't have that as 'Thunderball' was in fact one word and Jack was ruthlessly disqualified. The bass player, Eddie, was still trying to come up with the answer to one of Matt's tricky geography questions so he was a little preoccupied.

'The Hand that Rocked the Penis,' I enthusiastically shouted. Matt chuckled.

A few minutes passed then all of a sudden Ma B poked her head around the library door and proudly said, 'Gone with the Penis!' Everybody laughed.

Our games passed the time. Luckily most musos, along with entertainers, Matt aside, are by their very nature pretty feckless and they are well suited to the sort of inane games that we would play. It was all adolescent stuff but we had some really good laughs.

Matt had been booked to play sax through their dinner, before moving to the nightclub room, which was where we were performing. Matt went off about 7pm to play a couple of hours of mellow, background sax, which he was excellent at. We thought dinner would be the usual couple of hours or so and the organiser had told us that we would be going on around 10pm. We could hear Matt's sax and he seemed to be playing for an eternity. Ma B even crept into the back of the dining room to take a peak a few times, as she was in her Sunday best evening gear and at a push could try to mingle in with guests. This lot had absolutely no concept of time whatsoever. As is the case with a lot of the super-rich, they do exactly as they please and just love the sound of their own voices. The endless times that one after another they got up to regale each other with tales and anecdotes, was unbelievable. I think they had about 10 different courses of food and poor Matt had to keep stopping and starting, I think his lips were turning blue. At about midnight Ma B came back to the library where we were all struggling to keep awake as by this point we had been kept shut away for five hours.

'This is ridiculous, I am really concerned about Matt's lips as five hours of virtually non-stop sax playing is an awful lot,' she said.

At around 9pm the band had stood in the library, all present and correct in their tuxedos, bows all neatly tied, clutching their music sheets and keyed up for battle. Wind on four hours and the boys were lounging on the floor, bow ties scattered around drifting mentally away from the task ahead. With the exception of poor Matt who hadn't been seen by anyone, other than Ma B, since 7pm and could now possibly enter the *Guinness Book of Records* for sax playing. Ma B was sent outside again to find the Dutch agent and ask how much longer this was going to take.

I think it was 1am when he burst through the library door and barked, 'Ok, you are on! Quick, quick get yourselves down there, they do not like to be kept waiting.'

WHAT! Off we scurried and did our thing. They absolutely loved it all and, apart from a blue tinge to Matt's lips, we were a huge success. I had sat in the library in my dress from 9pm until 1am, bolt upright like Elizabeth Bennet waiting for Mr Darcy so the bodice had eased off and gave me no problems when singing. After the show a member of crew came to tell us they were ready to take us back to shore. We had been imprisoned for the whole night in the library so we had not seen the yacht and the shoreline at night. The whole yacht was lit up against a black, inky sea. The boys were super excited because a speedboat was taking us back. We all climbed in chattering excitedly and, in true James Bond style, we flew over the waves and headed back to the sparkling lights of the shore.

The fabulous yacht, Naples

The band boys on the yacht's deck

Ma B sampling a fine quality king prawn whilst on board

Surely Bassey's band being transported to the yacht, Naples

Matt in the library warming up for his marathon sax playing session on board the Naples yacht

A relaxed Matt being transported to the yacht.

Appreciating the Amalfi Coast scenery and the champagne with Ma B on deck

CHAPTER NINE

FROM DOWNTON ABBEY TO TRICKEY DICKIES

The year 2007 was great for us because the world and his wife were arranging 007 parties and, as a tribute act, Shirl was in great demand. We'd performed in France, Spain, Italy and Germany (Frankfurt was very pretty). We were flying in and out, driving up and down the country doing some fabulous Bond events. This one had to be up there amongst the most memorable ones.

It was the bleak mid-winter, 21st December to be precise, a cold, threatening, foggy early afternoon. We were making our way down the A34 to our next gig to meet up with Matt and the band. This was our final gig before we finished for Christmas and we all had a holiday feeling. We were excited to hand out our carefully chosen Christmas gifts to our staff. Yes the band would be getting their usual Christmas bonus, an extra £20 each, along with novelty bars of soap from Ann Summers, which were cleverly crafted into the shape of a penis. It was exactly the same present and bonus as they had been given the year before. They would love it. We were grateful for what had been a very busy year with some super bookings. You never took anything for granted in the entertainment business and we knew 2008 could be very different. To be doing the pre-Christmas gig with the band was great because we always had such a hoot. As was normal, whenever we were nearing our destination, we started to look at the paperwork in terms of where we were actually going, who we were working for and to try to get into work mode.

'This Innocent smoothie professes to be two of your five-a-day in every bottle, it's full of antioxidants and supposedly gives you the goodness of six different types of fruit along with being a great source of Vitamin C. What do you think?' I asked Ma B. We were around two miles away from the venue.

'I think they are very cleverly packaged,' She replied cynically.

It was strawberry and banana. I had decided that very morning to get a bit healthier so I gave the bottle an enthusiastic shake. It exploded. It exploded big. It went everywhere and I was covered. It went in my hair, all over my clothes, the car interior, the gig paperwork and it got Ma B. The car interior and I had come off worse and Ma B was just superficially splattered, although she appeared a little temporarily stunned.

'What the fucking hell just happened! It's exploded. How has it exploded? It's not even fizzy. I thought you were supposed to shake them. I'm covered in fucking smoothie. Look at the car! Jesus Christ!' I screeched. Ma B was quiet but her shoulders were moving up and down. 'You're laughing! How am I supposed to turn up to a posh castle with strawberry and banana hanging out of my hair? Eh? I already smell ripe and look at my clothes.'

The sat nav then proudly announced that we were reaching our destination in 400 yards. 'Piss off!' I hissed at the smoothie-splattered sat nav.

Ma B wiped some smoothie from her amused little face and said, 'Don't panic we're early. We'll have to find somewhere to clean up. Did you bring any spare clothes?'

I glared at her and said, 'Nope. Certainly no spare jeans, only pyjamas for later.'

Our destination was Highclere Castle, which meant absolutely nothing to us; it could have been any venue, anywhere. As we travelled up the long driveway the castle suddenly came into view. It was breathtaking, jaw dropping actually, and we were, for once, speechless. The grey winter afternoon, coupled with the descending fog, just added to the overwhelming beauty of the place. I was sure that arriving covered in two of the recommended five-a-day was not considered appropriate for a venue of this stature. We stopped the car in front of a huge, solid oak, unwelcoming and very imposing door and just sat staring at it for a few minutes. The smoothie in my hair was drying nicely.

I heard a loud bang and immediately thought the Lord of the Manor was doing a spot of peasant shooting, or is it pheasant? I hoped he was shooting pheasants because if he was blasting peasants, I didn't rate our chances. The aristocracy are a peculiar bunch, they don't have to conform to the code of morality that is imposed on the rest of us plebs.

Anyway, the bang wasn't His Lordship having fun. I looked in the rear view mirror and saw that it was actually the shambolic, backfiring excuse for a vehicle, which was, of course, Matt's green, smelly Maestro. Matt pulled up beside us, glanced up at the castle and simply said, 'I am sick of having to direct the brass, absolutely everywhere. All their fancy sat navs yet they cannot get from A to B without a million phone calls from me. (The brass, by the way, was not old gangster slang for prostitutes but short for the brass section, i.e. the trumpet and sax players.) They forget their sheet music and their bow ties. In fact it's a bloody miracle they remember their instruments.' He lit one of his long Superking fags and asked us, 'Have you knocked? Is there anyone about?'

He asked the question as if we had just pulled up to a working men's club not a castle. As if he had been heard, the door suddenly opened. We expected to see a butler or something of the like but it was just an ordinary female secretary. We told her who we were and she swiftly told us we had to go away and come back about 5pm and to park our cars around the back, not at the front of the building. With that she shut the door. Charming. That timing actually worked out fine for me as Matt had witnessed that I was a vision of strawberry and banana so promptly told us where there was a shopping outlet that was not far away. Ma B and I went off to buy clothes so I could get out of the smoothie outfit, leaving Matt to enjoy his fag and await the arrival of Paul the drummer along with the brass boys.

We arrived back at Highclere around 5pm and started to get set up with the band. The interior was, as you would expect from a huge stately home, fabulously grand and historical. Our performing area was to be in the library. It was a relatively small room as far as accommodating a live band and an audience was concerned and space was tight. We had to set up in front of a huge fireplace. To be honest, we could hardly fit the drum kit, together with Paul's belly, in at all. There were leads everywhere.

'Look how dated the interior is. You'd think they'd bring the bloody place up to date a bit,' Paul said sarcastically as we were setting up in the heavily ornate library.

'I know. If they've got no dough, they could do it up at Ikea for nowt. It's just laziness,' I retorted.

'Yeah I'd be getting a nice gas fire in here and I'd do away with that big fireplace. They want to get themselves a Kindle whilst they're at it and get rid of all those books,' he quipped.

I pointed out that that the place would benefit from a nice bit of maple and some chrome. Paul chuckled. Once we were all set up and sound checked, we were directed downstairs to the servants' quarters where we were due to be fed. It was truly *Upstairs Downstairs*; there was the original bell system that the lords and ladies used to ring for service from the upstairs rooms and bedrooms, then downstairs in the servants' quarters the bell rang under the relevant room. Being fed was always the most important part of the evening for Paul and the other musos, unlike Matt who, like myself, was content with a sandwich, a brew and a ciggie. The rest of the band could not function unless they were fed hot food. That's just how they rolled.

We ate and chatted. Matt went outside for a fag whilst Paul moaned that Matt was always moaning and before we knew it, it was approaching showtime. We were doing a Bond set for a group of Japanese businessmen. It was not a big audience but they were certainly enthusiastic. They were stamping their feet, banging the tables and shouting, 'More! More!' The Japanese did seem to love a good Bassey/ Bond set. We packed the gear down and started to stack it near the huge oak door when Matt looked up at a big portrait of a lady that was hanging on the wall and announced, 'I'm sure I just saw that woman coming down the stairs.'

'I think that's Lady Carnarvon,' Ma B said.

Then the front door opened and a man stood in the doorway. Matt looked at the man then glanced up at another large portrait that was hanging next to the picture of the lady. It was a picture of the Earl of Carnarvon, the same man that was standing in the doorway. Matt looked at him and simply said, 'I'm Matt. Is this your pad then?'

In 2010, nearly three years later, Highclere Castle, the ancestral home of the Earls of Carnarvon, became the setting for the enormously popular TV series *Downton Abbey*. It was surreal watching *Downton* and remembering our performance in the same library in front of that iconic fireplace.

By the time we had finished and loaded the vehicles, the fog had seriously descended – a real pea souper! The castle had taken on a scary look and we expected the hounds of the Baskervilles to appear at any moment. Matt was patiently helping everyone with directions and, as always, he had made sure that, as females, our car was packed up and we were safely on our way. He really was quite gallant in that respect. The times were endless where he'd ran from a venue, on foot, through a busy ring road in Leeds, located us and jumped in the back of the car to direct us. He looked at the fog and our worried faces and told us to follow him back up the A34 and he would get us to our next Travelodge. Those were the times we realised that Matt truly was a priceless gem.

***

As 2007 was coming to an end I was becoming painfully aware that Robbo was getting in a really bad way. His parents were scared, his colleagues were worried and I was shocked. Steph was trying to get him to go to AA for all she was worth. She left so many messages but he wouldn't return her calls. I had been told that he was not only pissed 24/7 but he was also taking cocaine. One of his closest and oldest work mates told me that he was downing vodka and snorting cocaine whilst at work. He was doing it on a daily basis, even in the mornings, and I was stunned. Robbo never did spirits or drugs whilst we were together (to my knowledge) and I couldn't believe it.

The drink side I had to believe because by this point I had endured around six months of drunken phone calls from him and his parents had told me the true extent of his alcohol problem. He would call me from various train stations or park benches with no idea where he was or what he was saying. I could barely understand him let alone decipher where he was slumped, in terms of getting him picked up. His mother told me to distance myself as only he could help himself and there was nothing I could do. He had received the money from our house sale, which for him was around £37,000, and he appeared to be merrily shoving it up his nose and down his neck. I sensed real trouble ahead and feared for his parents, Dave and Marie. They were such lovely people and had been part of my family for many years. I willed Robbo to recover for their sake as much as his own.

***

How do I describe The Braymont Society? How will I do this community justice? There was nothing different about this booking on paper. They simply wanted a Bassey tribute for a cabaret dinner dance at a hotel. The Braymont Society was named as the client on the contract and the name meant nothing to me. It was all run of-the-mill stuff. It was a very windy, dull, grey Saturday afternoon in late December 2007 when we pulled up on the hotel car park.

I was wittering on about somebody's poor parking when Ma B suddenly said, 'Oh dear. What is that over there?'

I followed her glance and looked over towards the reception doors. I saw a strange looking woman hobbling along the pathway that ran around the outside of the hotel. She was very tall and not walking very convincingly in her heels. She was wearing a beige tweed twin-set with a floral blouse underneath and carried a little cream leather handbag. As she approached nearer to where we had parked, I quickly noticed the masculine shoulders and the five o'clock shadow.

'Ahh... that's defo a geezer,' I replied with some certainty.

We chuckled and went inside to the reception area to inform the hotel staff of our arrival and find out the best place to unload. On my return from the second trip to the car, whist sharing the weight of a bass bin with Ma B, I spotted three women who were dressed in outfits that I suppose were similar to mother-of-the-bride wear. The women seemed to multiply in the reception and bar area until there literally seemed to be swarms of them; an infestation of two-pieces and frocks. There were pastels, florals and flowery hats everywhere. I was a little alarmed because the women appeared to be a tad bow-legged and their voices were quite deep.

At this point in time I feel the need to strongly express my firm belief in inclusion and diversity. I'm at one with absolutely everybody, regardless of their race, creed, colour, religious beliefs, background and sexual orientation – but somebody could have told me! The place was bursting to the seams with blokes dressed like Hyacinth Bucket. I scurried over to the reception and quickly asked whom I was working for. The lady confirmed I was booked to perform for The Braymont Society who had booked the entire hotel for their event. She said there were over 400 members attending that evening. Then she smiled a big bright smile.

Ma B and I set up the gear then went to the bar area. A group of the 'ladies' who I thought resembled The Golden Girls with an additional one that reminded me of Mavis from *Coronation Street* were gathered around the screen in the bar getting very enthusiastic about a rugby match that was on the big TV. Their fists were clenched tightly around their handbags as they punched the air. It was a strange sight indeed. Two straight, middle-aged, unsuspecting men wandered into the hotel bar to have a drink and watch the rugby. Ma B and I watched them, interested to catch their reaction. They scoured the bar area slowly then both of them laughed. They spent a few minutes doubled-up, shaking silently then left. They couldn't finish their pints.

Then my client arrived. A large, blonde, pot-bellied, bow-legged, portly creature dressed in a baby pink, netted, sleeveless dress waddled over to where I was perched. The fussy pink frock finished at her knees and there was a mass of hair poking through her tights (I do remember thinking at the time that the shade of pink lipstick she was wearing was actually lovely).

'Shirley Bassey?' She enquired with a big bright smile.

'Yes, hello,' I said enthusiastically.

'I'm Janet,' she replied.

We were such bullshitters. I was still sitting down at that point. Janet then hoisted her dress up and knelt down on one knee, legs apart in a similar way that a bricklayer would kneel if he was marking a line for his footings. Once she was at my level, she went on to inform me of the agenda ahead. I noticed that there were also a few 'real' women present, which confused me a little but I soon realised they were the wives. Janet informed me that they would all soon be retiring to their rooms for a while in order to change into their evening attire. I won't lie – alarm bells did ring. I couldn't understand the situation and imagined the bathroom scenario with them and their wives to be chaos. I sincerely hoped that Janet was going to shave her legs.

I started to ask myself questions. How would I address this audience? I always address my audience as 'Ladies and Gentlemen' but there were no gentlemen present, as such. Usually when I performed *Big Spender*, I would flirt with the men and perch on their knee with my boa coyly. I wouldn't be able to do that either. I was sure *I Am What I Am* would still go down a storm although in this case the lyrics were somewhat of a contradiction – or not. Before we knew it, evening was upon us. My intro played and I was on. I soon noticed that whilst the wives seemed to have remained respectable in terms of their chosen party wear, some members of Janet's crew had not.

I managed to get through the set without referring to any males in the crowd or offending anybody. I simply decided to refer to them as 'members of my delightful and immaculately turned-out audience'. I stayed on stage for *Big Spender* and just put more oomph into my own performance. They were a receptive crowd but so reserved. It was almost as if they wanted to be quiet, dainty ladies who clapped delicately and really appreciated the entertainment. I bet they were a different kettle of fish down the Cross Keys on a Saturday night.

Following my performance, it was party time. This would prove to be enlightening. Janet was wearing a white sequinned number. It was short, shiny and very tight and it made her broad shoulders seem even more exaggerated. She had gone for the very-large-silicone-gel-lumps-inserted-into-the-bra trick. In contrast to earlier, her wig, or should I say her long, curly blonde locks, were worn in an updo. She looked like a giant, inflatable Barbara Windsor. She had certainly loosened up by the time the DJ kicked off. She proceeded to tell me that the frock thing was really just a weekend pastime and most of the men were very happily married. She said their wives were very understanding. I was still a little confused. She said there were all sorts of industry professionals present, politicians, broadcasters and writers.

I glanced over at the full and excited dance floor, amazed at the mix. There was a very tall, long-limbed specimen sporting a leopard print skin-tight dress who had really big, bucked teeth. The frock was right up her backside, her chest seemed huge and her skin tone on the chest area did not match that of her face. Her hair was red and wild and although it was styled in an updo, she had long tousled bits hanging around her face. She was also wearing a studded dog collar contraption around her neck. She was all 'tits and teeth' and strutting around the dance floor like a hooker on acid. Janet told me Miss Leopard Print was a top solicitor in the City of London. That didn't surprise me. I was in fact scouring the dance floor looking for some representation from the church.

To Ma B's amusement, I was soon forced to dance with Janet and crew. I did party with clients on occasion following performances; sometimes I literally had no choice. This was a very funny dance floor indeed. Miss Leopard Print was soon upon me and really going for it. Once I was up close to her, I saw that the chest piece was a shiny, smooth, plastic torso that was fixed in place with a strap around her neck and one around her waist. I presume the dog collar neck piece was in place to disguise the join. I wondered where she kept her stash of crystal meth.

When Ma B and I returned home, Nan was there to greet us. We sat down for a brew and, as she usually did, Nan said, 'So how was the gig?' Ma B and I looked at each other and just replied in unison 'Oh fine'. Nan wouldn't understand. I didn't understand. Nan was very elderly. She hadn't got time for political correctness or the like. She would have looked very confused and said something like, 'So are they women?' No. 'Are they gay?' No. 'Are they lesbians?' No. 'Do they want a sex change operation to become women?' No, they are in fact married. Nan just wouldn't have understood some married bloke who wore his wife's frock and knickers at the weekend. It really wasn't worth the conversation. I won't forget The Braymont Society anytime soon. They were an eye-opener and thoroughly entertaining.

***

There was only ever one gig where I seriously didn't want to take the money. I felt totally guilty about being paid even though the client insisted. I had received a call in 2007 from a private care home for the mentally handicapped. The house was in North London and the residents lived on site on a permanent basis. A member of staff had found my website and he was calling because one of the residents had his 60th birthday in late December. He was a huge Shirley Bassey fan. The guy told me that the birthday boy was a little temperamental and could be very difficult to deal with. He said his name was Tony and he had a severe case of Down's syndrome. Apparently whenever he heard Shirley Bassey his eyes would light up and he would stand up excitedly and try to copy her hand movements whilst singing along.

The staff said they thought it would be a great idea to book a Bassey tribute act for his birthday. They said the families of the residents paid a lot of money to have them taken care of well and they also had a budget for entertainment so they wanted to pay the going rate. I didn't think too much about it at the time so I quoted them and said I was available. I had already been told that I would have to perform early so they could put the residents to bed at their usual time.

The house was big but not huge, a nice old-fashioned white building that, judging by the area, was probably worth a fortune. We pulled up on the driveway outside and I rang the doorbell. Two members of staff came to the door, asked if we needed any help unloading and led us to the room where I was to perform. It was absolutely tiny. It was literally a little living room with six chairs positioned in a half circle. There was a TV in one corner and a small Christmas tree in the other. The staff members told me that there were only seven mentally handicapped people living there and they all had different disabilities.

Whilst we were unloading the equipment a few of the residents started to appear. They seemed curious and wanted to see what was going on. The staff said they would probably get a bit excited so we would all have to keep an eye on them because they were likely to want to investigate the equipment and generally get very involved with the proceedings. There was a very cute, cheeky little woman called Emily loitering around the entrance to the house. She was only around four feet tall with wild, curly ginger hair. She was wearing a little grey skirt and green tights. She was probably about 30 years old but she looked just like a child. One of the carers told me she moved like lightning when she wanted to and they needed eyes in the back of their heads. It soon became apparent that she was into everything and needed constant supervision. Emily had a reputation for taking things apart because she was inquisitive and interested in how things worked.

I was informed that somebody would have to be in the room to watch over the equipment whilst we were still unloading it because Emily would have the mixing desk in bits before we could say, 'Christ what's happened to the desk?' There were two guys bringing the speakers in through the entrance area and Emily wanted to carry one. They tried to explain to her that the speakers were far too heavy but she was having none of it. She wanted to join in and I had to give her the little silver case that had the radio mic inside so she had something to carry. She wanted to hold my hand at the same time. I never found out what her condition was but she looked like a happy little woman.

When I got back into the room Ma B was guarding the mixing desk and trying to explain to one of the older residents who also wanted to help by enthusiastically unplugging every single plug in the living room including the Christmas tree, that we only required one socket because we had an extension lead. The guy was called George and he could speak but his speech was very affected and he just kept making funny noises and grinning. Every now and then he would blow me a kiss and giggled when I blew one back. As fast as I was plugging stuff in, he was unplugging it. One of the carers stayed to keep an eye on Emily who made a beeline for the mixing desk as soon as she entered the room. He had to tell her off and we had to cover the mixer with a tablecloth. I could see that setting up the gear and doing the sound check could take a long time.

Tony, the man I was actually going to be singing for, had not made an appearance at that point because he was busy eating his birthday tea in the kitchen. Adam, the man who booked me, said Tony was sometimes naughty and halfway through his dinner he would quite often throw the plate of food on to the floor. He explained that people with Down's syndrome were very affectionate and loving but they were also highly emotional and often had tantrums. He said Tony had good days and bad days and that he hoped today was going to be one of his good ones. Already I really admired how the staff handled these vulnerable people. They really knew what they were doing and did it in a firm but gentle fashion. Once we had finally set up and sound checked, the room had to be closed off so that Emily, George and their other friend, who was around seven feet tall but never said a word, couldn't get their mitts on the gear. The tall man just kept grunting and clapping his hands and the movie *One Flew Over the Cuckoo's Nest* sprang to mind.

Following the set up, I had an hour to go up into one of the little bedrooms to get ready. Before I went, Adam pulled me to one side and said that I would have to be careful with Tony when I was performing because they had never booked anything like a tribute show before and nobody could predict Tony's behaviour or his reaction. I was actually quite concerned because I didn't know what I would do if he didn't like it or if he got upset due to the fact that he knew I was not the real Dame Shirley. I got ready and told Adam to give me the nod when the residents were in place. I decided that I would approach it the same way as any other gig.

I made the biggest entrance I could, given the fact that I was performing in a tiny living room, and the show got under way. Tony and the other residents sat in a semi-circle facing me. They looked transfixed and I was pleased. Tony was wearing a bright red jumper and had a huge smile on his face. Towards the end of *Goldfinger* he jumped up and stood next to me mimicking my hand movements and shouting the lyrics. He looked really excited and the staff were standing at the back of the room laughing. Emily, George, the tall mute man and a cute little fat Chinese guy in a wheelchair started to laugh and clap their hands. They were making all sorts of strange noises and George kept blowing kisses and squealing.

The next song was Bassey's version of George Harrison's *Something* and after the first verse I glanced across at Tony and saw that he was crying but still trying to sing. For the first time during a performance, I nearly lost it and I couldn't look at him because I knew I would cry too. Ma B had tears in her eyes and had to look away. The staff gave me a look indicating that I should carry on, he was crying because he was happy. Adam put his thumbs up so I got it together and continued. To be honest, I could have cried during the entire gig but I didn't.

Tony loved *Big Spender* and got up to dance. He wanted to play with my red feather boa so I gave it to him and he put it round his neck whilst doing his little dance. It was too cute. During *I Who Have Nothing* the Chinese guy in the wheelchair started to pretend to play the drums. He then started to repeat the last word of the line I had just finished and did it throughout the entire song. It was very funny. I sang 'I' and then I heard a very loud 'I' then me again 'I who have nothing' then the echo 'nothing!' He did it on every single line I sang and although it was a little off-putting for me, he was having a ball.

I was coming towards the end of the set so I sang happy birthday to Tony and gave him a kiss. George didn't look too happy about that so I had to blow him two kisses just in case he got vexed. I had put the microphone back in the stand for the next song and it became apparent that somebody had obviously taken their eye off the ball because Emily shot up and took the microphone straight out of the stand. She was very quick and trying to get out of the room with it. The staff stopped her but she had already unscrewed the end and she was trying to take the batteries out. She really was a little tyke. We recovered the microphone and she was told to sit down and behave.

I was finishing the set with *I Am What I Am* and during the song Tony stood next to me and copied every gesture. He mimicked every single move I made. He sang enthusiastically and I was thrilled that he was enjoying it. There was another lady resident in the room with long dark hair but she didn't really make eye contact. I didn't think she liked it too much as she just sat rocking back and forth in her chair, looking at the floor and mumbling. Following the second verse of *I Am What I Am*, and while I was actually singing, the dark haired lady came up right in front of the microphone stand and shouted, 'Where do you come from?' I was trying to sing but I managed to reply 'Leicestershire' quickly between the lyrics. I could see Ma B laughing. The lady then came closer and gave me a hug and, again whilst I was still trying to actually sing the song, she shouted, 'You got enough petrol to get home?'

The residents were all so sweet and each one was different in their own way. I had to end the show on time because they had to go to bed and their routine was very important to the staff; they had a set time for everything. They were due to take their medication and put their pyjamas on and they did this in the same room while we were packing the gear down. They all sat in a little line ready to take their tablets. The chubby Chinese man in the wheelchair then called me over and said in a quiet voice, 'When you get in your pyjamas, can you come upstairs so I can teach you some tae kwon do'. I explained that I had to go home and he said, 'OK. You can come back tomorrow then. Promise?'

On the way home in the car, Ma B and I talked about what a truly humbling experience that gig was. I will forget some of the big, fancy, faceless, corporate events, but I will never ever forget Tony, his friends and that little care home. They were truly inspirational people.

***

'Jo come here, you're gonna love this one!' Ma B bellowed from her kitchen.

'I'm doing a stock check. I've got to get to Boots. We're nearly out of St Tropez you know. What is it?'

I arrived in the kitchen swiftly as she sounded enthused. 'Have a read of that. It's a juicy one,' Ma B exclaimed excitedly.

It appeared that I had received a prestigious invitation via email to a big event. It was going to be a grand occasion, officially endorsed by and arranged on behalf of The Diamond Dame herself! The email explained that Dame Shirley Bassey's chosen charity, Barnados, was putting on a large charity event called 'Hey Big Spenders!' in order to raise money. This fabulous evening was to be held at the world famous Café de Paris in London's Piccadilly. Dame Shirley was auctioning off some of her garments and shoes to raise money for charity and I had been asked by the Barnados event organisers to attend and perform at the event. In addition to this, they asked if I would model one of the Dame's glitzy gowns whist performing *Big Spender*. I said I would be delighted to wear one of her dresses and accepted their invitation to perform straight away. As I made my living paying tribute to the Tigress from Tiger Bay, to be asked to sing at an event organised on behalf of Dame Shirley was indeed an honour.

The evening was hosted by Julian Bennett, a well-known face from the TV show *Queer Eye for the Straight Guy* and Dame Shirley's friend and TV personality Christopher Biggins had been secured to take on the role of auctioneer. There were also going to be performances from Four Poofs and a Piano, the house band on *Friday Night with Jonathan Ross,* and I was excited at the prospect of performing alongside them. The pianist David had been in touch with me and decided that it would be a nice touch if we collaborated and performed a song together. We had chosen *Kiss Me Honey Honey.* Matt sent off my sheet music to him and we were all set to rehearse it on the day. David was confident that it would be a breeze.

It was always interesting to work with celebrities and they sometimes surprised me. I remember performing for a client in London who was big friends with Craig Revel Horwood who was hosting the very intimate party for them. It was a small and awkward sort of a gig, in terms of space and organisation but he was delightful and quite charming. The floor of their small marquee was very uneven and my microphone stand took a tumble so Mr Horwood shimmied over and picked it up for me mid-set.

I thanked him afterwards and said, 'You are so different from your TV persona Mr Nasty on *Strictly*, as I'm sure you've been told a tedious number of times, and you look far less orange in person.'

He took it in good humour as I could tell he would. It can work the other way though. I once sang for an Italian fashion designer at a swanky apartment near Hyde Park and his friend, who happened to be an extremely well known UK chat show host, was at the gathering. After exchanging pleasantries with this household name very briefly, it became apparent to me that he took himself very seriously indeed and was not a very likeable little chappie. I was, however, looking forward to the fabulous Café de Paris.

We arrived in the City of London late afternoon on the day of the event. Like so many iconic places in London, the entrance to Café de Paris was nothing spectacular. Once inside, however, one was transported back to a time of glamour and elegance. Ornate chandeliers hung over plush red velvet seating and there were lots of romantic, seedily lit alcoves where one could easily imagine an illicit affair taking place whilst a sultry lady sang Billie Holiday numbers. People were rushing around excitedly putting Dame Shirley's coats and dresses onto rails and sound people were setting up on and around the stage area.

On the walls there were wonderful photographs of the famous artistes who had performed there over the years. Sinatra was in a classic pose wearing his rakishly angled trilby, cigarette in hand… there were simply too many wonderful stars to list. Café de Paris created a bygone era. The Four Poofs were a dream to work with, we ran through our song and it was perfect. They were funny guys and we had a ball before the event had even gotten under way. When the guests started arriving, Christopher Biggins, the Four Poofs and myself, were ushered backstage where Julian Bennett ran through the running order. Ma B got me into Dame Shirl's gold swirly frock and I was ready to perform my 20-minute set. It was a strange feeling wearing one of her dresses but I loved the fact that I would be modelling it for the auction too. My show was well received and one of the organisers told me afterwards that the actress Brenda Blethyn, who was in the audience, had tears in her eyes during my rendition of *This is My Life*. The auction was a huge success and lots of money had been raised.

'That was fantastic Joanne. I really enjoyed it. It was strange watching you because you have the facial expressions to a tee, especially the sideways mouth! It was a great job.'

I turned around quickly to see a pretty girl in her late twenties standing at the doorway of my dressing room.

'Sorry, I'll introduce myself. I'm Jenny Kern, Dame Shirley's PA.'

I was surprised and delighted that Dame Shirley's PA had made her way backstage and introduced herself to me.

'Oh thank you Jenny. I'm so pleased you popped in to say hello,' I replied, still a little stunned.

I was thrilled by her flattering feedback – coming from Bassey's management it was praise indeed. We chatted about Monte Carlo where the great Dame resided and I mentioned that I was performing there again the following month. We looked at the dates and the very same day that I was flying out to Monte Carlo, Dame Shirley was flying into the UK to record the *Dame Edna Everage Show*. Jenny said it was a shame as I could have perhaps met her.

'Honestly, I really wish Dame Shirley would keep me informed regarding her movements because we seem to be like ships in the night,' I said to Ma B, tongue in cheek as we prepared to leave.

I bid the Café de Paris bon voyage and Ma B started the car as we were once again homeward bound. Barnados forwarded me an email the very next week from Jenny Kern saying that Dame Shirley had called her the following morning to find out how the event had gone because she couldn't be there personally. Jenny stated that during the conversation, she told her about my show and Dame Shirley thought my stage name Surely Bassey was very funny and it made her laugh. I remember thinking, 'that's good then, whilst she's laughing, she's not taking us all to court!' I admit that the last thought I had before I went to sleep that night was, 'Dame Shirley Bassey is actually aware of my existence!' As I've said before, I may have been a Shirley Bassey tribute act but first and foremost, I was a huge fan.

A few weeks later, Matt, Ma B and I were en-route to Monte Carlo. We performed in The Monte Carlo Bay hotel, along with our regular Oddjob and a new Daniel Craig. We were quite literally performing next to where Dame Shirley lived. It was such a shame that she was in the UK because I rather liked to pretend to myself that I could have popped in for a cuppa. It was quite amusing when we were at the airport for the return leg of the journey home because Matt, Ma B and I were trying to race Daniel Craig and Oddjob through Arrivals. It was a who-could-beat-the-queues-and-leave-the-airport-first sort of a scenario. I seem to remember that Matt won. He was outside lighting up a Superking fag before we knew it. Bond was no match for Matt and his blue bag.

***

'That's a bit over the top isn't it? I understand it's a Bond do but having our paperwork checked at the gates by seven geezers dressed as gurkhas! The pretend security here is tighter than real security at our Military gigs.'

We were a little tired and irritable upon our arrival at a large, gated property that was situated in the middle of nowhere in the Hereford countryside. A lady called Veronica had privately booked us to perform at a lavish Bond party she was throwing for her husband's 50th birthday. Her husband's name was Will. She had told me at the time of the booking that he was aware he was having a party but didn't know what entertainment had been booked so that element of it was a surprise. I had been booked alongside a Will Smith impersonator who would be performing *Men in Black* following my show. I thought that made a nice change from working alongside the 007 lookalikes.

Anyway, once our registration had been logged and we had been 'validated' at the gates, we were allowed to drive into the grounds of the property. The marquee was on slightly uneven ground and the positioning of one of the speakers was proving a little tricky. Whilst I was deliberating where to put it, a blond-haired chap walked over and introduced himself as Will. He was quite striking to look at with bright blue eyes. I introduced myself simply as part of the entertainment and told him that I was pondering on the speaker situation. It quickly became apparent that Will was a no-nonsense sort of man and without any fuss or dialogue he positioned the speaker safely in the most sensible position available. He lifted it up and swiftly popped it on the pole.

'That should do the job,' he said cheerily before wandering off to greet some friends.

I had been given a sort of library area apart from the main house, in which to change. There was a man outside the library stood permanently by a fancy car that had blacked out windows, which I thought was a little odd. As I glanced around what was to be my changing room for the evening, I noticed that all of the books that were stacked neatly on the shelves seemed to be military related. Many of them were books about the SAS. My mind began to wander. I popped outside for a ciggie and asked the man by the car how he knew Will.

He smiled and said matter of factly. 'I'm his driver.'

'Oh what does he do for a living? Is he military?' I asked inquisitively.

'Put it this way, I'm ready to drive him wherever he needs to be at any time and his passport is always at the ready,' he replied.

He was telling me no more. I went back into the library and glanced at the books. Will was clearly SAS. I smiled to myself at the thought of Will Smith performing *Men in Black*, what a nice touch. Ma B came to the library to help me into my dress carrying an envelope.

'We've been paid. I think this Will bloke is SAS,' she said.

The envelope bore an emblem of an SAS beret and winged dagger badge on the seal. I now recalled that the same crest was fixed on the security gates. The security was not pretend and the gurkhas were the real deal. My performance took place relatively early during that event but Veronica had insisted we stay for a drink afterwards. Will looked very precise in his dinner suit and I found him slightly fascinating. The Will Smith impersonator did a great job of *Men in Black* and the party got in full swing. I was having another cheeky chardonnay with Will Smith at the bar when the music suddenly stopped and the sound of loud gunfire came from a huge projector screen. A voice loudly announced:

'It was May 1997 and Will Scully was an ex-SAS soldier working in Sierra Leone. The country was thrown into anarchy and chaos after a terrorist coup and foreign nationals were being evacuated. Scully found himself in an hotel called the Mammy Yoko, managed by an American. It was located in the capital, Freetown, where there were over 1,000 refugees sheltering from the violence raging in the streets outside. Then the hotel was targeted by the terrorists. With the lives of over 1,000 men, women and children at stake, Scully took control of security and with a general-purpose machine gun taken from a Nigerian soldier, he single handedly took on the terrorists. What transpired during Scully's heroic solo achievement was described later by the American Ambassador as 'the biggest emergency evacuation since Vietnam'.'

There was more, much more. We were listening to some sort of mini documentary about Will Scully and this bloke was clearly no joke. Veronica got up to address the room. 'Your royal highness, ladies and gentlemen...' I was obviously in the presence of royalty. She went on to give a brief and humorous account of what it was like to be Mrs Scully and said that during their 15 years of marriage, she had probably seen her husband for around five of those years. It was an interesting evening and when I got home I simply had to Google Will Scully. He had written a book entitled *Once a Pilgrim*. His actions in Sierra Leone and his bravery were incomprehensible and in April 1998, William James Scully was awarded the Queen's Gallantry Medal. It seemed that on that evening, I had actually performed for a real life James Bond.

***

It wasn't always glamorous, though. Whilst doing this job I was sometimes, quite literally, launched from the sublime to the ridiculous. I was cruelly catapulted from working for the elite such as the SAS, performing amongst the sheer sophistication and class of Monte Carlo's finest folk and in venues like The Café de Paris, to the dark, oily, contrasting world of stag and hen parties. I am talking about one of Birmingham's finest night spots Tricky Dickies. This place was always heaving with oiled-up strippers, drag queens, shaving foam, odd lubricants and far too much exposed flesh. It was unbelievable. Tricky Dickies was a 400 capacity nightclub situated above Legs 11 (a well-known lap dancing joint) in the heart of Birmingham's China Town. At that time it catered for all genders and preferred sexual orientation but it did host mostly hen parties.

Unfortunately for me, it also hosted tribute shows amongst the rest of the 'entertainment'. The changing rooms at Tricky's were insanely busy. They were full, and I mean full, of male strippers changing into various costumes. There were the usual firemen, naval officers, policemen, US jail inmates, sailors, military soldiers and, of course, the Village People. The changing cubicles were covered in fake tan and squirty foam. They reeked of coconut oil and sweat. The noise of the over-excitable hens, constantly screaming for their next fix of flesh to paw and prod, was deafening. Poor Ma B would often be trying to do my sequinned frock up at the back whilst trying to avoid tripping over Stallion's mask and black leather codpiece and we literally couldn't hear ourselves think.

If there was a brief second of noise reduction, as one track faded into another, we could sometimes overhear conversations between strippers in the adjoining cubicle. 'Are you doing the sailor tonight?' One flustered, slippery stripper asked the other on a particularly lively Saturday night.

'No you do the sailor. I'll do the fireman.'

The resident compère was a transvestite called Miss Penny Tration who would randomly stalk the stage in stilettos and a black and white sequined dress.

'We all like a bit of Penny Tration now and then, don't we?' She would ask the crowd of drunken ladettes enthusiastically.

'Are we here to see cock? Are you ready for some more cock?' She would shout over the microphone before the next gyrating act was introduced and the hens would scream even louder. The first time I heard her say that, I was shocked. I just stood there with my mouth wide open.

'I'd shut that if I were you,' Ma B had said wisely.

They were being whipped into a frenzy and egged on by Penny's resident assistant drag queens Emma Roid and Anna Conda. A very greasy-looking Hot Chocolate or Cherry Popper might make a quick appearance in the changing area saying something to me along the lines of, 'Sorry love can you just pass me my truncheon? It's behind your foot. Thanks darlin.' Then everybody would be treated to a sterling performance from The Backstreet Buttfucks. As far as my show went, it seemed to go by in a blur for me. The Village People finished off the proceedings then Ma B and I would drive home totally deaf with *YMCA* ringing in our damaged ears. If we performed at Tricky Dickies on a Saturday night, our hearing would go back to normal around the following Tuesday.

Dame Shirley's 'gold swirl' gown, auctioned at Café De Paris, Piccadilly, London

Wearing Dame Shirley's 'gold swirl' gown

Wearing Dame Shirley's 'gold swirl' gown for the auction, with Christopher Biggins

Ma B taking in the views at a James Bond corporate event in Monte Carlo

Matt with cuppa in hand, standing proudly next to his green maestro, outside Highclere Castle

Matt dressed in his finery on piano at a 007 corporate event in Monte Carlo

Robbo happily sitting in a Spanish bar, in the days before drink became his arch enemy

Performing Kiss Me Honey Honey, Kiss Me *with the Four Poofs and a Piano, at Café De Paris, Piccadilly, London*

Performing Kiss Me Honey Honey, Kiss Me *with the Four Poofs and a Piano, at Café De Paris, Piccadilly, London*

In the backstage boudoir with Julian Bennet and the four delightful poofs! Café De Paris, London. Plenty of honey kissing going on...

In the backstage boudoir with Julian Bennet and the four delightful poofs! Café De Paris, London

CHAPTER TEN

THE PORT OF ABUSE

A t this point, I apologise that I have to break off but I must pen a note to Mr Cowell immediately. Yes I have to write a strong-worded, no-nonsense letter to the high-waisted, furry-chested, pop mogul that is Simon Cowell. In fact Ma B and I are considering taking out some sort of restraining order. I shall begin.

Dear Mr Cowell,

I am sorry to have to write this letter but you leave me no choice. You are becoming a nuisance. I have just put the phone down to another member of your Britain's Got Talent *team after 30 agonising minutes. Jez, Jaz, or whatever he called himself, was doing his best to convince me to come to Wales and do some filming performing as Shirley Bassey, which he insisted will be shown to millions on the opening credits of Britain's Got Talent Cardiff auditions show. He told me how career enhancing this would be. He seemed quite shocked when I told him that he was to save his breath and trot on as you have 'had me' on this scam before. This will be the fourth time that you have tried to stitch me up.*

I explained to him, as I did to the woman who called last year, that they need to find another unsuspecting Bassey as I have been there and done that. The first time your lot called I was already booked on the date in question, somewhere miles away and simply could not do it. The second time they called, the following year, they got me. I was told that I should come to Cardiff where I would perform as Bassey and be filmed in the scenic location that was Cardiff Castle.

They told me that they had secured a Tom Jones tribute act to do the same. I was promised that the footage would be delightful, well edited and shown at the start of the show to be watched by a huge Saturday night TV audience. I knew the

Tom Jones act so I called him and he told me that he'd agreed to do it. We had a brief chat about it and I then agreed. I will never do it again. Now let me tell you why.

The reality of the filming in Cardiff was this. It rained (that element was not your fault. You may control the world of light entertainment but even you cannot control our weather). Your film crew changed their mind about filming at Cardiff castle and decided that I should, in my sequinned dress and white fur cloak, be filmed singing a segment of I Am What I Am *whilst loading a washing machine in a busy Cardiff high street laundrette. As if this was not bad enough, your crew had not asked Mr Papadopolus, or whatever the owner's name may have been, to close the laundrette. Cardiff's 'great unwashed' kept coming through the door with bags of dirty skants, which I was then told to load, whilst taking* I Am What I Am *from the top again.*

This grisly episode in my career eventually came to end when your crew told me that they had everything they needed and it was all fabulous. They took their furry mics away and let me go home. I had a very emotional conversation with Tom Jones later that evening. He had been subjected to a ghastly afternoon of filming at a bus stop. He had to appear to be waiting for a bus on the high street, whilst belting out It's Not Unusual *(my mum thinks it was actually* The Green Green Grass of Home *but we're getting caught up in the details) in the pissing rain. He said he kept getting drenched by every passing vehicle, including the buses and people were looking at him as if he was on day release. We were both traumatised.*

So here you are calling me again. Your team are yet again trying to trick me into doing something hideous. Well not this time you don't! I do not wish to hear from you again Simon Cowell. If you want to come and hear me sing, get a ticket like everybody else. You're letting yourself down. Now hoist up your high-waisters, go away, think about what you have done and let that be it. If you continue to harass me, my people (Ma B) will be speaking to your people. Capiche?

Regards,

Joanne (Aka Surely Bassey)

As UK gigs went, I have to admit that I'd never quite gelled with Wales. I'd had plenty of bookings in Wales as this was where the Diamond Dame came from but there was something about the place. I sensed some sort of hostility. It was not Bassey related obviously but perhaps it was slightly, dare I say it, English related? I am aware that Scotland, and indeed Ireland, have had issues with good old Blighty since time began but the hostility is almost palpable in Wales. I have had some delightful gigs in Scotland and performing at St Andrews was a highlight. The people are passionate and the scenery is stunning (there is also some divine scenery in Wales).

Shows in Ireland were always a joy too. I performed in Belfast many times and I always found the Irish to be fun, cheeky and so poetic.

When I once asked a hotel manager in Belfast if I was allowed to help myself to a few nuts that had been placed in a bowl on a table, he replied, 'My dear, it is far better to beg for forgiveness than to ask for permission.'

Anyway, for whatever reason, I never really 'felt the love' in Wales. Celtic Manor was a nice venue but that aside, nothing stands out in my memory. That's actually a lie. Matt and I had been booked to perform for a restaurant in Cardiff Bay once (formerly Tiger Bay) and following our sound check, we wandered down to the reformed area of the docks, which by this time was looking rather swanky, with Ma B for a latte. Upon our return, we looked in horror and saw that the back window of our people carrier had been smashed and somebody had nicked our sat nav. It was a right royal mess, there was a mangled square where the window had been and glass everywhere. We just had time to sweep some of the glass up before getting on stage. Poor Matt had to spend the entire journey home covered in a blanket, listening to Bon Jovi with some polythene taping up the very noisy, draughty, window. Ma B said it could have happened anywhere in any city. It didn't, it happened in Cardiff. I know Shirley Bassey adores Wales, that's why she lives in Monte Carlo…

***

As the year was drawing to a close we were all gigged out so Ma B and I decided we needed a break. My back was not good and I felt like it needed some serious heat along with a few lengths in a pool in order to show any signs of improvement. I think the constant humping around of PA equipment over the years had finally strained it. We wanted a little sun and some well-deserved chill out time. We had earned well so we felt justified in treating ourselves and after sifting through a few holiday brochures, we made a booking to Marbella. Bazza had a little apartment there and he knew the place well. I didn't know it at the time but that was to be the first of many visits to Puerto Banús for me.

The easyJet queue to board the plane at Luton airport was a complete bore. What was it with this 'speedy boarding' rubbish? People apparently paid an extra tenner to become a speedy boarder. It appeared that these folk had kids and lots of baggage so they wanted to board the plane first before the rest of the passengers. The thing was, the whole queue of normal passengers, boarding group A, B and C had to wait around for the speedy boarders to arrive, even though the plane was ready for boarding. So there we all were, waiting for a bunch of late speedy boarders – what was so speedy about that?

Following a very cramped, turbulent, easyJet flight, during which passengers were subjected to a sudden overpowering stench of fuel (which panicked the life out me) we landed at Malaga airport.

There was no explanation given for the sudden fuel stench during the flight but easyJet are a budget airline so even if the cabin crew stank of piss and the pilot was late taking off because he was rolling a fat one, they would say that's why their fares were low and you get what you pay for. I decided there was no point kicking off about the fact that the entire plane smelled like the nozzle of a petrol pump at the Texaco garage.

The hotel was delightful and the weather was pleasant so it looked to be just what we needed. The first few days we just relaxed by the pool during the day and then had a few drinks in and around the hotel at night. We then felt like venturing out a little and made our way to Puerto Banús for a night out. The port is a lively strip on the front line where the rich folk moor their very expensive yachts. Bazza said that there was a piano bar where he had sang before. He couldn't remember the name of the place but he explained roughly where it was and told me that it was run by a guy called Paul, who was a great piano player/singer.

The port was a complete contradiction to me because it was expensive yet seedy. It was brimming with wealthy people who were obviously very fond of cosmetic surgery, fancy sports cars, designer shops, sleazy bars and Brazilian prostitutes. A Lamborghini or a Porsche passed by every three seconds, a hooker passed by every two. The place was alive with money, drugs, sex and entertainers, but dull it was not. To be honest, even on that first night I found the place quite intoxicating in a 'I better not stay here for more than a week or I'll be dead by the end of the month' sort of a way.

After walking up and down the front line for a while, Ma B and I asked a woman who looked like Ivana Trump, with lips the size of Gibraltar, where the piano bar was because we hadn't come across it yet. She directed us somewhat vaguely. Had I asked her where I could get a quick tit job, I'm sure her directions would have been spot on. We wandered into the bar that she pointed to called Old Joe's. Inside was a long haired bloke playing the piano and singing. His voice was amazing and he could certainly play. We stayed for a few drinks and soon realised that the guy was bit of a daft character. He was a mad jock, completely demented, and in true jock style drank like a fish. He knocked back large gin and tonics intermittently mixed with Sambuca shots. His name was Anthony Andrews and he had lived in Banús for 24 years. He was a talent but a proper party animal. He drank that amount every single night and had done for years. He put Keith Richards to shame. I fully realised this was the case after partying with him hard for the whole of the following week. He had a routine; he would finish his first set, order a round of drinks which were to arrive when we returned to do his second set then he would shout, 'Come on wee hen, put your drink in the safe. To Shenanigans!'

I had to put my drink next to his, which was hidden within a little fireplace in a corner of the bar, then hot foot it down the strip to another bar called Shenanigan's. We'd have a swift one in that bar and then shoot back to Old Joe's where Anthony began his second set. Most of the singers in the port hopped from bar to bar between sets and sometimes there was a group of us, depending on who was singing where and at what time. He got in some serious states due to the Sambuca shots but Anthony was fun to be around. Contrary to what he told people, there was never any funny business, we were just friends. If you were a close female friend of Anthony's you were actually quite lucky in a way because due to the amount of alcohol he consumed on a daily basis, he was always physically incapable of trying anything on. He would buy the drinks all night and then just collapse.

Anthony was very popular in the port and every night was party night. During the first trip, Ma B would go home around 1am and I would stay out with Anthony and a few other singers that we had met up with and we would party. The following day I would sleep by the pool and all was well. My back was improving too and I'd put it down to swimming in the pool but it could have been due to the copious amounts of alcohol that I was consuming as I was constantly anesthetised. I expected that just when my back was on the mend, my liver would pack up. Ma B was quite happy relaxing whilst reading by the pool during the day then having a few drinkies with me in the evening. She happily retired at night, leaving me to party with my newfound friends until the wee hours.

One of my new chums called Jane wanted to introduce me to Motown singer called Dan. She said he had a great voice so one evening I agreed to go and check him out. When Dan had finished his spot on stage he came straight over.

'Hey guys, you alright?' he asked, whilst putting a friendly hand on Jane's shoulder but making direct eye contact with me. We did the introductions and I immediately noticed the American accent and asked him where he was from. 'Philadelphia baby,' he replied in a cool fashion. I told him he had a great voice and I had enjoyed the set. We said our goodbyes and Dan asked if I was coming back the following night.

'Yep we'll be back tomorrow around 10pm,' I chirped.

I didn't have any intention of going back but I said it anyway. I even gave a rough time just for decoration. I was on my way out of the door when Dan shouted, 'See you tomorrow night then!'

I smiled and said, 'Yeah you will.'

'And your sweet ass,' I heard him say, although at a reduced volume.

I glanced back and he was smiling at me as we left. At the time I didn't know if he was one of those annoying, cocky, black Americans or just a bit of a cheeky one. Either way, I had rather liked his cheekiness. I smiled at him again and left. I also remember thinking that he was quite attractive.

Once home, gigging resumed as usual. The weather back in Blighty was its usual unpredictable self but I didn't care. We'd had a good break but my liver was glad to be home and it needed a good break from Smirnoff vodka. Drugs I didn't mess with but I had given the vodka and tonics a huge hammering over that past three weeks. I'd said I would stay in touch with Jane and a girl called Rhiannon who was probably the most genuine out of all of the portside entertainment crew. She was a lot quieter than the rest of them, and with that came far less bullshit. I had promised to send Rhiannon one of my demo CDs and when I posted it I popped an extra one in the envelope along with a note and asked her to pass it on to Dan. I was merely networking, you understand. I wrote down my website address so he knew that I was a professional singer and that my 'sweet ass' did not belong to some silly groupie who followed male singers around in holiday resort bars. One had to watch that the male singers did not start thinking that they were 'all that'.

By now 2008 was underway and really frantic in terms of performances. Rhiannon had asked me to join her back in Puerto Banús for another little jolly and, busy as we were, I said I was sure I could squeeze a cheeky visit in. I booked my flight alongside the 'lazy boarders' and was once more en-route to the port whilst Ma B held the fort at home. I only booked a one-week stay and although Rhiannon was lovely, I insisted on staying in a hotel. I had done the staying at people's houses bit and it really wasn't for me. At best it made me feel slightly uncomfortable.

Once back in the port I partied hard and abused my liver once again. We had spent quite a bit of time with Dan and on my last night we ended up drinking way too much. As a result, Rhiannon and I went back to his place for a bit of a party. He was well mannered and actually cooked for us. I soon started to think that he was kind of cool in a bad boy sort of a way. He was great at singing the Motown numbers and to be honest, after 20 vodka and tonics followed by his sterling version of *Nightshift*, I was anybody's. I had been single for nearly 18 months and I was simply having a good time. It made a change from listening to Robbo belt out Barry Manilow's *Mandy* after 12 pints of Carling, as amusing as that always was (although he was consuming far more potent stuff than lager at that time).

So another visit was over. I said my goodbyes to Rhiannon and my new singing friend from the USA and returned home. Ma B and I still had plenty of 007 events lined up and I needed to be match fit so I vowed to leave the port alone until the summer of that year.

It didn't happen. Dan and I spoke over the phone three or four times a week and emailed regularly. We were singers so that was a big thing to have in common and looking back I suppose a little relationship of sorts was blossoming. This progressed quite quickly and I visited what was commonly known as 'The Port Of Abuse' a few more times over that period, although I had agreed to stay at his apartment on those occasions. During those visits, I got to know him far more. I liked him and he interested me. He was quite charming at times but I was under no illusion that he was in any way without a chequered past. I knew he had a history with the law because he told me and it seemed the typical scenario. He was young, living in a rough, under-privileged area near Philadelphia and had got in with a bad crowd. He was doing what everybody his age around him was doing, which was basically hustling. He got involved with drug dealing, messed with guns and, by his own admission, generally began to fuck everything up along with the rest of them.

Time passed and the things he got involved in got a bit more serious. As he explained to me, there was nothing big or glamorous about leading that sort of a life. By the age of 20 he had taken a bullet in the leg, got a long razor wound across his back and he had been involved in gun crime. The inevitable happened and he was sentenced to a lengthy spell in Pittsburgh penitentiary. Dan did his time quietly and after serving a third of his sentence, he was given parole with a further probationary period. He was ordered to check in with his probation officer weekly to keep out of any trouble no matter how trivial it seemed and basically pray that trouble kept away from him. If they got a sniff of any wrong doing on his part they would simply lock him back up.

He said he couldn't handle the thought of that. He didn't think he could come out of prison, live in the same area and be subjected to the same influences without getting in trouble. He had seen it happen time and time again to other offenders. They would do their time, return to the streets where there would be a former gang member waiting, bearing a grudge, or an ex-girlfriend eager to report them for some form of violence that never occurred. Before they knew it they would get thrown straight back in jail.

It was at that time, during his late twenties, that Dan made the decision to skip probation and leg it to England. His father lived in London and was seriously ill. Dan had family in London and an aunt that worked in a US passport office so he, in his own words, 'got the hell out of the US'. I also knew he had been married and had an elder daughter. I suppose he told me as much about himself as he felt comfortable with at that time. Women didn't seem to be his thing and apart from a few casual encounters, he had been single and lived alone for quite a few years (I'd verified this was true with various people of course).

He just appeared to be a bit of a drifter to me. Hearing all of that whilst in my then 'fuck it, live for the moment' mindset, I still knew he was suspect. He said he wanted to change his life and he was in his early 40s so I think he saw our relationship as a bit of a 'last chance saloon' sort of a situation. Even though it had the ring of truth about it and I believed what he was telling me, I just had an overall wary feeling. There was a definite vibe that he was always ready to uproot and 'do one' at the drop of a hat. There were no roots there and no real feeling that his apartment was anything more than somewhere he stayed at that time. Yes there were pictures of his family and a few ornaments knocking around but nothing that couldn't be shoved into a case at the last minute. It wasn't a home and he came across as the type that was always in transit. Even I knew that usually meant trouble was eventually going to catch up.

To be honest, most of the entertainers in the port were on the run from something or somebody. They had something to hide and many of them were not merely part of the 'fun in the sun' brigade. They had pasts that they needed to get away from and whilst they were on stage singing, off their faces on drugs or drunk and generally partying in la la land, they could do it. With alarm bells ringing due to all of the aforementioned warning signs, did I hesitate to continue with the relationship? Nope.

Whilst I was on one of my little visits, Dan said he wanted to come back to the UK with me. He said he'd had a belly full of Spain and wanted a change. *Que sorpresa*! He said he wanted to see me properly, not just during my flying visits. I was sceptical about the whole idea but Dan explained to me that he wanted this to be his last move. He stressed that he was no longer interested in partying, drugs or any type of hedonistic lifestyle. I assured him that Hinckley was a very small, sobering little town and he could kiss goodbye to any excitement there.

He seemed to relish the prospect of a quieter life with no more country hopping. Dan saw the move like 'have voice, will travel' as I'm sure he'd done many times before. I believed his intentions were genuine but I was unsure that he would be able to just change his lifestyle. I'm unsure if I was on the rebound as such but I would like to think so as that would maybe have accounted for my impetuous behaviour. Although if I'm honest, I was probably just behaving the way I always had and there was no real excuse.

I agreed to Dan's suggestion and we made plans for the return to the UK together. The thing was, our plan wasn't actually a plan per se.

The idea was, as I was staying at Ma B's, I would simply move out and we would rent a place in Hinckley. Dan could earn money singing anywhere as could I. His show was not a 'tribute show' as such so he would earn less per engagement but his material was suited to pretty much any venue and was not as expensive or niche as mine so he would get more gigs. The idea was that it would all average out. We decided that Dan would get a ticket on the same flight as I had pre-booked for my return to the UK. I mentioned this plan briefly to Ma B over the phone before we left Spain but I was slightly hazy and didn't go into too much detail. Ma B took it that Dan was coming to the UK for a visit and I didn't put her straight. Subconsciously, I think I knew that she would have screeched something along the lines of, 'What the fuck are you on about you reckless fool? I don't even know the bloke! Have you been smoking crack? No you're bloody well not doing any of it.' She would have then possibly changed the locks before I landed. I selfishly and cowardly thought it was best that she be updated upon our joint return.

The end of that particular week had arrived and we needed to book the plane ticket. Dan had started to pack when he suddenly announced, 'I can't find my passport!' Alarm bells rang in my head once more.

'Ah that's a bit of a problem Dan. When did you last have it?' I asked dubiously.

'Around 12 months ago.' His reply was casual and quite ridiculous.

I told him he would have to apply for another one and come out to the UK at a later date. He said it was a UK passport not US so we could go to the town hall in Marbella and he would have to report it lost. From there he thought they might issue him a temporary one to get back to the UK. He said it was worth a try. We went to Marbella Town Hall that very day and, after waiting for around three hours, that's exactly what they did. They took a statement from him to say his UK passport had been lost and issued him with a temporary 24-hour passport. Scarily, it was as easy as that. Once back in the UK, he could then simply apply for a new one. We returned to Dan's apartment and he packed. When I say 'packed' I mean he threw his stuff in a couple of large suitcases and some big 'holdall' bags, all unsurprisingly very 'last minute'. In March 2008 Dan and I boarded a plane back to the UK. Ma B collected us from the airport, glanced in the direction of Dan's cases and said, 'Ooh that's a lot of baggage'.

Once we were back at Ma B's, I think she quickly processed the situation. After around two weeks, and once she realised I had actually lost my mind, she went ballistic. She boxed up my things, officially resigned from her post as Ma B, threw all of my singing files, along with her orderly account files, into boxes/bags and piled everything in either the garage or near the front door. She made it very clear that it was nothing personal as far as Dan was concerned (although she always found Americans to be a little noisy and over familiar) it was me. She called me a selfish, inconsiderate, crazy bitch and made it clear that I should 'do one' pronto. I thought her reaction was a tad over the top at the time but of course it wasn't.

Before Mum killed me stone dead I thought it best that we found somewhere to rent sooner rather than later. I feared that if we didn't vacate as soon as humanly possible, she really would resign her post – long-term. We had already looked at properties available to rent locally. There were a few possibilities but nothing great, and then we saw The Apartment (also the title of a great Shirley Bassey track by the way). It was delicious and in no way was it a flat. It was a modern, vastly spacious, open-plan, three-bedroom apartment and it was perfect. It was part of a brand new development right near the town centre and as soon as we saw it, we fell in love. We signed up and moved in immediately.

After a week or two, Ma B was beginning to thaw slightly and things began to settle. I admitted that I had behaved like a crazy arsehole and that helped. She agreed that the apartment was dreamy and actually started to warm to Dan. There were never any race issues as far as Ma B was concerned but it was a culture shock for her when he arrived. He was black, American and when he initially arrived he was very lively.

Ma B casually said to me one evening, 'Once he realises that this is Hinckley, it's cold and there is no party anywhere, he will have to get his slippers out, switch *Emmerdale* on and quieten the fuck down.'

He did just that and the sunshine and gaiety of Puerto Banús quickly became a distant memory for Dan. If he was not out on a gig, either with me or independently, he soon became like the rest of us; slightly depressed, waiting for a summer that never came.

We quickly settled into life in our apartment and work re-commenced. Ma B had resumed her post almost straight away and the Bassey machine was back up and running. I was due to perform in Italy within a week or so of being back in the UK so Dan came on that gig with me. He actually accompanied me on various Bassey gigs initially and got to witness my working life as a tribute act. Dan built up gigs of his own fairly quickly and although the money was less, there were lots of them.

There was a small issue with transport. As predictable as it seemed, Dan had lost his driving licence around five years prior to us meeting, due to being over the legal limit whilst driving après gig in Wales (yes he'd also resided briefly in Wales at some point). He hadn't needed a car in Puerto Banús as everything was either walking or taxi distance but this caused us a big problem in the UK. He applied for a new licence but because his old one had been revoked due to drink driving, the DVLA specified he would need to get a doctors certificate proving his GAMMA GT levels were low enough. Our GP told him to avoid spirits, cut back on alcohol in general and book the appointment three months later. As we were both singers, we were always out at the same time but in different places – mostly being Friday and Saturday evenings so during the three-month waiting period we needed some sort of chauffeur. Dan's past antics really did prove troublesome.

The weeks quickly became months and before we knew it we had been living in our apartment for nearly a year. During that time we had gotten to know our neighbours very well and it was quite a close-knit little community. Our apartment complex was filled with a cute and interesting mix of nationalities. It was quite cosmopolitan for Hinckley and Ma B used to say it was like the United Nations. Dan was Guyanese but as far as our apartment complex was concerned, he also obviously represented the USA.

There was Alex who lived in the two-bedroom apartment above. He was a 50-year-old black guy with a very gentle way about him. His roots were Jamaican and Ma B said he reminded her of Philip from Rising Damp. He was an intelligent, educated and sophisticated man and his accent was very upper class. It was almost a 'plumb in the mouth' job and some thought he was putting it on for effect. He lived alone but his 10-year-old daughter often came to stay with him. He was quite corporate in his ways and worked for BT. He was very generous and let us tap into his BT WiFi on a permanent basis. Alex seemed to love the fact that there were a couple of professional singers in the apartment below and he came with us on a few of our shows. He liked the whole music scene.

Vicky and Isaac lived in the tiny one-bedroom attic apartment just above Alex. It was the roof apartment and miniature. The ceilings sloped and everybody constantly banged their heads upon entrance. They were a young couple in their early twenties. Vicky was a pretty white girl with blonde curly hair. She carried a lot of weight but she had a lovely face. She was a teacher at an infant school in Leicester. She was a nice girl but a little naive. I always thought she had low self-esteem due to her size. Isaac was from Uganda. He was very small but had no problem with his size. He hadn't got a job as such, although he was trying to get into football coaching and vowed to get something permanent once his visa had been approved. His visa seemed to prove a problem. Vicky never really knew what Isaac was up to. He was a likeable little chap, although somewhat roguish and unreliable. He was so small that he was actually easy to misplace, which was just how he liked it.

Isaac often had some of his Ugandan friends/relatives come to stay with them at weekends. They would spend hours lying around on blow-up mattresses, mixing music and browsing Facebook to within an inch of their lives. Alex was also kind enough to let them tap into his WiFi. Vicky would complain about the Ugandan crew crammed into an already small space and the rest of our apartment residents would complain about the noise they made when they returned late at night from clubbing. At one point it seemed as if poor Vicky was funding a small part of Uganda all by herself. There was a lady called Bethany who lived in a two-bed apartment below us. She was a little eccentric and had short purple hair. She was probably in her mid-sixties and lived alone. She said that's exactly how she liked it. Bethany said she was determined to spend all of her money and intended to leave nothing to her kids. She had a very hectic social life and she was rarely in. She was very English and often said she despaired about the 'Ugandan situation' up above.

On the ground floor lived two Jehovah's witnesses. They were an English couple in their mid-40s with two kids around eight and 10 years old. The bloke seemed pleasant and looked fairly normal but the woman, although nice enough, looked completely raving mad. Her appearance was quite striking. She had dyed red curly hair and her makeup was clown-like. She always had bright red rouge cheeks, rather like the character Aunt Sally, along with red lipstick. She wore huge flower arrangements in hair and sported bizarre, outrageously colourful outfits. She was a case of 'once seen never forgotten'. She was a little feisty and unleashed a verbal attack on the Ugandans for being loud and intoxicated more than once. I was not sure what Jehovah made of her overall conduct but I suspected she required sectioning. Dan said she was 'crazier than a motherfucker' although she seemed to amuse him.

Our Estonian friends lived the other side of the underground car park. They were a young couple in their early 20s called Anna and Arvi. She was a trainee doctor and he worked for Triumph Motors. They had left Estonia a few years earlier and resided in a two-bedroom apartment. Anna and Arvi were probably our closest chums and we called them 'The Euros'. There were a few Polish couples on that side of the complex but we had little to do with them socially. All in all, everybody got along swimmingly (noisy weekend visits from outer Ugandans aside). We took it in turns to host dinner parties in our apartments and all called on each other for drinks. It was a very cosy and sociable environment to live in.

Isaac was probably the best cook and he knocked up some cheeky numbers. He explained that the Ugandan method was very much 'one pot cooking' but he was simply being modest. His dishes were spicy and delicious. Due to the size of their attic apartment, if everybody was due to attend, dinner parties at Chez Issac and Vicky were a little tricky in terms of space but Isaac prepared such delicious food, he was required to bring his 'one pot wonders' to whoever was hosting the evening. Our apartment was very popular when it came to hosting the United Nation soirées due to it being so large and such an open layout. Our hallway was a huge square area where people naturally congregated with drinks and the kitchen was also very spacious. Alex didn't cook so when he attended the soirées he would bring lovely red wine along with fine quality cakes and desserts. If Bethany's diary allowed it she always attended, bringing her vibrant hair and sharp wit.

The Euro's hosted a few social gatherings in their apartment and alcohol was plentiful but I always found the food to be a little odd. I recall one occasion there was no formal dinner date as such but the Euro's had been cooking so they wanted us to sample a traditional Estonian meal. They said they would bring their meal over to us. We got the beer and wine at the ready and awaited their arrival. What they brought to the table was rather strange. It was an array of cold cabbage, sausages, strange bread and rock hard potatoes. We said the right things, made all of the right noises, drank lots of alcohol and picked at what we could but it was hard work. Arvi and Anna said we should keep the left over food as they had plenty.

Once the Euro's had left Dan said, 'What the fuck was with that food? I ain't never seen no shit like that before. Cold cabbage and shit. Man!'

I said I agreed and we would not be 'hoovering up' the leftovers the following day. The very next morning our toilet blocked up. Now one may think that this was the result of a fully digested Estonian meal passing through the system and arriving at its final destination but it wasn't. Dan admitted that he had tipped the remaining Estonian spuds down the toilet the night before, flushed, then sauntered off to bed. He had a tendency to flush food down the toilet and I thought it had something to do with his life in Spain. I believed it was linked to not wanting to fill bins with unwanted food in the Spanish heat and the fact that people lived in upper level apartments, where bins started to smell. Regardless of the reason for his weird activity I had told him not to do it. It was a completely alien concept to me and I told him, in words that I thought he would understand, that, 'It was not how I rolled!'

Our toilet was completely blocked up and I pointed out that it was not merely a coincidence that he had lobbed a dish full of Estonian potatoes that were as hard as bullets down the trap the night before.

Dan said, 'Honey, it won't be the potatoes causing that shit. Food wouldn't block it up. That's a four-inch waste pipe there.'

'Yeah with a five-inch spud stuck in it!'

I reminded him that he was a singer not a plumber and said we needed to get some serious toilet unblocking agent down there quick because I did not want to have to use somebody else's loo every time I wanted a wee. It was at that moment that Arvi knocked the door. He had simply called to say hello. Dan told him about the blocked up toilet and Arvi swiftly said he had some powerful unblocking agent and a good plunger that he would bring over straight away.

'Bloody hell Dan, we don't want him freeing up his own potatoes. What if he wants to do it and he sucks up his own spuds? He may recognise them!' I hissed.

Dan assured me that he would persuade Arvi to leave the toilet unblocking gear with him and he would return it later that day. Luckily Arvi seemed happy with that and after a few unsuccessful attempts later that afternoon, the Estonian spuds finally shifted. It certainly was powerful stuff. The fumes were strong enough to break down a corpse, never mind stubborn potatoes.

We had asked the Euro's, along with Vicky and Isaac, to drive Dan to and from his shows that year while he was waiting for his driving licence to be granted. They had agreed a fee and as long as Dan booked them in advance they would share the work between them. The Euro's tended to be the more regular chauffeurs with Vicky and Isaac as back up. Ma B and I carried on gigging together and we seemed to always be at opposite ends of the country to Dan. The year was quickly drawing to a close and we had been busy with shows. Before we knew it, we were in the process of organising a big Christmas soirée with the rest of the United Nations and we were the hosts. Dan told Arvi not to worry about bringing any food. Nobody actually invited the painted lady from the ground floor to our gathering. It was nothing to do with religion. It was simply because she appeared unhinged.

CHAPTER ELEVEN

NEW YORK, NEW YORK

'Yo honey check this out, what's the name of that song that the Welsh band did?' Dan was on the phone to an agent.

'Which Welsh band?' I called back from the bedroom.

I had no clue which band he was talking about. He quickly appeared at the bedroom door holding his mobile phone in one hand and a roll-up in the other.

'Was it The Manic Depressives?' He asked with a slightly confused expression on his face.

Classic Dan. He genuinely got things slightly wrong. He meant The Manic Street Preachers and I laughed. I personally found The Manic Street Preachers very depressing so I thought The Manic Depressives was a far better name for that band. He often got things wrong in a funny way, like the time we were on a gig in Stratford-upon-Avon and, being an American, Dan wanted to, 'Swing by Shakespeare's crib,' as he put it. We took a few snaps of him outside 'the crib' and I suddenly couldn't remember the surname of Shakespeare's wife. Dan said surely it was Shakespeare. I explained to Dan that her surname was not Shakespeare.

Dan then asked enquiringly, 'Is it Ann Summers? I know that name from somewhere to do with y'all...'

I suddenly had visions of the world's greatest playwright sitting down to put the finishing touches to *Macbeth* when his missus Ann Summers enters the room and asks, 'Will dear, how's that play thing coming along?'

'Not bad love, how's work been for you today?'

'Steady. I've just had to personally test the prototype for the new Deluxe Rampant Rabbit, it's a bugger of a job. Once I get this last shipment of

Raspberry Dick Lick on the road I can relax. It's ever so popular you know. The Pussy Rub sold like hotcakes last year too.'

Will would then take a break from *Macbeth* to help Ann do a quick stocktake of her tubes of Slide and Ride lubricant before resuming work on his draft. I was enjoying my Summers/Shakespeare scenario when the name suddenly came to me. It was Anne Hathaway.

That particular morning Dan and I had been discussing holidays. A holiday was what we needed, a nice break. We deliberated and pondered for a week or so about which destination would suit us best. My aunt had a big villa in Corfu so we thought that sounded just the job. It was February 2009 and after some investigation via the internet we found that flights to Corfu only ran from May to October so we looked into taking a boat from Venice but it just seemed a bit of a hassle. We decided to go for a much more expensive alternative and at that point we didn't know just how expensive that alternative would turn out to be.

We decided Corfu could wait so we did a complete u-turn and decided on a trip to The Big Apple. I had never been to New York and although Dan had done New York before, he agreed that it would be nice to do the touristy thing for a week, just the two of us. We also decided that it would be a good opportunity for Dan to perhaps see some of his family as some lived in New York. Internal flights were no problem either if we decided to hook up with his brother Ivan and his mum who both lived in North Carolina.

Dan kept in touch with his brother via Skype and his mum via phone every few weeks from the UK and although I had spoken to them regularly on the phone, Dan really wanted me to meet them in person. The only member of Dan's family who had visited us at our apartment on a few occasions was his mother's sister, Aunty Marlia. She was a short, fat, old black woman with a heavy Guyanese accent that was so strong I struggled to understand a word she said. She lived in Walthamstow and would take a train from London to Nuneaton and we would collect her. To me, Marlia was an absolute culture shock.

Dan's mother still had a slight Guyanese accent but she was well and truly Americanised so I could understand her. She sounded more American to me than anything but Marlia was different. She always got off the train with too many bags for my liking and gave us both big kisses – her stays were always longer than planned and her ticket was always an open one. Once she was in situ in our apartment, she often called her brother Raymond and arranged to visit him at his house in Birmingham for an afternoon. During her stay she also liked to pop over to our local pub,

The Queens Head, and have herself a few rums. Naturally Marlia was partial to a little rum. She had hardly any hair at all and the bit that remained was grey, sparse and frizzy. For this reason Marlia wore a wig, only it wasn't actually a wig, it was a hat with the wig attached inside and I'd never seen the like. She simply popped the hat on and long flowing, greyish brown locks immediately cascaded around her shoulders. It never failed to shock me when she took it off.

She liked to go into Leicester with Dan to the meat market because her stay was never complete unless she had made Dan her famous Pepper Pot. I thought the ingredients that went into Marlia's Pepper Pot were bizarre. It took her at least four hours to get the right meats from the market and a good day for it to simmer away before she would let anybody at it. It contained some secret ingredients that she would never divulge but the general gist of it was to add the arse end of every animal that god had created, bones, knuckles and all, throw it into a big pot with some orange zest, talk to it a lot, give it a big stir and then add her 'secret stuff'. It was rich in taste, very black in colour and of a gooey consistency. I had never eaten anything like it before but as long as one did not dwell on the ingredients too much, it was actually very tasty.

Marlia had visited us three times and her 'weekend stays' had caused a little tension between Dan and I because on both of the last two visits the night before she was due to leave she suddenly announced that she was extending her stay for a few days. Marlia was quite a forceful woman to have around and she would take over the entire settee, not to mention my kitchen. Nan had not met Aunty Marlia, but the thought of that encounter amused me. I imagined Nan would look very bewildered and she would say something like, 'I can't understand what you're saying to me!' in a very loud, deliberate voice. Marlia would then reply equally as loudly but nobody would know what she'd said. I imagined that Dan would spend a long time trying to interpret between the two of them. We had seen a lot of Marlia but I had never met his mum so I agreed that it sounded like a nice idea.

We booked the flights along with the hotel in Manhattan, shopped, packed and within a week we were ready for the off. We flew directly from Heathrow to JFK, but what awaited us as soon as we landed at JFK airport simply defied belief. We filled out the relevant visa paperwork and stood in the queue at passport control along with the other arrivals. I was ushered to one queue and Dan to another. We gave our fingerprints in separate queues, as did everybody else, but immediately after we were printed, Dan was taken firmly to one side. At first we both assumed that there might have been something wrong with the British passport or that they may have had computerised records that flagged up the fact that he was an American citizen. We wondered if they had perhaps wanted to speak to him about why he didn't enter the States with a US passport, however, as we were led off to the immigration office, a far more worrying and frightening thought started to enter both of our heads.

We sat in the immigration room for what seemed like hours. First on their agenda was to establish that Dan was indeed a US citizen. In hindsight it would have been far better had he not been. He called his mum in North Carolina but she was out so he then called his brother Ivan to try and get his records along with the date that he was naturalised. Once they were happy with the information he gave them, a little podgy-faced immigration officer tapped around on his computer for a few minutes and then delivered an absolute shocker.

'Sorry, but there's an active warrant out for your arrest man.'

This was the very thing we didn't think was possible and we couldn't believe our ears.

'You must be joking. Jesus Christ. I did my time man back in 1986. How can it still be active?'

Dan put his head in his hands and just kept saying, 'Jesus Christ' repeatedly. I went a particularly pale shade of grey and my legs felt a little wobbly. The immigration officers were all looking bored and tired. It was 9pm when we landed but it was after 10pm by this point and it was clear that this 'active warrant' issue was an inconvenience to them. The bastards just wanted to go home.

'Yeah I hear ya man but it's definitely active. I ain't never heard of no warrant that goes back over 20 years but sorry man. The Pennsylvania police will have to pick you up.'

Dan was now looking as shocked as I was feeling. 'They're not gonna seriously arrest me are they?'

The podgy-faced officer sighed and said, 'It looks that way man. You need to get this sorted with the PA police department. We gotta hold you here until somebody comes to pick you up.'

Dan asked the guy what the warrant was for and, after a few phone calls, Podgy-face said it was for an old probation violation. Well this was certainly not part of our fucking travel itinerary. We had been there such a long time by this point that our baggage had arrived. A different officer escorted my increasingly wobbly legs to a separate area and proceeded to turf out everything that I had carefully packed from the suitcases. Although it was getting late and the New York immigration officers obviously wanted to get home to eat huge buckets of fried chicken and catch highlights of the game, this officer had a surprising amount of energy. He emptied out our entire luggage contents with mucho enthusiasm. I think he was hoping to find something slightly more incriminating than my Oil of Olay face cream and a small tube of Blisteze but he sifted through every toiletry bag regardless.

He fired a few questions at me such as how and when Dan and I met, how much money we had on us and where we thought we were heading once we left JFK. I answered all of his questions to the best of my ability then told him that I had no chance of shutting the suitcase that he had just emptied because it had been packed very methodically and it had taken me an hour to actually close it the first time. He smiled as if that was the least of my worries. I asked if I could go to the toilet and he said I would have to be accompanied by an officer. When I was led back to the office, Dan had been told that the New York Police Department were on their way to arrest him.

Podgy-face then said, 'You will be placed under arrest and then taken to a holding room.'

He then pointed at me. 'She's free to go.'

These Americans truly had no manners. Dan was clearly panicking about me being left alone in one of the world's scariest cities with two heavy-duty suitcases and a laptop. At that point, just like something from the movies, two very tall, very big, New York police officers burst on the scene. They had all of the relevant necessaries for the role, everything one would expect from a couple of power-crazed New York cops. They had keys, guns, handcuffs, clobber and an attitude. I just couldn't believe it was happening. What were these crazy Yanks thinking? This was Dan, my boyfriend, not John Wayne Gacey.

They arrested him and cuffed him on the spot. They bluntly instructed him to take off any jewellery and his watch and told him to give any money that he had on him to me. They said he could keep no more than $20 on his person. It all happened so quickly and I wanted to scream at them. Dan hurriedly told me to get a number for the holding room where they were taking him to; he said immigration should give it to me. He also told me not to panic and to get a cab straight to the Radisson Lexington Hotel on 48th street. I wanted to cry but I didn't. He told me he loved me and asked the two burly cops if he could give me a kiss before they took him away. They grunted and nodded. He gave me a kiss then he was gone.

So that was that and I was alone in New York. Once I had located a luggage trolley, negotiated my way out of the airport, fought to make it down an incredibly long, windy ramp towards the cab area and chuffed two Marlboro Lights in quick succession, I was ready to get to the hotel. I sat in the back of the cab completely stunned. I had known about the history of Dan's US probation violation pretty soon after we met and regardless of whether it was the right or wrong decision at the time, I understood his reasoning. Before we decided to book a trip to the USA, this issue was obviously something we needed to look into. This is where we both made a big mistake, huge.

It had been nearly two decades since he had violated his probation in the US, one could assume that the details would have been wiped as it was such a long time ago. Dan had asked his brother Ivan, who had a connection with an attorney, to check and establish if the case had been closed in the US and he was told that it had been. The attorney had checked some computer system and said the case had been closed years ago. We also filled in the online ESTA document, which had to be done a week or so prior to our departure where background checks are carried out and visitors are permitted to enter the USA. The email came back with no problem. Little did we know that they were probably rubbing their hands together, eagerly awaiting our arrival. I couldn't believe we had been so stupid and that the extent of our investigation into whether it would be safe to return to the USA or not merely consisted of a message from some attorney that we didn't even know who clearly had the information wrong. Well we were about to pay the hefty price for our negligence.

I had a number for the holding room and prayed that after an hour or two I would be able to call and speak to Dan. I thought the whole sorry mess would surely be cleared up the following day so I checked into the hotel, had two glasses of Chardonnay in record time then called. The abrupt, rude wanker manning the phones finally put me through and we spoke. Dan was of the same opinion as me; yes it was a shock but he would get some representation of some description the following day and we would sort it out. He said we must not panic and told me he was more concerned about me.

The following day was frustrating as I was unable to call again so I had to wait in the hotel room because he was only allowed to make one phone call. Dan called later that evening and said he had been taken to Queens Central Booking where he had to wait to see a New York judge. The phone calls had to be really brief. He told me he had been given some sort of legal aid so at least that would be something. He was left in Queens Central Booking all night and had to sleep in a chair. He didn't get to see any judge and the next day went by in a blur. I couldn't leave the room just in case he called and I was updating Ma B using my mobile because I couldn't risk taking up the landline.

I didn't want to eat or to sleep so I just sat around watching crap on the TV in a daze. The following evening the phone finally rang. Dan told me New York had no charges against him but the judge said he couldn't release him. They would hold him for the state of Pennsylvania and he would be transported there in due course. The attorney that he had been assigned advised him to sign the paperwork saying he agreed to be transported to PA. He really didn't have a choice and the situation was getting worse. Dan told me that it was going to take a day or two and they were taking him to Rikers Island jail where he would be locked up until the Pennsylvania police came for him. I winced as soon as I heard the words Rikers Island because even I had heard of that fucking hellhole. I was sure it had featured on *The World's Worst Prisons* a few times.

At that point I burst into tears on the phone. I couldn't help it. It was turning into a nightmare and fast becoming the holiday from hell. I did all I could the following day. I called Queens Central Booking but I couldn't get through so I repeatedly called the New York attorney. When she finally called me back she said there was absolutely nothing she could do and we just had to wait. Dan was taken to Rikers Island jail and I felt like a prisoner in the Radisson Lexington Hotel. I only left the room to run down to Starbucks and get a cup of Earl Grey tea, praying that I didn't miss a call when I'd gone.

The next few days were spent waiting for the phone to ring, speaking to Dan's mum and his brother, crying on the phone to Ma B and generally feeling totally helpless. Dan could only make one phone call per day and he never knew when that would be. He was sharing three public phones with 800 other inmates so I didn't want to go anywhere or do anything at the risk of missing a call. As far as I was concerned, New York could fuck right off and I didn't want to see any of the sights. I wished we'd never arrived at all. Dan was running out of money and he needed to be able to call me once a day.

The prison had told him he needed certain prison clobber, such as a plain, grey tracksuit, Jesus-style sandals, socks and underwear. He was instructed that the tracksuit was to have no hood, ties or pockets and nothing could be branded with a name or sports logo. By this time, he had been at Rikers Island for three or four days and there was still no sign of the Pennsylvania crew. Dan called me on the Sunday morning, asked me to get the prison clothes for him and said he had found out that his visiting day was a Sunday. I could actually visit him that day but could only see him if I got there before 2pm so I had to move quickly. It was already around 11.30am and I had to try and find unbranded prison gear, locate Rikers Island jail and get in that queue well before 2pm. I still couldn't believe the situation we had found ourselves in. I had to dig deep as I was about to make my way to a jail in the Bronx completely by myself. I cursed the crazy Yank legal system once more, picked up my bag and left the hotel.

I managed to find a big sports shop a block or two away from the hotel but every single item was branded with Nike or Adidas logos and I couldn't even find plain socks. I moved onto a big department store but that was much the same. I was about to lose it completely and ask an assistant where the bloody hell they had put the 'non-branded prison wear' section when I spotted a plain grey tracksuit with no hood and no pockets. Hallelujah! That was a start and I scooped it up quickly. That was, however, to be the highlight of the shopping event. The socks I had found had tiny Nike symbols on the bottom but time was running out so they would have to do. The closest things to sandals I could find were some plain, black flip floppy things.

I needed to get a cab to the prison sharpish. The jail was a good 40 minutes away and the robbing cab driver told me it would cost at least $60 to get there. Rikers Island was situated in the heart of the Bronx and the Bronx didn't fail its reputation for being a complete shit tip. As we passed decaying car repair garage after decaying car repair garage, I realised that the journey was taking forever. The cabby was probably taking the piss but this was not London and it was no time for a row with a New York cabby. I got to Rikers at around 1pm. The queue was huge and it was pissing it down.

This queue of people was like no other queue I have ever stood in during my entire life. It was dark, wet and everybody looked like they had lost the will to live. I was the only white person there. The queue was a mix of big, black women who appeared to represent 'the projects', a scattering of Mexicans and a few Hispanics.

I boldly joined the queue while everybody proceeded to stare at me. After five minutes my mobile phone rang and when I answered it they all turned and looked at me again. I decided it was probably due to my accent so I got off the phone quickly. I'll admit that I was slightly fascinated by them and they looked very inquisitively at me. They looked totally at home standing in that queue and they probably stood in it once or twice a week. I, on the other hand, probably appeared petrified.

At that point the chattering between the women in the queue started. It felt surreal and even in the midst of the horrendous situation I found myself in; I couldn't help being amused by their accents. I listened while I waited and the queue was barely moving so we were going to be there for some time. Woman One was probably only in her late 20s. She had quite a pretty face but she must have been 18 stone and no more than 5 foot 2 inches. She had shiny, jet black hair that was cut into a very precise bob with a heavy straight fringe. She was standing right behind me.

In a heavy accent that I can only describe as 'purest black street' she said, 'Gurrl you ain't gon' get a booth visit in that hoodie.'

'I'm sorry, did you say boob visit?' I didn't quite catch what she'd said.

She rolled her eyes. 'What? No baby, a *b-o-o-t-h* visit. You know, glass, behind the glass, where you can't hear a motherfuckin word yo' man say. A booth visit.'

I really hadn't thought about what I was wearing. I prayed that I wouldn't get turned away because of my stupid tracksuit hood. I hadn't got anything on underneath so I couldn't take it off.

'Oh thanks. I didn't know that.'

She nodded and quietly said, 'Well then yo' man ain't gone see yo' pretty behind today. Go to yo' vehicle baby, get yo'self dressed for prison. I'll keep yo' place in line.'

Did this woman actually think I kept a spare prison-visiting outfit in my car? I didn't even have a car. I moved a little nearer to her and bravely said, 'Actually I came in a taxi. I had to get a taxi from Manhattan.'

She looked shocked right down to her little black furry boots and exclaimed, 'Excuse me? Are you out of yo' motherfucking mind? That gotta be $50. I wouldn't pay $3.50 to see my man. Damn gurrl, a cab from Manhattan?'

I explained that it was $60 each way in the cab and I'd just spent $95 on prison wear that would be probably be rejected because the tracksuit was the wrong shade of grey. She appeared to be totally astounded at what I was telling her. We then heard voices and a bit of commotion coming from the other end of the queue, which was still trying to shuffle forwards. Everybody in the desperately sad line was wet through. We both looked towards the front of the long line of women and a huge black guy in uniform was informing everybody in a very loud, don't-fuck-with-me voice that it was now past 2pm so nobody else would get in.

That's when Woman Two piped up. Woman Two was a tall, skinny woman dressed in a red tracksuit – with no hood. She was probably in her mid-40s but looked old and drawn. She looked like life had dealt her a few shitty cards.

'Hell no! No you didn't motherfucker! What he just say to me? I ain't here for no damn visit. I'm here to leave that cocksucker some money. Got himself locked the fuck up again. What do I wanna see that no good motherfucker for?' She shouted at the top of her high-pitched voice.

The whole queue was beginning to get very unsettled. Woman One nudged me and whispered, 'Close yo' purse honey. I mean get a lock on that motherfucker. If you do get in next time, these fuckers search yo' shit, take stuff and keep it for their damn selves.'

I immediately closed my handbag properly as everybody started to make their way back towards the heavily guarded front gate.

'That nigga smoking crack. It only five minutes after motherfuckin 2. Motherfucker.' Woman One hissed.

I made my way out with the rest of them and yet again I had a strong urge to kill myself. I made it back to the hotel and promptly took two Nurofen. It seemed the whole experience had given me the mother of all headaches. An hour or two passed and Dan called to see what had happened. I tearfully told him I'd made it there, only to be turned away. I didn't know which one of us sounded more deflated. Monday and Tuesday passed by in a haze and there was still no sign of the Pennsylvania police. We were both feeling very desperate and I hadn't been out anywhere apart from to the bar in the Radisson lobby.

The guy behind the bar had started to look at me in an oddly sympathetic fashion. He tried to make the typical conversation that a barman would make with a tourist but his attempts failed with me. I think he thought I was some sort of saddo who pretended to have a boyfriend that didn't actually exist. I couldn't tell him the truth so I would just sit in silence staring at my glass of very expensive Chardonnay, mumbling total rubbish about why I hadn't yet seen the Empire State Building or Times Square and muttering on about how I was going to get around to it.

I had been in constant contact with Dan's mum and Ivan. I was due to fly home on the Thursday but I couldn't stand the thought of leaving Dan in jail and returning home with no idea of what was happening. If I stayed, I would miss a gig or two but I didn't care. Dan was worrying about me and he wanted me to return home where at least I would have family around me. He said I should take care of the apartment and keep my gigs going. I spoke to Ivan and he told me if I wanted to stay on for a while he would collect me and I could stay with him and his wife in North Carolina until we knew more. That sounded like a more bearable alternative to me at the time and I felt a small amount of relief. I had been in that hotel alone for a week so the thought of some company and some support from Dan's family was much welcomed.

I was due to be collected on Wednesday by Ivan and his wife Irene. Ivan was making the 10-hour drive from North Carolina to New York to pick me up. I still needed to get some money and the prison clobber to Dan but this meant going back to Rikers Island, which was not an appealing thought. We agreed that Ivan would take me to Rikers and we could drop off the clothing and the money together. I was sure that having an American physically by my side would help with the next dread filled visit to Rikers 'motherfucking' Island.

To be honest even though our American cousins and we English are supposed to speak the same language, it was becoming clear to me once again that in fact we did not. I had only been there a week, yet the times I said something to either a hotel staff member or just a girl serving behind the counter at Starbucks and was met with the following sort of response, 'Huh? Sorry Ma'am, say that again' were countless. I tried to speak slowly and never used any English sayings or slang but it proved futile. I may as well have spoken in Swahili and, yet again, you couldn't get a decent brew anywhere. Not a good cuppa in sight.

I was beginning to dislike the USA in a big way. Not just because they refuse to spell words like 'colour' and 'flavour' correctly, or because they mispronounce 'aluminium' and make spurious claims about landing on the moon. Mostly I was beginning to dislike them because they were not sincere. They would be rude and shitty on the phone, but always end the conversation with, 'Have a great day'. What was that about? They didn't give two small turds if I had a great day so why say it?

I decided that the only thing the USA truly did best was host the world's most impressive serial killers. I had to give them that one. I knew my serial killers and they had some true gems. If I hadn't been a singer I'd always liked the idea of being a serial killer profiler, similar to the role Sigourney Weaver played in the movie *Copycat* – I thought I would be quite good at that. I have always had a fascination with the macabre but please don't judge me. I believe I'm not alone. It sounds pretty sick to say I admire certain serial killers but if you're going be one, at least be a little flamboyant like the damn Yanks.

I checked out of the Radisson Lexington Hotel and Ivan collected me as arranged. It was strange to meet my boyfriend's brother for the first time under such horrible circumstances. It was certainly not how I envisaged meeting Dan's family. Ivan said he was going to try and get us a visit with Dan before we left New York, even though I explained that his day for visits was a Sunday. I tried to tell Ivan how strict these bloody prison geezers were but he was having none of it. He said he had a plan. This I had to see.

Although I didn't know it then, Ivan was about give me a personal demonstration of what he did best in life, which was to bullshit. He explained his plan and although I could see a few potential flaws, I had to agree that it was worth a try. Ivan was ex-military and he had an old military ID. He hadn't been in the military for years but the ID card displayed no expiry date. His plan was simple. He would wait until the registration point and when they informed him that Dan could only receive visitors on a Sunday, he would flash his ID then explain that this whole thing was a mix-up concerning incorrect paperwork and old computer records. He would tell them that he had been sent from North Carolina to explain the legal situation to his brother before taking me to the airport and flying me back to England.

As I said, I spotted a few flaws in his plan, such as the fact that they were likely to say, 'We don't give a fuck, he gets no visits until Sunday' but I didn't want to appear negative so I went with the plan. It took hours before we even got to the registration desk as the waiting room was full. The general bodily searches and checks went on for an eternity and the whole thing seemed to take forever. Airport searches were nothing in comparison. These people were one step away from taking a DNA swab and shoving their hand up your back passage. After an eternity, we finally got to the point where Ivan's plan was to be put into practice.

He began quite confidently. 'We are here to visit Daniel Goodman.'

'Passports please,' the prison woman barked in an abrupt and hostile manner.

She looked Hispanic and had a face like a smacked arse. We handed over our passports and once our ID had been checked the shrivelled up little woman punched some details into a computer.

'The initial of his surname is G. Visits for G are Sundays not Wednesdays. You can't see him today. Check before you leave next time.' She handed us back our passports.

Ivan began to perform. 'Yeah I'm aware of that but I have been sent from North Carolina to visit today. Do you wanna see my military ID? My people have already called in advance to arrange this. My brother is only here temporarily until some paperwork has been put in place.'

Ivan handed over his military ID. 'I have to visit my brother with his English fiancée before we fly her back to London.'

He handed over my passport again. 'I have been driving for 10 hours so I really hope your people have arranged this your end.'

The woman looked slightly concerned that she should perhaps be aware of something that she actually she knew nothing about. I was surprised and, dare I say, a little hopeful, although something told me that the sort of scenario I was witnessing, the 'my people, your people' attacking kind of trick that Eddie Murphy would pull in *Beverly Hills Cops*, would soon be uncovered. If that was the case we, or should I say Ivan, would be in real trouble. The woman told us to wait where we were and shuffled off to talk to her colleagues.

After a couple of minutes she came back and said, 'I have to speak to my superior. Who did your people speak to here?'

Ivan pulled his best bored/slightly irritated face and sighed. 'I have no idea Ma'am. I'm just told where to go. They told me that you guys would know all about it. Now I haven't got much time before I need to get this lady on a flight to London so can you get your superior down here fast?'

Power was shifting between Ivan and the she-devil. He was doing well but he still had the superior to deal with. I was sure that's where it would go on its arse and Ivan would be swiftly taken into another room, only to re-emerge in the full Rikers prison gear. We were told that we would need to wait for the superior and in the meantime we were to get in the queue where the prison staff checked any clothes or items that were to be left and passed onto inmates. There was a small hatch where people had to hand their stuff over and it was then checked by two guys who informed people whether the items would be accepted or not.

This was the time when my choice of prison clothing would be validated and I was feeling the pressure. There was a lady in front of us who was frantically trying to rip the back pockets from a pair of grey tracksuit bottoms. She was trying to do this with her bare hands and her teeth, as there was nothing else she could use. She could hardly ask if they would mind lending her a pair of scissors. She had obviously been told that the tracksuit would be rejected because it had pockets. She was tearing at the tracksuit bottoms like some beast that had just caught its prey on the Discovery Channel.

Meanwhile other people were allowed to move forward so we were next. We handed over the bag to the guy behind the small hatch. He said nothing and started to examine the items. My pocketless tracksuit bottoms were a huge success and he put them to one side. My hoodless tracksuit top swiftly followed. He took one look at the socks, handed them straight back through the hatch and said, 'No sports symbols'. He mumbled something else but I couldn't quite catch it. The Nike symbol had meant my white socks were the first to be rejected. Next up were the sandals/flip flops. He handed them straight back to me and barked, 'No Velcro'. Well that was just silly. I had never heard of an inmate on

suicide watch who took his own life with the aid of a Velcro strip. I know
that Velcro can hold well once attached but surely nobody could hang
themselves with it, or indeed cause bodily harm to another human being.

He looked at me like he believed I had intended to try and smuggle in
Velcro whilst knowing how deadly it was. Anybody would think I had
just handed over two Stanley knives, a meat cleaver, a bottle of Sambuca,
some nice Columbian hashish, a small revolver, a nail file and a long rope.
Either way, along with the socks, my sandals were also cruelly rejected
and I probably had a guilty look on my face even though I had no reason
to feel guilty. We walked away from the queue, leaving the woman on the
left of us a little bit more room to wrestle with the pockets of her man's
tracksuit bottoms.

Ivan tried to comfort me by saying that two items out of four had been
accepted so that was not too bad. I was more concerned about what Dan
was going to put on his feet. The system obviously provided some sort of
prison issue footwear but I imagined it was basic and very uncomfortable.
I knew Dan well enough to know that even locked up in the big house,
he would cringe at the thought of prison issue footwear. He was into his
footwear in a big way and he would probably prefer to go barefoot than
wear anything less than brown, leather, Prada Jesus sandals. We made
our way back to the desk where Ivan had originally performed his best
Axel Foley pulling a fast one impression and waited for the superior.

We were only there for a few minutes when a big unit the size of
Professor Klump approached us and I knew immediately that this was
the superior. The two women from the front desk had obviously already
filled him in. He asked a few questions (I think he just wanted to check out
my English accent) and Ivan basically delivered the same lines as he had
earlier. To my absolute and utter fucking shock, the superior checked our
passports and said we could see Dan. Not only that, he told Ivan that he
had arranged for the visit to be extended so we could see Dan for one hour
and 15 minutes. I didn't know whether to kiss him or laugh at him for
being so intensely stupid. This was supposed to be Rikers Island jail, the
mother of rules and security. This man had just fallen for a complete pile
of horseshit and he obviously hadn't even attempted to check who 'Ivan's
people' were because I knew they didn't exist. Had I not seen the events of
that day unfold with my own eyes, I would never have believed it.

Ivan looked very pleased with himself and whilst we were in the
visiting waiting area, I had to congratulate him on his performance. The
surprising result was not so much down to Ivan's Oscar-winning acting
skills, although he did a fine job, it was due to the fact that the superior

had clearly had his brain removed and it had been replaced with a KFC Bargain Bucket. These Americans really were something else. They looked at you like you had walked into their house on Christmas day and pissed on their kids for trying to bring in a pair of Velcro sandals, yet they allowed a bloke who had nothing more than an expired military ID card, some flimsy story about incorrect paperwork and a nervous British woman an extended visit on a non-visiting day with no problem at all. It really was priceless.

It took another hour or so before we were led into a huge area where the inmates sat at little tables awaiting their visitors and after a few minutes, I spotted Dan. All of the inmates were dressed in grey all-in-one prison issue suits and they all had plastic tags attached to the suits. We went over to the table and Dan asked one of the supervising members of staff if it was OK to give us a hug and make physical contact. She said it was OK but we must keep our hands above the table at all times. I had already decided prior to entering that room that no matter how hard it would be I would not cry. Dan gave us both a hug and he was very emotional.

We were all aware that the guards were watching everybody closely. Dan hadn't seen his brother for years and I think he felt guilty about putting his mother through something like this again after such a long time. We didn't know when we would see each other again after that day so he tried to keep it together but it was hard. It was probably a good thing that Ivan was there because I think I would have lost it if it were just the two of us.

CHAPTER TWELVE

ALL RISE

Prior to visiting Rikers, I had been online looking for contacts within Erie County Police Dept. I needed to establish when the Pennsylvania crew intended to collect Dan. He felt like he was being left in New York indefinitely with no proper attorney. I found a list of email addresses and copied in everybody I could find. I sent what I hoped would sound like a desperate woman asking for help and that was actually the truth. I said he was my fiancé in some pathetic bid to make us sound established, adult and stable.

Hello,

Please can you help me. My fiancé (Daniel Goodman) and I arrived into JFK from England on Thursday 19th February. I am English, my fiancé is a US citizen and was naturalised in 1985. He is also a British passport holder. We were due to spend a week on vacation in New York but he was arrested as soon as we landed in JFK.

Erie police have detained him in Vernon C Bain Centre of Rikers Island New York for over a week. We were informed that Erie police had an active warrant out for his arrest for violating probation in 1992, 17 years ago. He left the US because his father was seriously ill and apparently he violated his probationary period. He has been in no trouble since that time.

Once detained last week, he signed a waiver immediately, agreeing that he be taken back to Erie to be dealt with. New York has no charges against him and is merely holding him for Erie Police. He has been told on three occasions that Erie police will collect him and take him back to Erie to appear before a judge. So far this has not happened and he is still being held in New York.

His brother (Ivan Goodman, a US citizen residing in the US) and I are trying to arrange for an attorney in PA but I am increasingly worried that my fiancé is still stuck in jail in New York with no real representation. He is not a hardened criminal and he has not been in any trouble since 1992 for which he served his time. His only crime is violating probation 17 years ago to see his father who was sick in the UK. His father did pass away. We both live in England and we have jobs there. We have missed our plane home and I don't know what to do. I am panicking.

I'm sorry if I have sent this email to the wrong person and I apologise if I have taken up any of your time and you are not the person to speak with. I do understand that he will need an attorney but I just wanted to know why he has been held in New York for this length of time and why he has not been taken back to Erie.

Please help me. Ivan Goodman's number is: 555 832375. If somebody from your department could reply to my email it would be greatly appreciated because I don't know what to tell our employers in England and this whole episode is making my fiancé and I sick with worry. He just wants to put things right in Erie for something he did so many years ago.

His booking case number is: 555 9021490 and his date of birth is 11th July 1966. His full name is Daniel Goodman.

Thank you for your time,
Joanne Copeman

I received a reply from Randy... what a ridiculous name.

Joanne,
I contacted Ivan Goodman and also spoke with Dep. Sheriff John Loomis regarding the arrest of Daniel Goodman.

Deputy Loomis confirmed that Daniel was arrested on an outstanding warrant for a probation violation. Daniel will be transported to the Erie County Prison (16 Ash St., Erie, Pa. tel: 555-451-7500) sometime in the next 24 hours. At some point in time he will appear before an Erie County Judge. Your best bet is to contact the Erie County prison for further information.

Dep. Chief Randy Flowers
City of Erie Police

I was almost relieved to hide my face behind my jacket in the back of Ivan's car for the long journey to North Carolina. I just wanted to cry. I had tried not to cry all day and my head was pounding. The journey from New York to Charlotte was around nine hours and feeling totally exhausted I probably slept for five hours and cried for four hours. I was trying to keep Ma B fully informed but due to the time difference and the cost of calls, I was keeping in touch via email.

We have just arrived in Charlotte at Ivan's place. It's about 4.30am here so Ivan, his wife and I are all knackered. Ivan managed to get us both in to see Dan today. It wasn't his day for visits so we were lucky. Ivan pulled some bizarre shit to get us a visit! We got Dan some white t-shirts and a grey tracksuit, which is all they are allowed to wear on their own wing. He got upset when we went in the room, which was awful, and I hated seeing him in that prison suit. He's not eating. He has bite marks on his arms because he reckons the beds have nasty bugs in them. I just hope they deal with him quickly when he leaves for Erie on Friday/Saturday.

I will text you Ivan's landline tomorrow when I wake up (may be later in afternoon) and I can talk to you then. Ivan is doing his best. He is sorting Dan out with an attorney tomorrow, not some legal aid fool.

I'm nipping outside for a ciggie then bed. I'm not sure I'll make it past the hostile looking Husky that is sitting guard by Ivan's front door though. It's a strange dog. Ivan says he's fine once you get to know him but I'm unconvinced. Irene told me that a neighbour is taking them to court because the dog has bitten a child who leant over their garden fence. Anyway, the dog has form and I'm a stranger so the chances of me getting past him both ways, without being mauled, are pretty slim. I'm risking it though and to be honest, the mood I'm in, my money is on me!

Jo x

'Big Momma' cruelly woke me early the next morning. Ivan and Irene had gone to work so I was left alone in an unfamiliar big house with an unhinged Husky. The house was lovely and very big. Suddenly a booming voice came drifting across the house from the kitchen area.

'Where are you my poor child?'

I got out of bed and shuffled across to the kitchen where Dan's mum, Maria, was boiling the kettle.

'Good morning sweetheart, I've brought you some London tea! With all that trouble that my boy is in, you need your English tea,' she said cheerily.

I had not had enough sleep so I knew this first meeting was going to be hard. I tried my best to look pleased about the teabags and actually I was a little uplifted by the thought of an English brew. Maria was a big woman. She seemed very pleased to finally meet me. She was not as mobile as Marlia and had terrible trouble with her knees. Dan had told me that she'd had a few operations but with little success. Her car had been modified due to her disability but she still struggled to drive and she was unable to walk very far at all. She was also diabetic and had been told by doctors that she would be unable to have any future surgery unless she lost weight.

She was just pouring the water over my brew bag when the dog jumped up at Maria excitedly and scratched her nose with his big paw.

'Benny!' She shouted as he clambered around her shoulders.

'Get down!'

So that was the fucker's name. We spoke about the horrid situation that Dan was in and although she was very upset, I soon remembered that she'd been in that situation before. After my 'London cuppa', which had come out of a box that had a picture of Big Ben on the front and had no doubt sat on a shelf in her kitchen since her last trip to London 20 years ago, she asked if I would help her go shopping. I was unsure what she meant by that and I was not quite awake but I agreed because I could hardly say no. After my tea, I got dressed and we left.

She drove slowly to an Aldi supermarket, parked the car and promptly pulled out a list. She began to explain how bad her knees were and how helpful it would be for her if she could stand at the top of each aisle whilst I went and fetched her individual items. She said it would save her legs. I just nodded in a bewildered fashion. I would rather have had a little more sleep, woke up alone, gathered my thoughts and indulged in another brew before the day got under way but it was not to be. Here I was, straight out of bed, in Aldi, doing 'supermarket sweep' for a woman I had only just met.

She said that once we had done her shopping she would take me to church. I smiled agreeably but thought, 'for fucksake no. Not the church thing'. I wasn't ready for it. Luckily, once I'd flown around Aldi, collecting her diabetes-friendly provisions, Ivan called just as we were loading the car and asked her to bring me back to his house as he wanted to speak to me about Dan's chosen attorney. She was a little disappointed but agreed and said she could take me to church another day. Ironically, I thanked the Lord. Once I had been deposited back at Ivan's, Big Momma said her goodbyes and said she would come back tomorrow with some goat curry. I kept thinking I must be having a really weird dream. I fully expected to wake up in my apartment and realise that the whole sorry episode had just been a nightmare but I was not waking up and it was really happening.

I had witnessed first-hand in Rikers that Ivan was a master bullshitter. He said he was in the investment business and his line of work was all finance-related, which didn't surprise me. Somebody was earning a good living if his house was anything to go by. I was quickly introduced to Ivan's somewhat permanent lodgers, Ed and Davey. Ed was Ivan's business partner. He had been staying with Ivan for some time and Irene said he was there indefinitely. He was always on the landline phone and when I say always I mean 90% of the time, day or night. Ed said that's how it was when dealing with investments globally, due to time differences.

Ed was a little, thin, black man in his late 40s and he had one discoloured brown tooth at the front (they obviously hadn't all got 'pearly whites' in the US). He seemed very intelligent and, unlike Ivan, he didn't appear too shady. Davey was a chubby young bloke in his early 20s. He seemed a little on the feminine side to me. Apparently he was a godson of Irene's. Over the following week or so, I tried to establish why he was actually living there but I couldn't quite fathom and Ivan appeared to be equally baffled as to why Davey lived with them too. Davey was not the sharpest tool in the shed but he was turning out to be a good runner. When I say 'runner' I mean I was starting to find my feet in Ivan's gaff and I'd began putting Davey to use in terms of fetching me wine and cigs whenever he went to the shops. He seemed eager to please and I needed things bringing back. He went to the shops most days and always asked me if I wanted anything. It was nice and discreet too. I was the only drinker and smoker in the place so Davey nipping to the shops on a daily basis was far better than me asking Ivan and Irene to get me five bottles of Chardonnay and 100 Marlboro Lights whilst on their weekly shop.

I'd been there a while before the attorney had been put into place and Dan had been transferred to Erie County Jail. He was calling as much as he could and Ivan was topping up his phone credit whenever it got low. The whole thing was turning into a really lengthy process and one that would not be rushed. I was keeping Ma B fully informed regarding the whole frustrating business because she was still manning my emails and calls at home for gigging purposes. We were lying to people through our teeth about mine and Dan's whereabouts and Ma B had to tell some giant whoppers to agents and bookers regarding gigs back in the UK.

As far as my family, our friends and entertainment agents back home were concerned, Dan's mother had become unwell and we had extended our stay. It was a terrible lie and one that had the potential to run away with us but what was the alternative? We could hardly tell people the truth. Emails were being sent to and fro by Ma B and I constantly, along with phone calls where possible. Calls via the landline were far cheaper but we could hardly ever use Ivan's landline because bloody Ed (the brown-toothed one) was always occupying it. There was a window of around 10 minutes where it would be free at around 4.30am and that was not ideal.

Lawyer says he won't see a judge tomorrow. Apparently the parole officer has to review the case before it goes before the judge. Won't be able to speak to the lawyer properly until tomorrow. Only found this out today because Dan's mum is a friend of a woman who knows the lawyers wife. It's ridiculous!

If I were Dan I'd be about ready to top myself. He will probably call tonight. He's going to be proper pissed off.

Don't know what to think now… I feel the need to speak to this lawyer creature myself and not keep getting things relayed back to me via other people.

Jo x

Oh no another set back, can't believe it! Poor Dan. It is not looking good for getting back for this weekend is it? I know what you mean about men – enough to drive you to drink. On that note it will soon be bevvie o'clock – how are you getting your quota? You didn't have to go to church today did you? Why can't you speak to the lawyer yourself? You must be tearing your hair out again. It must be hard keeping your cool in someone else's house – I would have been mad about Ivan going out as well – this is when you have to start talking to yourself about these people just to vent and keep sane.

Will be going to bed soon. It is 10.45pm but I will wait for your reply.

Ma B xxx

Yeah the whole situation is doing my head in now. I will speak to the lawyer tomorrow myself. No it's not looking good for the weekend but don't do anything until I speak to this lawyer prick myself tomorrow. I want to hear something from the horse's mouth. I have sent the godson Davey to get me wine and chuffs. Big useless cretin just stands around looking stupid all day so I sent him out. Think he likes my accent. Fool. Anyway, Dan will be suicidal. I almost don't want him to phone because he will be really deflated.

Anyway have a good sleep and I will speak to you tomorrow,

Jo x

Maybe the parole officer reviews it to see if it warrants going to court at all, so perhaps it may still be OK tomorrow. My poor little Miss Bassey, I am really feeling for you. Please God this has to end soon – I am going to bed to say a prayer for you!

Love you loads and missing you even more.

Ma B xxx

Love you too!!!

I'm going have to speak to this attorney myself. I just spoke to Dan. It's horrible. I can't do anything to help him. I'm fed up of everybody going about their business like he's not locked up. He's starting to get negative now. Why is everything so fucking slow? He hasn't raped, murdered or kidnapped anybody.

Bastards! Will keep you updated tomorrow. I will pray tonight too.

Jo x

I agree with you, get the number and ring this attorney, hope she is not just mate/ favour arrangement. It is worse for you than anyone, except Dan. He will obviously be more upset with you than anyone so you are taking all that on and you are in someone else's house so can't vent and kick ass like you need to. Very, very hard for you.

Rang Regal this morning, spoke to Joy, she said they do not take cards. I told her you would be back this weekend. She said she would pass message to AJ – I asked to speak to him but he wasn't in. I will ring him later.

Is Dan getting any feedback from inmates, etc., in Erie – sometimes inmates seem to know the law better than the supposed experts. I still feel they will chuck this out with a fine but today was a psychological deadline for everyone and we need some urgent action from that attorney today. Get a list of questions together and speak to her yourself if you can.

Steph has just rang and can't get her breath that you have no more clear info and said to tell you she is thinking of you and praying.

Speak or email soon – let me know the minute you know something.
Ma B xxx

Dan was struggling and so was I. Time was passing and nothing concrete was happening. The female attorney was actually more like an assistant to the real attorney, who was a guy called Jed Carlton. He was a rude, arrogant, busy, expensive tosser. He was the typical American lawyer. I just hoped he was as good as he seemed to think he was. The ultimate problem was getting hold of him for any updates. That was driving us insane. Dan had been asking about his daughter in Erie and due to a strange and twisted set of events, he had managed to get an address for her but his spirits were lifted only briefly. It really seemed like we would never get home. The emails flowed and in between updates regarding Dan's incarceration, Ma B kept me updated on the mundane things at home, such as how many toilet rolls her golden retriever Amber had chewed up and which rogue ingredient of Ma B's baking had wreaked havoc with Nan's colostomy.

The attorney called Ivan this morning at 8am! Everybody still asleep so I am speaking with him after 2pm today. Dan just called and he told us that last night he asked his councillor in prison to try and find his daughter. He knows/thinks she is somewhere in Erie. The councillor found out that Sandra's brother (remember Sandra is Dan's ex-wife and the mother of his two kids) is locked up for a few days due to non-payment of child support and he's in the same prison as Dan! Priceless isn't it? The brother gave the councillor an address for Sandra and Dan's daughter, Cissy. He now knows where they live and it's not far away from where he is. He hopes that when we are on our way to get him (10-hour drive for Ivan again) he will be able to see his daughter and his little grandbaby (granddaughter!). Anyway it's the little fat baby in the picture that Nan says she could eat. The main thing is he now knows where his daughter is because he has been trying to find her for the last year. He says perhaps that's why God locked him up in Erie. Freaky.

They have moved him to a trustee wing and he doesn't want to get too hopeful but the guards told him that is where they hold people before they get sent home. It's the last place they are before they get released. He's hoping they are right. We just need him to see the judge before Friday. He was a little better this morning because of the news about his daughter and because they moved him to that wing.

Keep praying. I'll email again when I have more news and I have spoken to that robbing lawyer. He wants $1,000 before he'll even get a pen out. Dan is wittering on about needing his hair cutting. I spoke to his cousin Pete today who said, 'Why the fuck does he want to look so tidy? He really doesn't want to look too pretty in jail!' Ivan keeps telling me how he should be a millionaire within the next few months as he and Ed have a big deal going down. He actually said he'd give us $50,000 and we could have his house. I think he's losing it. I better go now. I can hear Big Momma's voice. She's arrived with more fried chicken.

I emailed Steph last night. She replied this morning and her language regarding the US justice system was choice!

Jo x

Indeed, the Lord works in mysterious ways. The situation is now looking far more promising if they have him in the trustee wing. You almost dare not think that he will be released before or by the weekend – keep praying. You just might be able to get on a flight Sunday/Monday – just want you home now. I will understand if you want to stay into next week though so no pressure – thought you might both just have had enough of 'The Land of the Free'!

I have just been down to the bank to get the cash and paid it to Regal. They wouldn't take a cheque – reckon they must be on their uppers. Called into Nan's to take her some chicken pie and cheesecake I had cooked. Told her your gig in Devon had been cancelled for this Friday so you were staying on a few more days. She said, 'Oh how lovely they must be having a wonderful time and how nice for Dan to be able to see all his family.' Bless her, she will never know he has been locked up in a variety of cells since you arrived there! In the time it took me to go down town and Nans, Amber had done a couple of loo rolls. She had also chewed up one of the books from the bookcase. The title of the book she had chosen to rip to pieces and distribute all over the hallway this time was Dog Behaviour Explained.

I am with Pete on why would you want to look nice in the pen! He only had his hair cut before he left – it surely can't have grown that much.

Feckin hell – Old Jed Carlton wants $1,000 upfront, what a wounder! Still as you say, everyone will be in clover when Ivan's big boat comes in – are you getting $50,000 plus the house?

Shall I leave it until Thursday and then email L Productions and tell them you have a cold? They might wonder why you can't ring them if I ring. As for Barry at Stream Entertainments, when and what do you want me to tell him re. Dan's gigs?

Email me back with any other news or stateside gossip.

MB xxx

I am praying! I hope something happens before the weekend. Thanks for taking the dosh in to Regal. I will give it straight back to you upon my return to Blighty.

Don't know why he was flapping about his bloody haircut, think he kept expecting to see a judge or probation officer or some fecker but nobody ever came.

Yeah $50,000 plus the house apparently. Strange!

We need to tell Barry that Dan's mum is seriously ill and he can't leave until next week. Say he's really, really sorry. Tell him the passport thing is sorted though. Can you phone him for me?

Maybe L Productions should be told because if they just think I'm ill they may ring my phone and hear the overseas ringtone. Maybe you should say my mother-in-law is on her last legs in the States, what do you think? Terrible I know. Actually her legs are completely fecked!

Jo x

Had a conversation with Jed Carlton. He says this should all get sorted out with no difficulty in a few days and the judge would be insane to impose any further custodial sentence, taking into account the time Dan has already served. I don't dare be too hopeful but I have been looking at flights back from Charlotte to London. I've found a fax number for the judge's office. I'm going to send him a fax, pleading for mercy. I'll send you a copy. Can't hurt.

Oh, Dan's mum has asked me to go over to her house tomorrow and help her with some hoovering. Great!

It's all go…

Jo x

My but you have been busy! I thought the fax to the judge was a great little touch and he would have to be a hard-hearted old man indeed not to feel sympathy — that's if it gets to him of course, but definitely worth a try. Let me know if you hear anything else.

I have had Nan and Bernadette up this morning – told them you were going from North Carolina to Erie as Dan wanted to see his daughter and told Nan your gig had been cancelled in Devon. Had to then go straight to hairdressers where I told Nicky Dan's mum is not well and he wants to try to see his daughter. Been pretty much bullshitting all day really. Oh and emailed L Productions and Barry. LP emailed back to say hope Dan's mum recovers and haven't had a reply from Barry yet but will ring him tomorrow if I don't hear. Would be great if you got back into

Birmingham – Erica does – might be worth emailing her – her and Maureen are experts! First things first, let's get him bloody out of there.

The cheesecake I did for Nan gave her the runs again – must have been the hazelnut yoghurt in it – who would have thought just a nut flavoured yog would cause that – anyway she had plenty to say today (I haven't 'fessed up' to hazelnut yog – just said must be the richness of the cream). It's a bit of a shame really as she is likely to give up fresh cream cakes now and I know how she likes an eclair.

I will call Gemma at Dansatak about your other gig tomorrow. Oh Robbo has been causing carnage again by the way. He's pissed, or worse, from dawn til dusk apparently. I spoke to Marie and Dave yesterday. Marie said he's lost so much weight. As a mother, it must be so painful for her.

What have Gordon Gekko and his sidekick Ed been up to today – I would start earwigging if I were you – might learn something!

Email back.

Byeeeeeeee...

Dan was becoming frustrated. I mentioned to him during one very limited phone call that Ivan said his ship was well and truly coming in so we shouldn't worry about finances.

Dan replied, 'Honey Ivan has been saying that for the last five years. Don't hold your breath. I was excited the first time he said it to me too. He's my brother but that motherfucker ain't in the real world. Mom said a long time ago that she thinks there's something wrong with his head. Irene was going to divorce him a couple of years ago. I think he's caused them some big debts. Scrap that thought cause that shit ain't gonna happen!'

It was a shame as I'd had big plans for that house. Later that afternoon I had some bad news from Billy Big Balls the attorney. He said the date for the court case had not been 100% confirmed but it looked like it would be set for two weeks from then. It was not as soon as he'd have liked. The bloke had been talking like it would all be rectified in a few days. He was obviously as deluded as Ivan. What was wrong with these people? I felt deflated and I knew Dan would be more so. So no $50,000 from that crazy fantasist and we were not going home any time soon either. It appeared that Dan would remain in Erie County Jail until further notice.

I informed Ma B straight away that we would not be coming home as soon as we had hoped and told her that Ivan was officially a lunatic who had obviously been residing in cloud cuckooland for some time so there would be no financial help either. Ivan had initially said he wanted to pay for the attorney for Dan and he had done so but then that very morning Ivan had asked if we were OK to reimburse him as he was struggling for cash. That was more like it!

Every day I was listening to him and the brown-toothed one with three or more phone calls on the go at once, snappily speaking in that 'buy coffee, sell tea' Wall Street fashion and they were beginning to grate on my nerves. I felt like the novelty of the situation had worn off for Ivan. He wanted to bask in the glory of getting his brother out of a situation, celebrate his genius with a family party and move on. It was not panning out that way and he was bored.

I had also noticed that he was looking at me in a different way. One morning when I went into the kitchen he was making coffee and asked if I would like a cup. I smiled and said, 'Yes please.' He looked at me in a funny way and whispered, 'That was a sexy smile'. I acted like I hadn't heard him and just pretended to look for something in my bag. I bloody well had heard him and unfortunately I'd heard him correctly. I tried to ignore the way Ivan sometimes looked at me because I felt bad about believing that my boyfriend's brother was a lecherous bastard, but my instinct told me I was right. It was making me slightly uncomfortable and I felt the need to get out. His womanising aside, and in fairness to the crazy man, along with his suffering wife Irene, they'd had a stranger staying in their house and I was not their responsibility or indeed their problem. I told Ivan that I would mention the attorney money to Dan on his next call, gave the Husky a filthy look as I passed and retired to the spare room to email Ma B's oldest friend Erica.

Erica and Ma B had worked together for many years and had been best friends since I was a little girl. Erica was around 12 years younger than Ma B, she was from Atherstone and we knew each other inside out. She had terrible luck with men but after a few relationship disasters, she met an American whilst on a night out with me to celebrate my 19th birthday and they started a serious relationship. His name was Gus. He was over in the UK working for General Motors on a short-term assignment. After a while, Erica and Gus got married and she moved to the US where they went on to have two kids. We always kept in touch and she came home a few times per year.

Erica knew me very well and she was a really good sort. She lived in Blandon, Pennsylvania at that time so I emailed her and filled her in on the situation. She immediately emailed back and told me to call her. I managed to plead with the brown-toothed one to free up the landline for ten minutes and called her that evening. She had already spoken to Ma B and they thought it would be a good idea to for me to stay with her for a week or so until we found out the exact date for Dan's farce of a court hearing. I'd had a belly full of Ivan and Ed so I agreed. I informed

Ivan the following day that whilst they had been very accommodating and I was very grateful, I thought that (like a stray dog) it was time I moved on.

I explained that my friend lived in PA and I would visit her whilst waiting for the outcome of Dan's court appearance. Ivan seemed slightly put out that I was moving on. Ed was indifferent and I imagined Irene was quite relieved, although she didn't say as much. Davey appeared to be disappointed and I think my daily shopping requests had given him purpose. Erica had informed me that she and her family were visiting a place called Quantico on that very Sunday. Prior to working for General Motors, Gus had been a US marine and he was still a reserve. Quantico was The National Museum of the Marine Corps situated in Virginia. Ivan said he, Irene and myself could visit his cousin in Washington DC on the Saturday, stay overnight and he could then drop me off at Quantico on the Sunday morning to meet Erica as it was kind of half way. It was all arranged so I said my goodbyes to Davey along with the brown-toothed one and we left for DC on the Saturday.

Ivan's cousin was a big woman called TC (no idea what's with the Yanks and the initials). She was a nice girl and her little house was cute. She had a small, white dog who, unlike the Husky, was delightful. We had a few drinks with her and I was wondering what the sleeping arrangements were going to be that night as she only had two bedrooms. Luckily at around 11pm the sleeping situation was addressed. TC said Ivan could sleep downstairs in her attic room on a blow up bed and I could share a room upstairs with Irene. It was not ideal but hey ho. During the night I needed to make a trip to the ladies, which was situated downstairs on the middle floor.

As I was leaving the bathroom, closing the door behind me, I heard a voice say, 'How you doing?' Ivan was standing in the hallway.

'Erm. I'm fine,' I mumbled. He was standing in my way just enough to make it awkward.

'Yeah I couldn't sleep either,' he quickly said.

I had no issue sleeping, I just needed a wee so I didn't know what he was on about really. I was half asleep so I didn't respond.

He then whispered, 'It will be OK you know, this thing with Dan.'

I just nodded and started to walk past him towards the stairs. It was at that point that Ivan made an attempt to hug me. He didn't lunge at me as such but he put both arms around me and then he tried to kiss me. I think he aimed for my lips but he actually got my cheek as I was turning my face away from him. I woke up pretty fucking quick and made a break for it. Once back in bed with Irene, I reflected on Ivan's clumsy pass because that's what it was. It was soap opera stuff really. The brother takes the vulnerable girlfriend in whilst the boyfriend is in custody awaiting sentence, then he makes a pass at her in the middle of the night whilst she is sharing a bed with his wife. I suppose he was running out of time so the cheeky bastard just went for it. I turned over in bed, prayed Irene didn't try and squeeze my arse in the wee hours and tried to go to sleep. At least by the following day I would be delivered to my English friend Erica.

I hardly said a word the following morning and I was very quiet during the car journey to Virginia. Ivan was wittering on about all sorts of nonsense but he didn't get much of a response out of me apart from the odd 'yep' 'nope' or 'not really'. I still couldn't believe his chutzpah the previous night. Irene was blissfully unaware and chatty. I would never have told Dan about Ivan's attempted fumble so I put it out of my mind. He was a shady, untrustworthy geezer in every way and that was that.

I arrived at Quantico at around midday. It was a joy to see Erica and I felt like a toddler about to run over to its mother. She put my bags in her car, eyed Ivan up and down quickly and said, 'Thanks for looking after her.'

Ivan replied, 'Yeah you can take it from here. Take her, she's been nothing but trouble.' Then he laughed his totally false laugh and gave me a big cheesy grin.

I simply said, 'Thanks Ivan, you've been great. I don't know what your brother would have done without you. I'll be sure to tell Dan how much you've looked after me. I'm sure we'll keep each other updated in terms of his court case.' Ivan looked slightly uncomfortable for around a millisecond then he got in the car. I said my bon voyages to Irene and off they went.

Erica looked at me and said, 'So how are you? What a bloody situation.'

I told her I felt better having gone from Ivan's. She looked me in the eye, offered me a ciggie and asked, 'So was everything OK with the brother? What's he been like?'

She wore a knowing expression like she already knew the answer. I told her I would fill her in over a cuppa.

She lit my ciggie and said, 'Well whatever the story it won't surprise me. He looked as uncomfortable as Katie Price at a Mensa convention.'

Once we had met back up with Gus, Erica's mother Maureen and the kids, we all went for lunch. Once sat at the table, Maureen opened her bag and said, 'Do you want one of these kid?' She then offered me one of the tea bags that was poking out of the top of her bag, like it was a shipment of Columbia's finest cocaine. I'm not going to lie I was excited. That fucker was a PG Tips brewbag baby!

'They can't brew up Jo. The tea bags are vile, the water is never hot enough and the milk is odd. I'd bring my own water if I could,' she said.

I quickly took her up on her offer. It soon became apparent that whilst Gus was enjoying his day at Quantico, Maureen and Erica were bored shitless so they were happy to hear my tales of woe.

'I knew Ivan looked shifty,' said Erica. 'Bloody men, I tell you no female is truly safe. I've experienced the brother thing myself... and the father... and the uncle... bastards.'

Maureen nodded and added, 'Oh that they are.'

Dan called me as much as he could whilst I was staying with Erica and at least he could call a landline. Jed Carlton and the dream team still had no firm date for Dan's court case so after a few days relaxing and reflecting upon the situation with Erica and her mother, Maureen, I decided that as much as I wanted to await the outcome, I needed to get home. I couldn't wait any longer without any date even in place.

Ma B said gigs awaited and I needed to get back to the UK. I couldn't cancel any more and I needed to get back to earning money. Dan completely understood. We had a life back in the UK and that needed tending. The trip had truly been the holiday from hell and it was still ongoing but I'd had enough of the US. The attorney assured me that the judge would not pass any custodial sentence once he had heard the case so Dan should be following me back to the UK fairly swiftly. I booked my flight for the following Thursday. Two days after I had booked my return journey to the UK, Billy Big Balls called me to say the date had come in for Dan's hearing and it was set for the following Thursday. The big man upstairs was certainly playing with me. I had no choice but to accept the fact that during the car journey to Newark airport, I would be told of Dan's fate. I couldn't be there and I wouldn't be able to speak to him.

Ivan sent me a text saying he would be there at the court case but I didn't trust that he would be. I packed and got prepared to leave. Erica had been a true friend and she had kept me sane but I was now ready for departure. I was nervous during the car journey to the airport and to say I had my fingers firmly crossed was an understatement. We had been in the car for around 40 minutes and it was approaching midday when my mobile rang. Erica looked at me, smiled and nodded prompting me to answer it. It was Jed Carlton.

He cleared his throat and said, 'Yeah hey it's Jed. I'll get straight to the point. The judge didn't swing the way we wanted him to Joanne.'

I took a very deliberate, deep breath and quietly replied. 'Right. What's the situation?'

He paused and then just hit me with it. 'Daniel has been sentenced to a 12-month custodial term to be served in Erie County Jail. At best, he may get parole after three months if he behaves, but the chances are he will have to serve the remaining nine-month parole period here in the US. The court has also imposed a heavy fine that must be payed to the state of Pennsylvania before he would even be eligible for parole. The amount of monies owed to the state has not been confirmed yet as they are also adding transportation costs for shipping him from New York to Pennsylvania. It's not the result I was hoping for Joanne but these things can happen. It's sometimes the luck of the draw on the day,' he replied.

Erica was driving but she looked at me and knew it wasn't good news. I was silent for a few seconds then I just barked, 'Twelve bloody months? How has this happened? It's ridiculous? That's not a slight variation on the expected result is it? Jesus Christ!'

I fumbled around in my bag for my cigarettes. Billy Big Balls simply said, 'I know. I'm sorry. It's a bit goddamn harsh. I'll keep you in the loop on everything else via email.' With that he was gone.

I was in shock. Erica passed me her lighter. I had a tear in my eye. Erica said gently, 'Jo you need to get home now and gather your thoughts. That was a nasty shock. I can't believe they gave him that! Don't panic though. Perhaps he could appeal.'

I immediately sent a text to Ma B to inform her of the fucking horrible outcome. I didn't really remember the rest of the airport journey, checking in, the departure lounge or even the flight (I didn't even recall the take-off or landing). Once I had touched down in Blighty, Ma B was there at Heathrow to collect me. I got in the car when my phone beeped and I saw there was a text message from Ivan. I had sent a text asking him how Dan had coped with the news before I left New Jersey. Ivan's text reply said unfortunately he had been unable to attend the court case as something had come up but the attorney had called him with the outcome. He went on to say I shouldn't worry too much as he was sure Dan would be fine and he would speak to him later. Fine? How would he be fine? I didn't reply. I knew that slippery fucker had no intention of making the court case.

Life had to resume quite quickly for me in the UK. I arrived back at home on the Friday morning and I had a gig on the following night in Bristol. Ma B and I batted the horrid situation back and forth but it really didn't help. I spoke to Dan as soon as I got back. I had called Erie prison and somehow managed to persuade the guy who answered the phone to let me speak to him. I pretty much explained that I had used my mother's landline to call the US from the UK and due to us being in different countries Dan and I wouldn't be able to keep in touch other than in writing. I pleaded with him to just let me speak with Dan for a few minutes. He did and when I spoke to Dan I found him to be surprisingly accepting of the situation. He said he'd had his 'moment' following the sentencing but there was nothing anybody could do. He told me to try and keep everything together for when he got out.

Over the next few months Dan and I kept in touch via mail. The letters were regular and lengthy as this was our only means of communication. As far as work was concerned, I threw myself straight back into it. Ma B and I continued to lie to all and sundry regarding Dan's whereabouts and we were telling people that his poor mother (who I did keep in touch with throughout) was getting more poorly by the week. We had to tell people that he would be there indefinitely.

Back at our apartment, our UN chums couldn't understand why Dan wasn't replying to emails, texts or Facebook messaging. I said he was keeping his phone off to avoid costs plus the signal was poor where he was based in North Carolina and they seemed to accept it. I avoided speaking to Ivan as much as possible and although it was tempting to believe him when he told me that he would pay the court fine, I knew he wouldn't. That would be down to us and it was substantial. I knew that I would need to sing like a fucking canary and perform like the bastard child of Beyoncé and Michael Jackson to cover it. I did just that as there was no alternative other than to leave Dan incarcerated for 12 months. Constant emails flowed to and fro between the PA justice/collections department and me. I was desperately trying to secure a parole date and a highly unlikely pass for him to return to the UK after the three months was up. It was proving very tricky indeed.

After I had been back around seven weeks I had a call from Robbo's dad, Dave. I had been aware that Robbo had recently been into a rehab unit for a month in Southampton. His parents had been warned that he was in a bad way and he needed serious professional help before he killed himself. They had to re-mortgage their house to fund it. Dave said that Robbo had completed his rehab stint, was sober and wanted to meet me (with his Dad in tow to keep an eye on him) for a coffee. He said it would mean a lot to them so I agreed. I did not want anything horrible to happen to my former partner of over a decade and I wanted to see him sober. I desperately wanted Robbo to recover and to be happy.

I met them in the Red Lion Hotel in Atherstone and Robbo was thinner than I expected. We sat in the bar area but in the lounge seats where they served teas and coffees. Once the hellos and cheek-kissing bit was out of the way, I said to Robbo, 'You don't look too bad. How are things?'

He shuffled nervously in his seat and replied, 'I could murder a pint but other than that… anyway, how are you? What's been happening with Ike? I hear he's in the big house.'

Robbo had referred to Dan as Ike before, as in Ike Turner. Dan and I were both in the entertainment business and as far as Robbo was concerned, he was a black American bad boy so that was enough of a similarity to Ike Turner for him. I knew Ma B had confided in Dave about Dan's predicament but I didn't know how much Robbo knew. He obviously knew most of it and found it rather amusing. Due to his mental state, along with the fact that he was a piss taker by nature, I let him revel in my misfortune. After two coffees and some chitchat, Robbo admitted the true extent of his illness to me. It transpired that the rumours had been somewhat accurate and it had been drink and drugs.

He started getting a bit twitchy and all of a sudden without warning he said, 'I want to go to the garden centre.' I nearly spat out my coffee.

Robbo had always hated garden centres. For the whole time we were together, he would do anything to avoid having to go to a garden centre at the weekend.

I looked at him as if he had lost his mind and said, 'Why now? Why do you want to go to the garden centre? This is the only time we haven't got a fucking garden?'

He looked confused and muttered, 'I don't know really. I just do.'

So we wandered aimlessly around the local garden centre for what seemed like hours and Robbo looked extremely troubled to me. I thought he looked wobbly mentally and he didn't appear to know where he wanted to be. I don't think he wanted to be anywhere unless it involved a drink. Dave said he was doing well but I feared for his recovery. It came to a point where we could peruse the shrubs no longer and it was time to say our goodbyes. Robbo asked that I stay in touch and I said I would. I told Dave to keep me informed and I hoped to god Robbo could come out the other side.

As we parted company to walk to our cars Robbo shouted, 'I hope Ike ain't been bummed in the big house. Tell him I said 'Wassup!''

I turned and smiled at him then got in my car and left. I had visions of him necking vodka and snorting a few lines before the week was out but I really hoped that wasn't going to be the case.

The weeks passed quickly and soon turned into months. I don't know how it happened but with Ma B's help we paid the fine. The judge in PA said Dan had served his three months with good behaviour so he could return to the UK. Once he was released, Ivan collected him from Erie and he spent a few days with his family in North Carolina before returning home. I didn't know what they fed them in prison but Dan boarded the plane to New York with the physique of Eddie Murphy, yet when he plodded into arrivals at Heathrow on collection, he resembled Biggie Smalls. I pointed this out to him quite quickly and he replied, 'The cocksuckers like to keep us fat, we're less mobile.' Life got back to normal and Dan returned to his normal size in record time. We gigged hard and began to relax, although I vowed never to step foot in the US again.

Robbo remained sober for a few more months and then all hell broke loose. He went on an almighty round of benders and his parents thought he was a gonner. It was so frightening for them. They found out about a rehab facility in South Africa and it seemed to be their only hope. They said it cost a fortune and he would be there for months but it had a high success rate and they were very desperate. They did their research and once they had made the decision to go for it, Dave had to accompany the troublesome pisshead on the plane all the way to South Africa. They knew he wouldn't get there unless he was personally delivered. What a year it had been.

EPILOGUE

I have to say, it's nice to get back to some sort of normality. The last 12 months have been a bit crazy to say the least. I am sitting in my office with a nice cup of Earl Grey tea, putting the finishing touches to this little book. Dan is in the kitchen slurping on a can of Stella, complaining at the TV about this year's choice of nominees for the Sports Personality of the Year award. He has just recommended that the award should be given to the gold medal winners of this year's 'paralegal Olympic team'. Of course he actually meant the paraplegic Olympic team. His error must have been due to all of the talk of the US legal justice system over the last few months. Once again an amusing vision is creeping into my head. I am picturing a team of young trainee attorneys legging it around the track in their suits, doing the relay using brief cases and mobile phones as batons to pass onto the next fuckwit attorney.

That would be reminds me of a comment Nan made to Dan a while ago. Remember that she is in no way racist but for somebody of her generation (born in 1925) from a small town such as Atherstone where there were only white folk, Dan was different. She liked him but he was different. She used to say things that made me cringe but it amused Dan. After watching the athletics with him one afternoon, she exclaimed, 'Can't your people run fast?' Coming from her, it didn't offend him in the least. On another occasion, not long after we first got back from Spain and we were on the way to my aunt's house for dinner, completely bypassing Dan who was sitting in the back, she asked, 'What do they eat Joanne?'

Dan smiled and said, 'Oh I'll just have a couple of bananas Nan,' but his comment was wasted on her.

So what does the future hold? I really don't know. Will Nan live long enough to get a telegram from the queen? Will Matt ever develop any social airs and graces? Will Steph stay off the pop? Will Robbo make it back from the rehab unit in South Africa and if so, what will the new Robbo be like?

As far as Ma B, Dan and I are concerned; we will continue to gig like trojans. Maybe one day I will actually get to meet the great Diamond Dame in person. I would like to think that she'd find this book a tad amusing. If I feel brave enough I may send her a copy.

We are hosting a UN gathering tonight in our apartment and Dan is keen to get cracking on the food. He will soon be throwing potato salad all over our kitchen worktop. We then have a show to do tomorrow for the *Daily Mail's* advertising department at some swanky hotel. Dan will be opening with his Motown set, then I'll be giving them some serious Bassey and we have Matt on piano. It's nice and busy.

I can promise you that everything I have written happened exactly as I have described it. Nothing has been fabricated or indeed remotely exaggerated and I didn't need to embellish any part. Life is indeed stranger than fiction. There are mysterious and unknowable forces at work in our lives and I am happy to report 'it's a madhouse out there!'

So far, it has all turned out a little differently to how I expected it to. Fifteen years ago I made a decision to become a professional singer and it's a decision I certainly don't regret. The last 15 years seem to have flown by and now a new year is just round the corner. I may not have hit the big time and I'm certainly no millionairess. I haven't got a platinum selling album and I have no pop videos showing on VH1 or MTV. I will never collect a Grammy and my house will never appear on *Celebrity Cribs*. What I do have, however, is the privilege of earning a great living, being flown half way around the world doing what I adore doing and being paid good money for doing it. Don't get me wrong, being a tribute act can sometimes be challenging. In my case, it does, on occasion, take bling, boas and balls!

So that's that, in the words of the great Dame 'This is my life!'

YOU AIN'T HEARD
NOTHING YET

During the course of writing this book there has been so much more craziness in my life, I had to start to jot it down. I soon realised there would be far too much for just one book so I would like to tell you all, dear readers, that I have decided to start my sequel. Once again, I have found myself in truly bizarre situations. Some desperate, some sad, some hilarious, some frightening and some that I still cannot believe have actually happened to me again! A birth, a death and yet another prison visiting line. Anyway, I will save that, along with further Surely Bassey adventures and the antics of my friends and family, for the next book.

Note to the rich and famous:
Could I respectfully ask the icons and legends to whom we pay tribute and on whom our livelihoods depend, to refrain from indulging themselves in any nasty shenanigans. It would be appreciated if you could keep your name up there with the odd bit of naughtiness i.e. drug offences, quad bike accidents, affairs, oily threesomes and the accepted bit of tax evasion but please no real nastiness!

You think Cliff Richard was relieved when those charges were dropped? There was nobody more relieved than 'Quiff Richard' believe me! It was touch and go for him for a while. At least Cliff could continue to pay his bills. Poor Quiff could have been in arrears. Just think before you act. That's all we ask.

As for the poor Michael Jacksons, they haven't known where they stand for decades...

Printed in Great Britain
by Amazon

33658787R00140